WOMEN, WORK AND THE FAMILY IN EUROPE

Edited by
Eileen Drew, Ruth Emerek and Evelyn Mahon

ROUTLEDGE

London and New York

First published 1998
by Routledge
11 New Fetter Lane, London EC4P 4EE

Simultaneously published in the USA and Canada
by Routledge
29 West 35th Street, New York, NY 10001

© 1998 Eileen Drew, Ruth Emerek and Evelyn Mahon

Typeset in Baskerville by
J&L Composition Ltd, Filey, North Yorkshire
Printed and bound in Great Britain by
MPG Books Ltd, Bodmin, Cornwall

British Library Cataloguing in Publication Data
A catalogue record for this book is available from the British Library

Library of Congress Cataloging in Publication Data
Women, work, and the family in Europe/edited by Eileen Drew, Ruth
Emerek, and Evelyn Mahon.
p. cm.
Includes bibliographical references and index.
1. Work and family—Goverment policy—Europe. 2. Family policy—
Europe. 3. Women—Employment—Europe. I. Drew, Eileen P.
II. Emerek, Ruth. III. Mahon, Evelyn.
HD4904.25.W655 1998
331.25—dc21 97–45075
CIP

ISBN 0–415–15350–6 (hbk)
ISBN 0–415–15351–4 (pbk)

WOMEN, WORK AND THE FAMILY IN EUROPE

INGHAM COL

This book provides a new and timely analysis of major changes in society within the extended European Union by addressing the consequences of altered family forms, the restructuring of labour markets and the conflicting demands of family and working life. As well as providing an up-to-date survey of many of the current areas of debate across Europe, *Women, Work and the Family in Europe* reviews new developments and initiatives being taken in an attempt to reconcile men's and women's roles in the family and at work.

Bringing together many of the leading experts in social policy across Europe, the book covers subjects as diverse as family policy, gender roles and the care of the elderly. Contributions set out the major demographic and labour market trends which are critical in understanding the sexual division of labour, occuring in relation to both paid work in the labour market and unpaid work at home.

Clearly written and arranged under general headings and individual chapters, *Women, Work and the Family in Europe* will appeal to students as well as researchers and professionals and will be an essential addition to the material available to students of cultural studies, women's studies and social policy.

Eileen Drew is Senior Lecturer in the Department of Statistics/Centre for Women's Studies at Trinity College, Dublin, **Ruth Emerek** is Associate Professor in the Department of Development and Planning, FREIA, at Aalborg University, Denmark, and **Evelyn Mahon** is Lecturer in the Department of Sociology, at Trinity College, Dublin.

CONTENTS

CONTENTS

FIGURES

TABLES

CONTRIBUTORS

Ulla Björnberg is Professor in the Department of Sociology, Göteborg University. At present she is leading a research programme focusing on the theoretical and methodological development of gender and family sociology. She has been engaged in several international projects on family policy, on the reconciliation of employment and family life and on lone mothers, in Eastern and Western Europe. She is a member of the European Observatory on national family policies.

Julia Brannen is Reader in Sociology at the University of London, Joint Director of Centre for Research in Employment and Family Life at Thomas Coram Research Unit, the Institute of Education. She has carried out research in the following areas: households and family life, dual-earner households, marriage and partnership, young people, health and help-seeking behaviour. She has an interest in methodological issues, especially the combination of qualitative and quantitative methods.

Daniela Del Boca has a degree in economics from the University of Turin, and was awarded a Ph.D from the University of Wisconsin, Madison, in 1988. Since 1991 she has been an Associate Professor in the Department of Economics, University of Turin. She has also held posts of Visiting Associate Professor, at New York University, 1990, 1991, 1992, and Visiting Fellow, Cambridge University, UK, 1987. She has been a member of the editorial board of *Economia e Lavoro* since 1993 to the present, a Research Associate at the Agnelli Foundation Turin, 1982–9, and a Council Member of the ESPE (European Society for Population Economics) from 1995–8.

Eileen Drew is a Senior Lecturer in the Department of Statistics and Women's Studies, Trinity College, Dublin, where she teaches in the areas of management, quality, data analysis and communications. Her research has included an examination of part-time working in Ireland relative to other EU countries, the issue of low pay for women workers, women and rural development, demographic change in the European Union and EU-supported research on the 'Integration of Women into the Irish Labour Market'. She has published extensively in the areas of women and employment, flexible work practices, reconciling work and family life and IT innovation. Her current research projects relate to collaborative research into gender inequalities in Europe and on an international comparative leadership survey. She currently holds the post of Chairperson, Standing Committee One, of the National Economic and Social Forum and is a member of the Scientific Committee of IRIS, the European Network on women's training.

Ruth Emerek is an Associate Professor in the Department of Development and Planning at Aalborg University, Denmark. She graduated in statistics from the University of Copenhagen in 1973. Her specialist fields are data creation, measurement and modelling, labour market research and equal opportunity studies. Current research areas are: women's working and living conditions in a gender segregated labour market, education and equality and the creation of new data and development of new methods of measurement, for example, in relation to comparisons of working conditions and workload.

Jeanne Fagnani is Research Director at the Centre Nationale de la Recherche Scientifique, Paris, and Scientific Adviser at the Caisse Nationale des Allocations Familiales. She is an Expert Member of the European Observatory on National Family Policies, DGV, Commission of European Communities, Brussels. Her principal research interests and current work relate to family policies in the European Union, social protection and the economic activity of married women in Europe and research on childrearing benefit in France – take-up, impact and the implications for gender roles.

Dino Giovannini graduated in educational sciences in 1970 from the University of Bologna, Faculty of Educational Sciences, in the Department of Psychology and Department of Educational Science. Since June 1994 he has been full Professor of Social Psychology, teaching social psychology at the Faculty of Sociology, Department of Sociology and Social Research, University of Trento (Italy). He is interested in issues concerning social interaction and communication (experiencing and recognising emotions, social competence), identity, social comparisons and social representations of social practices, and fathering today (fathers' involvment in childcare, fatherhood and models of fathers, family responsibilities and intersubjective relationships).

Yvonne Hirdman was a member of the Swedish Power and Democracy Committee during 1985–90. She formerly held the post of Professor of Women's History at the University of Gothenburg and is now Professor of the Swedish Centre for Working Life, Stockholm, Sweden. She has undertaken extensive research on state policy and gender contracts.

Lis Højgaard is Associate Professor in Sociology at the Institute of Political Science, University of Copenhagen. Her main research areas are gender culture and organizations, involving empirical research on workplace culture and gender differentiation in terms of leadership positions and wage-differentiation in public and private corporations, and the changing relations between working life and family life, welfare state policies and labour market regulations.

Arnlaug Leira is Professor of Sociology, University of Oslo and Research Director at the Institute for Social Research, Oslo. She has published widely on gender issues in sociology and social policy. Her recent research deals with women's work and care formation and with the gendering of citizenship in modern welfare states. Presently she is conducting research for the European project, 'Defining Family Obligations'.

Susan McRae was formerly Senior Fellow and Head of the Employment and Society Group at the Policy Studies Institute. Prior to joining the PSI in 1986, she was a Research Fellow at Nuffield College, Oxford. Since January 1996 she has been appointed Head of the School of Social Sciences at Oxford Brookes University and Director of the ESRC Research Programme on Population and Household Change.

Evelyn Mahon is a Lecturer in Sociology and Women's Studies in the Department of Sociology at Trinity College, Dublin. She was formerly employed as Director of the postgraduate degree in Women's Studies and the Centre for Women's Studies at the University of Limerick, having been employed as a Researcher by Combat Poverty. She is Consultant to the European Commission DGV and the Irish national contact for the European Network of Women's Studies. Formerly she has been an expert with UNESCO, consultant to the Radio Eireann Series on Women's Studies, editor of the Sociological Bulletin/Newsletter, secretary of the Women's Studies Association of Ireland, editor of *Women's Studies Review* and secretary of the Galway AIM group.

Theodoros Papadopoulos holds a degree in sociology from Pantion University (Greece), an MSc in Social Research Methods from the University of Surrey and a Ph.D in Social Policy from the University of York. He is now a Lecturer in the School of Social Sciences, University of Bath. His research interests include comparative research methodology, Southern European family policy and the welfare arrangements for the unemployed in the European Union member states. He has been involved as the national respondent for Greece in the Support for Children in Fifteen Countries project and the Comparative Study of Social Assistance Arrangements in Twenty Four Countries, both undertaken by the Social Policy Research Unit (SPRU) at York.

Judith Phillips is a Lecturer in Social Work and Gerontology in the Department of Applied Social Studies, Keele University. Her research interests relate to the issues around social care and community care, worker carers and research methodology social work in the independent sector, particularly in relation to services for older people. She is Chairperson of the External Relations Committee of the British Society of Gerontology and is currently engaged on a research project on 'Kinship and Household Change: The Experiences and Responses of Older People', funded by the ESRC.

Sheila Rowbotham is the author of several books on women's history as well as on women's contemporary moments and conditions including *Hidden from History* (Pluto 1973), *Women in Movement* (Routledge 1993) and *Homeworkers Worldwide* (Merlin 1993). She edited *Dignity and Daily Bread* (Routledge 1994) and *Women Encounter Technology* (Routledge 1995) with Swasti Mitter. Sheila Rowbotham's most recent work is *A Century of Women. The History of Women in Britain and the United States* which was published by Viking/Penguin in 1997. She was awarded an honorary doctorate from the University of North London in 1994 and is a University Research Fellow in the Sociology Department at Manchester University.

Jane Tate has worked with homeworkers in West Yorkshire since 1988. She is a founder member of the West Yorkshire Homeworking Unit, which acts as an advice and support centre for homeworkers in the area. She has written several reports on homework. In 1992–3, Jane acted as the reporter for an *ad hoc* Working Group on Homeworking in the EC and wrote the final report for this group. She currently co-ordinates a European Homeworking Group. Jane also has contacts with homeworking groups in Asia, such as the Self Employed Women's Association in India and the ILO-DANIDA project on homeworking in the Philippines, Thailand and Indonesia.

Els Veenis studies social pedagogy at the University of Leiden in the Netherlands and worked until 1994 as a Ph.D student at the Utrecht University, Department of General Social Sciences. She is preparing a dissertation on the position of male and female employees in two Dutch retail companies (supermarkets and bookshops).

FOREWORD

Sylvia Walby

The reconciliation of family and working life is one of the most pressing policy and political issues facing all European societies. This volume is a timely collection of up-to-date theoretical and empirical work on this issue from all corners of the European Union. There are rapid and dramatic changes in the extent to which women, and men, engage in caring in families and participate in paid employment. The elucidation of the reasons for such changes is important for both social theory and public policy.

The balancing of intimate personal life and the production of the means to live has always been an issue for society and social scientists. The care of the young, the old and those unable to look after themselves has often been performed by women in families and communities outside of the market economy. What makes this question of such pressing concern today are the enormous changes that have been taking place in gender relations in society, in particular the rise of women's employment and the declining significance of marriage. Whether these changes are giving rise to greater social justice for women, or merely greater poverty is one of the questions to be addressed.

The balancing of family and working life is very different in the various countries of the European Union. These differences are not simple – it is not that women either do paid work or housework. Rather, there are extremely complex patterns and rapid previously unpredicted changes. For instance, the countries where women are having the fewest babies are not those where the rates of women's participation in paid employment are highest, but rather among the lowest, that is the southern European countries of Italy, Spain and Greece. The forms of household and family structure are both varied and changing, with an increasing tendency for women to live outside of marriage. The nature of employment is changing with the rise of 'flexible' or casualised forms of employment, for instance, part-time work among women. The forms of patriarchy are changing in complex ways.

There are a range of state policies which potentially affect the balance of domestic activities and paid employment including: those which provide an infrastructure facilitating the employment of carers, such as socialised forms of child and elder care and parental leave arrangements; as well as natalist policies, for example, the provision of financial benefits for motherhood by the state. There are policies which affect the income and employment levels of women as either carers or workers including: equal treatment regulations affecting employment and related issues such as pensions; employment protection such as that against unfair dismissal; the presence or absence of a minimum wage which especially affects the wages of women who are disproportionately among the low paid.

Increasing European integration impacts on these processes. The increased regulation of working life and the economy from the newly developing central institutions of the European Union affect both working and family life, even though most EU level policies are aimed at only working life. The strategic balance between deregulation of the economy in order to increase competitiveness or greater regulation in order to create social cohesion is one of the major political and economic questions of our day (as indicated in the two White Papers of the European Commission: *Growth, Competitiveness, Employment: The Challenges and Ways Forward Toward into the 21st Century,* 1993a, and *European Social Policy: Options for the Union,* 1993b). This choice is acutely gendered, even though it is rarely analysed in this way. Policies to increase economic growth by increasing competitiveness impact severely on those who are marginal in relation to employment, including not only those in regions with declining industries, but also women who commit time to caring as well as paid work. Whether the compensatory development of policies for social cohesion is sufficient to counter-balance this impact is a question. Yet a fully efficient economy needs the skills and contributions of all workers, and society as a whole suffers if some are unable for structural reasons to participate and their skills and energies are underemployed.

One of the questions for the European Union is whether its policies can deliver efficiency and justice simultaneously. Can the Single European Market deliver an economy which is competitive within a global arena which includes trading blocs based on the USA and on Japan, while social policies deliver social cohesion and justice? One issue which potentially connects both policies is that of the notion of a 'level playing field' within the EU, for example, the equal treatment of companies of different member states, and the equal treatment of women and men. The equal treatment of women and men was laid down in Article 119 of the Treaty of Rome, the founding treaty of the European Union, and underpins many of the directives and rulings of the EU about justice for women. But can it be effectively implemented in a fiercely competitive economy if women more than men attempt to combine work with caring?

In order to answer these questions and understand the implications of the EU we need to both gender macro-economic analysis and to develop a theory of gender relations which is able to deal adequately with macro differences between societies. Macro-economic policy is too often considered to be gender neutral, despite its implications for the extent to which women participate in the market economy. Gender relations have too long been considered within bounded national societies.

The analysis of comparative systems of gender relations demands a renewed understanding of the variation and changing nature of families and employment:

the new forms of household in which life-long marriage is no longer such a frequent occurrence; and the new forms of employment which are more 'flexible' need new forms of conceptualisation. Further, the analysis of gender regimes is more complex than simply asking about the extent to which women care or work. It demands analysis of state policy, both at national and EU level, and a gendered analysis of welfare state regimes. A full theory indeed would engage with all dimensions of women's lives, not only families and work, but also violence, sexuality and culture. Such a theory needs to be able to deal with change at the level of a system of gender relations, not only in specific local situations.

This volume is important in providing both empirical research which addresses these concerns from the viewpoints of many different European countries and in providing contributions to the theoretical debates needed to explain these differences. The work is both comparative and particular, empirically grounded and theoretically informed.

Despite the protestations of some postmodernist theorists against the use of many macro-level concepts, most analysts of gender at the comparative societal level agree that there is a need for gender concepts at the level of the social system. This recognition is noted by the use of terms such as 'system' or 'regime' and by terms including 'gender', 'sex-gender' and 'patriarchy' – all of which are intended to convey the notion of gender and structured inequality (see Hirdman 1990b; Ruben 1975; Sainsbury 1994; Walby 1990, 1997). It is now recognised that we need to develop such theoretical tools to deepen our understanding of the macro-differences between gender regimes.

Feminist theory has lively debates about how to conceptualise women's agency in the context of structural constraint. I have preferred to recognise the simultaneity of structure and agency within the concept of social structure (cf. Giddens 1984 on the duality of structure). Hirdman has preferred to use the term 'gender contract' in order to emphasise the bargaining between women and men, although some might think that this over-emphasises women's active consent at the expense of structural constraint. Further, this term lends itself awkwardly to differentiating types of gender system, because of its emphasis on individual agency. I prefer to distinguish between public or domestic gender regimes. However, Hirdman and I agree that one of the crucial features of these systems or regimes is that of the extent to which women are excluded from and segregated within paid employment and that gendered political struggle in relation to the state is a factor of major importance in structural change.

This book demonstrates the need for the development of these theoretical debates and for the comparative empirical studies in which they are grounded. While European data sources have considerably improved over the last few years in terms of their reporting on gendered distinctions, there is none the less still some way to go before the data needed to assess contemporary changes in gender relations, and in particular the reconciliation of family and working life, can be considered readily available. The need for further research on the impact of European integration on the specifically gendered aspects of social exclusion is clear from this volume. The problems of combining both care and employment have marginalised the many women, and some men, who care, in Europe. Only when there is a full reconciliation of domestic activities, of family lives, with those of paid employment, of working lives, will European societies become both efficient and just.

INTRODUCTION

Eileen Drew, Ruth Emerek and Evelyn Mahon

The objectives of this book are to focus attention on the interaction of major societal changes within an extended European Union, by providing a platform for authors to consider the consequences of altered family formations, the restructuring of labour markets and the conflicting demands of family and working life. These are examined in the context of similarities and differences between member states. The book reviews new developments and initiatives which might contribute to a new agenda for reconciling men's and women's roles in the context of sharing economic and social responsibilities.

The book is divided into three parts according to its major themes. Part I is on reconceptualising families. It examines demographic changes in Europe and the implications of this for family types and gender roles. It reviews caring responsibilities and family policies in some EU countries. Part II relates to restructuring labour markets. It is in this context that flexible work schedules and the adaptability of the labour market, through adjustment to regulatory frameworks, are examined. In particular, the (dis)advantages of working in 'atypical' jobs and homeworking are explored in terms of their gender implications. Part III deals with reconciling family and working life and considers gender differences in the adoption of 'family-friendly' options as attempts to reconcile family and working life.

Context

Within the European Union the traditional nuclear family type, considered as two adults with dependent children and a sole male breadwinner, has declined dramatically. Dual-income and one-parent families, predominantly female, are increasingly common. Such variation in family structures, makes the term 'families' rather than 'family', with its traditional stereotypical connotations, the major focus. It is important to examine the implications of variations in family structures within the context of employment in the European Union.

The participation of married women in the labour market has changed husbands' traditional responsibility of primary breadwinner in two-parent families. As a result of de-industrialisation, in some countries men have lost their jobs while

1

women have gained jobs in the expanding service sector. An increase in divorce and a rise in the number of lone parents make it imperative for women to be economically active. If not, they run the risk of being long-term dependants on social welfare. Research has shown that women have increased their labour force participation by availing themselves of part-time and other forms of 'atypical' working throughout most member states.

This redistribution of economic responsibility has not necessarily been accompanied by a redistribution of domestic and caring responsibilities in dual-income families. Men have been slow to accept parenting and other caring obligations. In theory these new social arrangements should provide men with a more varied life: combining parenthood/caring and employment with a shorter working week and yielding opportunities for increased leisure.

The book focuses on international comparisons, national reports and case studies in EU member states. The rationale for including national case studies is to provide examples of new ways of working and living. It is also important to discuss and compare national case studies since family structures, the state and the labour market have different forms as well as recognised similarities.

The book emphasises the interaction of the labour market and gender roles in families. To understand this interaction it is necessary to study it as a part of a triad of family, labour market and state. Without understanding the different influences of the state within the EU it is impossible to understand and explain inter-country variations in the combination of family life and working life.

The relationship between family and working life within the EU has changed radically within recent decades. Some changes have led to a convergence of patterns across member states, while others have resulted in divergent behaviour. The concept of 'family' differs between member states. National history, religious hegemony and structural development have shaped family formations and models

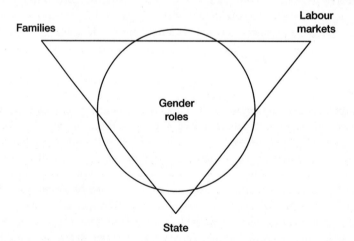

Families, labour markets, the state and gender roles.

of family life. The labour market is different because of varying levels of development in manufacturing, services, public sector expansion and expenditure. These factors have also influenced state policies on employment and the family. Some states have stressed the man's economic role in a primary 'breadwinner' model with dependent wife and children. Other states have adopted a 'dual-earner' model which includes a working mother. This book addresses the different ways that the state regulates and intervenes in the interaction of families and labour markets, for instance in the provision of childcare facilities and supports for carers of other family members.

Over the last two decades EU countries have experienced a decline in fertility rates and an increased participation of women in the labour market. Contraceptive practices have enabled individuals to plan their families and to decide if and when they wish to have children. While the labour force participation of mothers varies between countries, in general there has been an increasing tendency for women's working lives to begin to resemble those of men.

Cross-national variation in the labour force participation of women can be generally explained in terms of 'gender contracts' (Chapter 3). These concepts refer to a composite of national characteristics including state policy on taxation, childcare provision and services and gender equality in employment. The formation of these national gender contracts has been brought about by a series of historical, religious and cultural factors.

Some countries adopted a 'familistic' traditional gender regime based on a family model of a male 'breadwinner' and a dependent domestically based 'housewife'. Such countries offered a very low public provision of childcare or eldercare since the assumption was that these needs were or could be met within the family (Chapter 4). This is in stark contrast with 'individualistic' gender regimes which assume that everyone will be in paid employment, hence there is state provision of care for children, the elderly and disabled. The Scandinavian countries are the appropriate examples of such regimes.

In general, there has been a gradual transition from 'familistic gender regimes' towards more 'individualistic regimes' in many countries. The overall EU orientation in terms of social policy and employment are in the same direction. However, as women have generally assumed responsibility for caring within the family, the replacement of a 'familistic' regime by an 'individualistic' one may be problematic for women, and in some cases not promote women's participation in the labour force unless there is formal state or other support for care for children, the elderly, sick and disabled. It is mothers, daughters (and daughters-in-law), sisters, as well as wives (more commonly than husbands), who have to adjust their lives (particularly their professional working lives) to caring responsibilities. Unlike childcare, eldercare and care for persons with a disability, can last for an indeterminate time. For some carers, the duration could extend well beyond the time required to rear several children (Chapter 6).

Changes in family forms and the breakdown of traditional families by death, divorce and separation along with the growing proportion of births outside

3

marriage, can accentuate divisions between families. Differences in family incomes are widening between the 'work rich/time poor' dual-income households and 'work poor/time rich' households in which no one may hold a job (Chapter 7). This pattern is more acute in countries experiencing high levels of unemployment.

There has been an increase in the proportion of lone mothers and an increase in divorce rates in most European countries. In the case of single parents and divorcees, the cost of childbearing and childrearing is often borne solely by the mother. Marriage rates have declined in many northern European countries and the marriage contract is being replaced by consensual unions, which can be viewed as a rejection of the traditional marriage in favour of more individualistic cohabitation agreements. While there has been a great increase in births outside marriage, a very high proportion of such births are registered by both parents. In practice a pattern of individualised marriage and non-marital unions is emerging but is occurring at different rates in different countries (Chapter 1).

Along with lower fertility and smaller families in the EU, there has been a rise in women's, and men's life expectancies. This means that, due to demographic trends, a growing proportion of the population will be approaching retirement or retired, a situation which has associated problems, as well as opportunities. This situation is accentuated by the demographic consequences of post-war 'baby boom' giving rise to a new generation of elderly people who will expect to have a more active role in society in a voluntary or paid capacity.

Research has shown that women's employment is already highly concentrated into the service sector, including the caring professions in health and education. This means that women's paid labour in these professions mirrors that of unpaid carers within families, since women dominate as nurses, paramedicals and home helps. A further extension of public sector care provision could lead to further segregation in the labour market. This book raises the issue of how to promote 'sharing of the caring' (Chapter 2). This emphasis on individualism and on the reconciliation of care for dependants with paid employment necessitates changes in work practices and inevitably the demise of traditional gender-segregated practices within both the employment and domestic spheres.

Internationally, the shift towards labour market restructuring, involving part-time and other flexible patterns of work must be seen in the overall context of a reduction in working hours. The current average full-time hours of c. 35–40 hours per week represent less than half of the working week during the nineteenth century.

Technological change has been, and will continue to be, a prime factor in influencing work and its place in society. It has served as a catalyst or vehicle for change in how (degree of automation), when (working time), where (location of work) and by whom (allocation between men and women) work is undertaken. Society is now in a position to take an active rather than a passive role in determining changes in patterns of work, the location of work and working time. It should now be possible for women to act as 'change agents' in bringing about a better balance in the use of time.

Women's integration into the labour market is still hampered by their caring obligations and individual family circumstances such as the presence or absence of a 'male breadwinner'. Predictably, women who face caring obligations have sought ways of 'reconciling work and family life', through flexible working practices and, where available, formal childcare. In some countries, the strategy for many 'working mothers' has been to opt for part-time employment, particularly when their children are young. In other countries there has been a longer tradition of women, including mothers, holding full-time employment, facilitated by state childcare provision and allowances, particularly for children who attend school (Chapter 5).

Allied to technological change there is increased demand for labour in service industries and service occupations. At present, the service sector is still relatively labour intensive but unlike the manufacturing sector it requires different forms of work scheduling and use of labour to meet irregular demands, e.g. in retailing, financial and personal services. Hence it is particularly in the service sector that demands for a different arrangement of labour inputs have occurred and this has led to the search for 'flexibility' and recourse to 'atypical' forms of work. These forms of 'atypical' working can be advantageous for some workers who seek alternatives to full-time hours (Chapter 9). They may also have the adverse consequence of marginalising such workers and segregating them into low-paid, low-status, occupations.

External flexibility requires improved geographical mobility through improvements in the accommodation market and making available more advanced vocational training. This is advocated without reference to the possible negative impact on family life. Internal flexibility is sought via adjustments to the workforce which would avoid making people redundant. Initiatives under this form of flexibility relate to staff versatility, the integrated organisation of work, flexible working hours (including part-time working or job-sharing) and performance-related pay (Chapter 8).

In countries where demand for female labour has remained low, women's participation has been restricted due to a range of adverse conditions. In Italy's tightly regulated labour market of the 1980s, women were marginalised or excluded, and opportunities to work part-time remain strictly limited (Chapter 11). Ireland's taxation policy (based on joint assessment) for married couples (Chapter 16); lack of childcare facilities or allowance by the state; and, until recently, limited access to part-time jobs have meant that women had to make difficult choices when faced with childbearing. These countries are beginning to see a belated rise in married women's participation in the age range 24–40 years, mainly in full-time employment. These are also the countries (with Spain and Germany) where fertility rates are falling most rapidly in the EU.

Homeworking also supports flexible work structures since it departs from the rigidities of fixed hours of work for everyone with the associated disadvantages of time lost in getting to and from the workplace. If sought by positive choice, such work from a distance can be combined with flexible working time schedules which suit the worker, as well as employers. Against this must be weighed the problems of isolation, low pay, lack of employment protection, disruption by children (if present), additional safety and health risks, any of which could adversely affect family life. Research on workplace culture and gender differences is also included to illustrate its impact on families (Chapter 10). As Danish labour market research shows, there is a radical need to adopt alternative and more realistic forms of measuring employment in terms of its intensity (hours worked), duration of job-holding and continuity of employment (Chapter 12).

The relationship between family and working life within the EU has changed radically within recent decades. The participation of married women in the labour force has increased more rapidly in some member states, compared with others. At the same time the fertility rate has declined in all member states. The latest trends in Scandanavian countries show an increasing fertility rate suggesting that it is possible under certain conditions to combine participation in the labour market (albeit part-time) with childrearing and family life. To understand why the interaction between labour market and family formation moves at different speeds and in apparently different directions in different member states it is necessary to compare the influence of the state and its policies towards family and work in different countries in Europe (Chapter 15).

Part III seeks to examine how individuals, including fathers, combine family and working life, in countries as diverse as Ireland, the Netherlands, Sweden and Italy (Chapters 13, 15 and 17). It includes discussions of new experiments and research on the creation of family-friendly working places. It examines some of the obstacles to combining work and family and the barriers created by workplace cultures. In response to employers' needs, women adjust their working (produc-tive) time to their reproductive/caring obligations because they feel responsible for the daily well-being of their families. Despite gains in labour force participa-tion, cross-cultural research findings suggest that mothers/carers still remain fundamentally involved in parenting and other domestic work. In contrast, research findings in Sweden and Italy highlight the fact that men's role as fathers/carers has not altered substantially over the last three decades.

The structuring of everyday life: shopping hours, banking hours, school atten-dance hours (including lunch breaks), transport services, working hours, crèche opening times, differ between member states. Some structures facilitate the com-bination of family and working lives while others make it more difficult. Greater flexibility, e.g. extended service provision helps, rather than hinders, this combina-tion. One of the benefits of a shorter working day is to enable workers to engage in family life and leisure pursuits, to enhance their lives. The reallocation of work and family life between men and women is a first step in this longer process and would also help to promote desegregation in the labour market and require 'sharing the caring'.

Across the EU, it is mainly women who seek to balance work and family life, through part-time and other forms of 'atypical' work. This creates a vicious circle in which, for example, part-time/job-sharing is perceived as a female option, signalling that the woman lacks commitment to the job, has limited career aspirations and hence the practice is an unattractive option for men who might otherwise seek to spend more time with their partner/family (Chapters 18 and 19).

Perspectives

In labour market terms we can observe a gendered polarisation in relation to reconciling work and family lives. Men, including fathers, retain the primary breadwinner role, display stronger and continuous attachment to the labour market, in a full-time capacity. This working time commitment may increase rather than diminish when children are born. They are free to pursue their careers, adopting a fast track model. However, this pattern could be significantly altered among subsequent generations (Chapters 18 and 19). Women, particularly mothers, face the dilemma of juggling with the dual burden and stress associated with being workers and parents and resolve this by opting for 'atypical' working practices, adopting a slow track model (Chapter 17). Increasingly, women are not prepared to make such adjustments, given the adverse consequences for their careers.

As this book shows there have been considerable political, economic and social changes throughout the EU, but gendered divisions of labour have not kept pace. Although there have been observable shifts from the 'breadwinner'/'housewife' contract to an 'equality' contract, this has served to force women into a dual role, and there is an evident lack of adequate change in men's behaviour. Despite their professed desire to spend more time on family/child-related activities, their professional obligations do not allow this.

Experience from some member states illustrates the importance of the state as a mediator and activator of changes traditionally sought by women activists and their supporters. If men will not/cannot choose to adjust their working time to ensure a better balance between personal and professional life, the answer, in the long term, may lie in the extension of the fatherhood quota of parental leave (Chapter 19) to all EU countries in the implementation of that unfulfilled demand for a compulsory 6-hour day, as standard EU practice. In tandem with this it will be necessary for society to re-value the caring work which is essential to the survival of human society.

Part I

RE-CONCEPTUALISING FAMILIES

1

RE-CONCEPTUALISING
FAMILIES

Eileen Drew

Introduction

This chapter charts the demographic changes characterising the last three decades, which have resulted in a diversity of family forms. It marks the magnitude of some of these changes, the exceptions to general patterns and how these may be combined to offer a new perspective on how we might view 'families' and 'households' in Europe. Macintyre states:

> Though sex, marriage, and reproduction may be linked empirically in a particular society and its dominant ideology . . . . We cannot assume *a priori* that people have babies because they are married, or marry in order to have babies; nor that people have babies because they have had sex, or that they have sex to produce babies.
>
> (Macintyre 1991: 3)

The chapter provides a backdrop to the theme of Part I, 'Re-conceptualising Families', illustrating how the concept of family differs between member states for historical, religious and developmental reasons.

Demographic trends

Demographically, Europe has experienced a reduction in infant mortality, increasing life expectancy and decreasing fertility. Not only have the number of births (particularly third and subsequent births) been reduced, there has been a postponement of first and often subsequent births and a rise in childlessness. In tandem with these trends, there has been an alteration in the choices available to individuals and couples, exemplified by the lower marriage rates, higher levels of cohabitation, increased divorce and re-marriage rates and births outside marriage. There is no longer adherence to permanent monogamous family units as the basis for family life.

11

Life expectancy and ageing

General mortality rates declined steadily between 1960 and the 1990s leading to improvements in life expectancy which have continued in most countries of the European Union. Table 1.1 sets out the life expectancy[1] at birth for women and men in the European Union and how these have altered since 1960.

By 1994 women's life expectancy was 80 years or over in France, Sweden, Italy, Spain, the Netherlands, Greece and Belgium. Male life expectancy was highest in Sweden, Greece, Italy, the Netherlands and the UK, where it exceeded 74 years. Since 1960, the former north–south differences in life expectancy have largely disappeared or reversed. Women's life expectancy continues to exceed that of their male counterparts and in some countries the gap is widening. In the early 1960s, female life expectancy exceeded the male rate by an average of 5.2 years and this rose to 6.5 years in 1992. The differential varies country by country. France has the largest male–female life expectancy gap of 8.1 years.

Declining fertility rates and higher life expectancies contribute to an altered age structure, resulting in an 'ageing of the population' throughout Europe whereby an increasing proportion of the population consists of people over 75 years, a trend which is set to continue into the next century. Table 1.2 sets out the proportion of the population which is/will be aged 75 years and over. In 1960, only 3.6 per cent of the EU's population had reached 75 years, the level rose to

Table 1.1 Life expectancy at birth in the European Union (14) 1960–94

Country	1960		1994	
	Women	Men	Women	Men
Belgium	73.5	67.7	80.1	73.4
Denmark	74.4	70.4	78.1	72.7
Germany	na	na	79.6	73.1
Greece	72.4	67.3	80.2	75.2
Spain	72.2	67.4	81.1*	73.8*
France	73.6	66.9	81.9	73.8
Ireland	71.9	68.1	78.7	73.2
Italy	72.3	67.2	81.2	74.7
Luxembourg	72.2	66.5	79.7	73.2
the Netherlands	75.3	71.5	80.3	74.6
Austria	72.7	66.2	79.7	73.4
Portugal	66.8	61.2	78.6	71.6
Sweden	74.9	71.2	81.4	76.1
United Kingdom	73.7	67.9	79.4	74.2
EU (15)	72.7	67.5	80.5	74.0

Source: Eurostat (1996a).

Notes:
* Refers to 1993.
na – not available.

Table 1.2 Percentage of the population aged 75 years and over in 1960, 1990 and 2020

Country	1960	1990	2020
Belgium	4.2	6.4	9.9
Denmark	3.7	6.8	7.5
Germany	3.7	7.1	10.1
Greece	3.0	5.7	10.2
Spain	2.7	5.2	9.3
France	4.3	6.4	9.5
Ireland	4.2	4.0	6.3
Italy	3.1	6.1	9.4
Luxembourg	3.5	5.7	8.3
the Netherlands	3.1	5.4	7.3
Portugal	2.7	5.1	7.0
United Kingdom	4.2	6.7	8.7
EU (12)	3.6	6.3	8.6

Sources: Commission des Communautés Européennes (1992); Eurostat (1995a).

Note:
Comparable data for Austria, Finland, Sweden are not available.

6.3 per cent in 1990 and will be nearly 8 per cent in the year 2020. This represents a major shift in the population structure compared with only a century ago.

Combined with the decline in marriage and increased divorce, it is likely that an increasing number of elderly people will live alone and to varying degrees this could place a burden of responsibility for caring on offspring, other family members and/or the state.

Fertility rates

The trend towards fertility decline has been traced back in some parts of Europe to the end of the eighteenth century. With the exception of the period 1945 to 1965, which witnessed a rapid increase in births, the general trend has been one of steady decline during this century. Figure 1.1 shows the rapid rate of decline in fertility since 1960 throughout Europe, and the considerable variations in the geographical patterns of fertility decline.

It is in Germany, particularly the former GDR[2] and southern EU countries that fertility decline is most dramatic. In 1994/95, apart from Germany's GDR, Spain had the lowest total fertility rate in Europe (1.24), followed by Italy (1.26), Germany (1.35) and Greece (1.35) (Table 1.3). In contrast, it is in the northern and western EU states that higher than average fertility is recorded in recent years. Based on recent Eurostat forecasts of total fertility up to the year 2020: Sweden and the UK are expected to maintain a fertility rate of 1.90; followed by Denmark, the Netherlands and France with a fertility rate of 1.80, compared with a rate in Ireland of 1.50 and Spain of 1.13 (Eurostat 1995a). Fertility in Sweden never fell to very low levels (the lowest was 1.56 in 1983) and the social policies

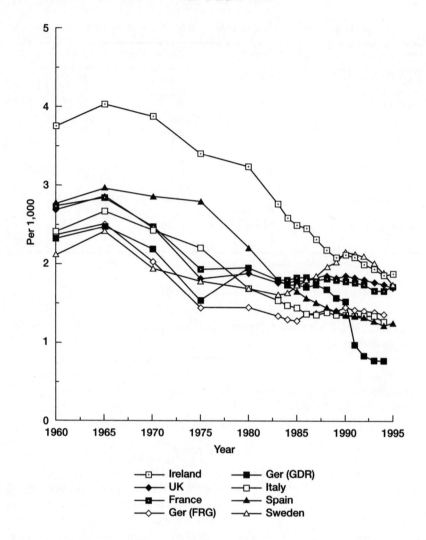

Figure 1.1 Total fertility rate in selected European Union countries.
Source: Eurostat (1996a).

pursued by the Swedish government have (somewhat uniquely) 'tried to facilitate women's entry into the labour market and their continued attachment to it at minimal cost to childbearing and childrearing' (Hoem 1990: 740).

The link between fertility and social policy intervention is extremely important. One of the themes for further and urgent research is whether rapidly declining levels of fertility (as experienced in Spain and Italy) represent freedom of choice by women, or a pragmatic response to the lack of social supports (separate taxation, childcare, flexible work practices, parental leave). The Swedish example represents

Table 1.3 Trends in total fertility rate[3] of the European Union (15) 1960–94/5

Country	1960	1965	1970	1975	1980	1985	1990	1994/5
Belgium	2.54	2.71	2.25	1.74	1.69	1.51	1.62	1.56
Denmark	2.54	2.61	1.95	1.92	1.55	1.45	1.67	1.81
Germany	2.37	2.51	2.02	1.45	1.45	1.28	1.45	1.35
Germany (GDR)	2.33	2.48	2.19	1.54	1.94	1.73	1.52	0.77
Greece	2.23	2.32	2.43	2.28	2.23	1.68	1.43	1.35
Spain	2.78	2.97	2.86	2.80	2.21	1.64	1.36	1.24
France	2.73	2.84	2.47	1.93	1.95	1.82	1.78	1.70
Ireland	3.76	4.03	3.87	3.40	3.23	2.50	2.12	1.87
Italy	2.41	2.67	2.43	2.21	1.68	1.45	1.36	1.26
Luxembourg	2.28	2.42	1.98	1.55	1.49	1.38	1.61	1.72
the Netherlands	3.12	3.04	2.57	1.66	1.60	1.51	1.62	1.53
Austria	2.69	2.70	2.29	1.83	1.65	1.47	1.45	1.40
Portugal	3.01	3.08	2.76	2.52	2.19	1.73	1.57	1.41
Finland	2.71	2.47	1.83	1.69	1.63	1.64	1.78	1.81
Sweden	2.13	2.41	1.94	1.78	1.68	1.73	2.14	1.74
United Kingdom	2.69	2.86	2.44	1.81	1.89	1.79	1.84	1.69
EU (16)	2.59	2.72	2.38	1.96	1.82	1.60	1.57	1.45

Sources: Eurostat (1995a), Council of Europe (1996).

an interesting alternative model to those states experiencing rapidly declining fertility rates. Norway's response to the prospect of population decline from 4 million to 3 million by the year 2010 was to appoint a Population Committee in 1981. The Committee concluded that a stabilisation of fertility, near to replacement level, should be sought and recommended radical improvement in the living conditions of families with children. It sought an extension of paid maternity leave from 18 weeks to one year; an adequate supply of kindergartens; public care arrangements for children entering school and improved living standards for families with small children through public transfers (Jensen 1989). The author notes that there has been little sign of radical action following these proposals.

Hall has concluded that given the availability of contraceptive technology, higher levels of education, rising living standards and how these impact on women's lives in terms of labour force participation, 'it seems unlikely that fertility will rise much, unless a wide range of public policy measures is introduced to help parents combine parenthood with paid work. Even then it is unlikely that fertility would rise significantly' (1993: 7).

Maternity – to be or not to be a mother

Folbre (1994: 111) has contested that fertility decline is not due simply to an aggregation of individual choices, to conceive or not, but is a 'circular process of struggle over the distribution of the costs of children [which] accompanies the technological changes associated with fertility decline'. Throughout western Europe, women born after 1945 have increasingly altered their reproductive behaviour by controlling their fertility and delaying childbirth. Women can make more deliberate decisions about whether to have children; when to commence, space and complete family formation. Part of this exercise of choice relates to the number of children, whether they are born within marriage or a stable union. The overall rise in childlessness suggests that women now have the means to make real choices rather than to accept some form of reproductive imperative, should they wish to be sexually active. Childlessness in Denmark, Germany, Italy, the Netherlands and the UK had been 10 per cent for women born in 1945, rising to 18 per cent for those born in 1955 (Hall 1993).

A key indicator of preference being exercised by women is in relation to the age of mothers when their first child is born. In the 1960s there was a pattern of women having their first child at an earlier age of 26 to 27 years, coinciding with the 'baby boom'. During the 1970s this trend reversed in all countries so that by 1993 the mean age of first time mothers was 29 years (Eurostat 1995a).

Another trend which has manifested itself to varying degrees in Europe is in the rate of legal abortions. Figure 1.2 shows that Denmark's abortion rate[4] was 5 per cent in 1960. Along with other countries (including the UK and Italy) freer access to abortion in Denmark was introduced in 1973 by legislation, following which the abortion rate peaked at 41 per cent in 1980, when the fertility rate was very low. This rate was almost matched by Italy in 1980, following legalisation. During the 1980s there has been a decline in the abortion rate in all the countries for which data on legal abortions are available (Drew 1995a).

Further evidence of women's exercise of choice is in relation to the marked and rapid decline in third and subsequent births. These had formed one-third of births in the European Union countries in the mid-1960s but fell to just one-sixth of births in the 1990s. Higher levels of third or higher births are still found in Ireland (35 per cent), Finland (26 per cent), the UK (24 per cent), Sweden (24 per cent) and France 22 per cent) compared with lower rates in Denmark and Greece (17 per cent) and Italy and Portugal (15 per cent) (Eurostat 1995a).

Marriage rate

According to Boh (1989: 276):

> changes in marriages in European societies were first marked by a dramatic swing to higher incidence of marriage and to falling age at marriage, to be followed by an inverse trend characterised by a decrease in marriage rates and an increase in the age at marriage, a growing number of divorces and cohabitations.

The total number of marriages peaked in 1970 with 2,625,503 in the EU (15) and fell to 1,939,279 in 1994. All EU states experienced a decline in marriage

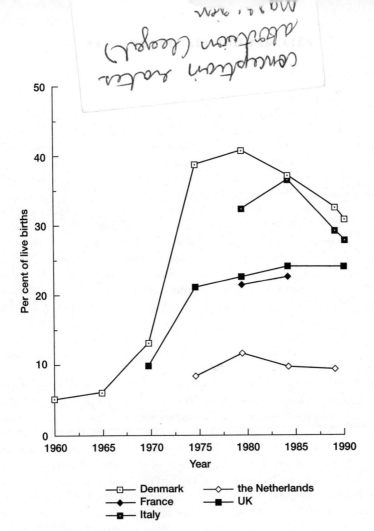

Figure 1.2 Legal abortions in selected European Union countries.
Source: Eurostat (1993a).

rates from 1970. Within the EU, the highest marriage rates in 1994 were in Denmark (6.8 per 1,000) and Portugal (6.7 per 1,000), followed by the UK (Eurostat 1996a).

Alongside this trend and the tendency for women to postpone the birth of a first child, the average age at marriage has increased for women by between two and three years since 1970 in many countries. Denmark switched from having the youngest mean age for women at first marriage of 22.8 years in 1960 to the oldest, 28.9 years in 1994. The mean age at first marriage of women in the European Union was 24.1 in 1960, 23.2 in 1970 and 26.1 in 1993. Among men there has been a similar shift towards marrying later with a mean of 26.7 in 1960, 25.9 in 1970 and 28.5 in 1993 (Eurostat 1996a).

Cohabitation

The postponement of marriage is related to the increased popularity of cohabitation which often precedes and in some cases replaces marriage. As Hall (1993: 8) states 'no longer is marriage seen as the only organising principle for relationships'. Boh (1989: 277) points out that in Europe cohabitation was not unusual in rural regions. However it now represents a newer trend whereby legal marriage has 'given way to a variety of optional non-traditional forms of "living together"'. This pattern was more frequent in the Nordic countries and has also increased in the Netherlands, France and the UK, but is still less frequent in Belgium and Italy (Boh, 1989). Boh (1989: 279) also claims that cohabital unions 'have everywhere functioned more as a trial marriage than as a more permanent alternative to formal marriage', since 'most cohabiting couples marry once they have children'.

Although EU data on cohabitation are not readily available, figures for Ireland suggest that fewer women were in non-marital unions compared with the Nordic countries. Cohabiting couples in Ireland accounted for 3.9 per cent of all family units in 1996 (Central Statistics Office 1997). Given the quite steady rise in births outside marriage in Ireland since 1980, it is likely that the situation in relatively 'traditional' and Catholic societies such as Ireland and Italy are moving towards the Nordic and European pattern of cohabiting.

It is difficult to gauge the rate of long-term consensual unions which do not result in marriage. However there is evidence of a growing proportion of older age cohorts among the 'never married' in some countries. Although fewer than 9 per cent of women aged 35–39 in Denmark had never married in 1984, the proportion for men was 18 per cent. It is in Sweden that there has been a steady rise. In 1970, only 11.6 per cent of women aged 30–34 years had never married, a level which increased to 36 per cent in 1984. There was a similar rise among 35–39-year-old women and the proportions for 'never married' men in these age cohorts was even higher (Hoffmann-Nowotny and Fux 1991). In Ireland, 43 per cent of women and 55 per cent of men in cohabiting unions were aged 30 years or more, confirming that cohabitation is not just a precursor to marriage but a more permanent form of union (Central Statistics Office 1997).

One further pattern which represents another alternative to marriage and cohabitation is of 'living apart together' in separate households. Hoffmann-Nowotny and Fux (1991: 51) have identified this option which accords with 'societal ideologies of individualism and equality, and becomes structurally more feasible with an increasing material independence of women'.

Divorce rate

Since 1960 there has been a rise in European divorce rates[5] (Figure 1.3) from 0.5 per 1,000 to 1.7 per 1,000 in 1993 (Eurostat 1996a). At current rates, it is estimated that 40 per cent of marriages in the UK will end in divorce (Hall, 1993). There has been some stabilisation of divorce rates in the later 1980s but this may be due to a rise in cohabitation and lower rates of remarriage among divorced people. Within the EU (12) divorce rates were highest in the UK (3.1), Denmark, Sweden and Finland (2.5) with lowest in Greece (0.7), Spain (0.7) and Italy (0.5) in 1993 (Eurostat 1996a).

Part of the increase in divorces has occurred in response to a liberalisation of divorce legislation away from a system based on matrimonial offence, guilt and punishment to one based on irretrievable breakdown, mutual responsibility and need. It is also argued that the rate is high due to the democratisation of relationships and the increased independence of women. Other social factors which are

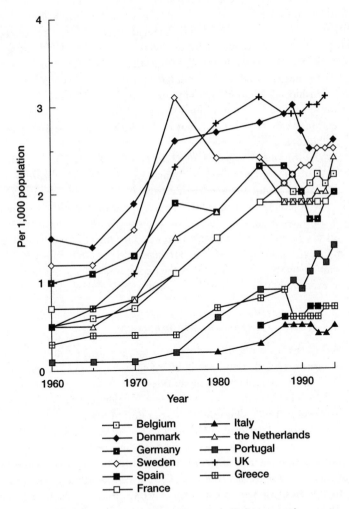

Figure 1.3 Crude divorce rate in selected European Union countries.
Source: Eurostat (1996a).

19

commonly cited are the individualisation and privatisation of marriage, with individuals seeking higher expectations of personal happiness and self-fulfilment. These break with the traditional adherence to conformity and duty (Boh 1989). With the rise in the rate of divorces there has been a removal of the stigma attached to being divorced, particularly for women. Gittins (1993: 9) posits the view that the divorced state now displaces the experience of widowhood, a much commoner event in centuries past: 'the common-sense notion that all families in the past were much more solidaristic and stable institutions cannot be borne out – death saw to that'.

Another feature of the higher divorce rate is the pattern of remarriage and step-families. In most countries there has been a rise in the number of marriages by divorced women and men from 1960 to 1990/1, when this increase was halted. The exceptions are in Spain, Finland and Portugal where the number of remarriages continues to rise. Remarriage by divorced persons is higher among men than women, reflecting a possibly greater reluctance among women to remarry and the higher probability that women will have responsibility for children from a previous relationship (Hoffmann-Nowotny and Fux 1991). Gittins (1993) again reminds us, by the all too common appearance of 'wicked stepmothers' in fairy tales, of the common practice of remarriage and children living with step-parents/siblings throughout recorded history.

Delphy (1991: 46) would argue that while at an individual level a divorce signifies the end of *a* marriage, 'it by no means implies the end of *marriage* as an institution. Divorce was not invented to destroy marriage since divorce is only necessary if marriage continues to exist.' Commenting on the virtual monopoly women have over assuming care for children after divorce, Delphy (1991: 56) places this on a continuum of women's responsibility for children 'which exists before the marriage, is carried on in the marriage, and continues afterwards'. For Delphy this responsibility can be defined as the exploitation of women by men and the collective exemption of men from the cost of reproduction.

Births outside marriage

Closely related to the increase in cohabitation has been the rise in extra-marital births which have increased dramatically in many European countries, particularly in the Nordic countries but also in countries like Ireland with formerly low levels (Figure 1.4). The EU (15) level in 1960 was 5.1 per cent of all births which rose to 21.8 per cent in 1993. This masks the considerable variation within the EU from a current level of 2.9 per cent in Greece to 51.6 per cent in Sweden. The rise in births outside marriage, which began in Scandinavian countries, has been followed about a decade later in other northern and western European countries. In France births outside marriage rose from 6.1 per cent in 1960 to 34.9 per cent in 1993; in Ireland from 1.6 per cent in 1960 to 19.7 per cent in 1994. Similarly in the UK the level was 5.2 per cent in 1960 rising to 32.0 per cent in 1994. In contrast, Italy's rate of births outside marriage increased slightly from 2.4 per cent

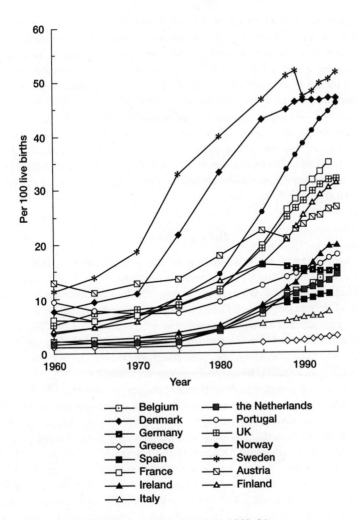

Figure 1.4 Proportion of live births outside marriage 1960–94.
Source: Eurostat (1996a).

and for Greece the figures are 1.2 to 2.9 per cent over the period 1960 to 1994 (Drew 1995a).

Diversity in family/household forms

The differentiation of household types reflects major social, cultural and demographic changes. Along with demographic trends, Schmidt (1992) identifies four factors which have altered household structures, through changes in women's working lives: the decline of conventional security-affording institutions making it necessary for women to become financially independent; new options and dependencies which have shifted the focus of women's lives from neighbour-hood/community towards greater personal autonomy and market consumption; women's identity and self-fulfilment increasingly sought, and obtained, outside the home in the male domain of employment; women's qualifications and career aspirations which enable them to improve their position in the labour market, particularly following the 'feminisation of education' by the 1980s.

This has resulted in an overall growth in women's labour force participation and a corresponding rise in dual-earner households compared with single-earner households. As Brannen's work shows (Chapter 7) this trend masks the divergence which exists between households, as well as the unequal distribution of earnings between and within them.

Lone parenting

Higher divorce rates are contributing to the increase in one-parent families (mainly headed by women). Hoffmann-Nowotny and Fux (1991) state that far from being an abnormal family type, one-parent families have become a wide-spread and permanent way of life for many women, stemming from the break-down of the 'conjugal family' or an alternative consensual union. The dramatic increase in the number of one-parent families where a divorced, or married but separated, mother is the household head has increased by 118 per cent in France between 1968 and 1982 (Hoffmann-Nowotny and Fux 1991).

The highest percentage of lone-parent families[6] within the EU is found in Ireland, where 10.6 per cent of private households consisted of lone-parent families (compromised of 1.8 per cent headed by fathers, compared with 8.8 per cent headed by mothers). Countries with a higher than average proportion of lone parents are: Belgium (9.2 per cent) and the UK (9.0 per cent). Lone parenthood was a less common family form in Sweden (3.9 per cent), Finland (4.1 per cent), Denmark (5.8 per cent) and Greece (6.0 per cent). It is interesting to note that while Greece has a low level of births outside of marriage, its level of lone parenthood is higher than that of Sweden, Finland and Denmark where there are high levels of births outside of marriage.

Part of this apparent paradox is explained by Ermisch (1990) who has pointed to the popular misconception that lone-parent families comprise young unmarried mothers and toddlers. The data for all countries conflict with this and indicate that the majority of lone parents are mothers, of whom the vast majority are divorced or separated, followed by widowed, commonly with older children.

One shift which appears to be well established is towards a greater diversity of family forms, which can be seen clearly in Figure 1.5. This emphasises a far from static model and suggests that during any person's life span they may move from, and/or return to, 'conventional' family forms, via transitional states of separa-tion/divorce, into one-person households, marriage, cohabitation and lone parenting. In examining trends in the data available we find only a 'snapshot'

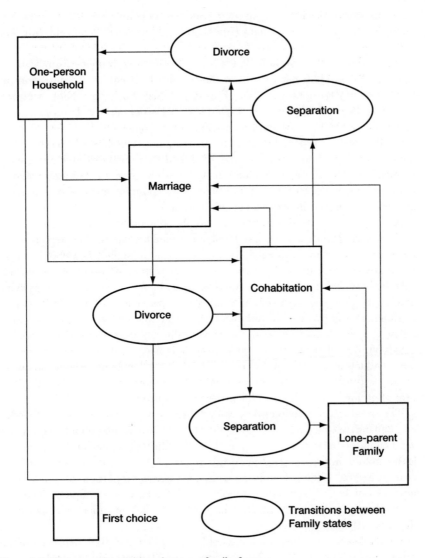

Figure 1.5 Choices and transitions between family forms.
Source: Commission des Communautés Européennes (1992).

picture at any one time. It is likely that with the current rates of demographic and social change, there will be more flow through a greater range of family forms.

Another strong trend which has become established is towards smaller households. In 1960 21.4 per cent of households in the current European Union had five or more family members (Commission des Communautés Européennes 1992). By 1990/91 this had fallen to 9.3 per cent (Eurostat 1995a). In Ireland 26.7 per cent of households had five or more members, followed by Spain with

20.3 and Portugal with 15.4 per cent. Such households were least common in Denmark (4.8 per cent), Germany (5 per cent) and Sweden (5.2 per cent) (Eurostat 1995a).

The rise in one-person households has been similarly dramatic from 15.0 per cent in 1960 to 33.6 per cent of all households by 1990/91 (Commission des Communautés Européennes 1992; Eurostat 1996a). Such households are commonest in Sweden (39.6 per cent), Denmark (34.4 per cent) and Germany with 33.6 per cent in 1990/91, and least common in France (12.1), Spain (13.4 per cent), Portugal (13.8 per cent) and Greece (16.2 per cent) (Eurostat 1996a). This increase in single households may be attributed to a number of factors: greater financial independence, individualism and less recourse to multi-generational family forms, lower fertility, marital breakdown, postponement of childbearing, childlessness, higher life expectancy and widowhood.

Although even official definitions of 'family households' vary (Eurostat 1995a) some patterns can be discerned in family/household structure. The percentage of the population living in 'family', as opposed to 'non-family'[7] households ranges from 83.4 per cent in Portugal and 83.1 per cent in Spain (these would include extended families in which there could be more than one/two generations living in a household) to 60.4 per cent in Sweden, 61.2 per cent in Greece, 61.9 per cent in Denmark and 62 per cent in Finland (Eurostat 1996a). If household structures follow the Nordic pattern, as occurred with diminishing fertility, rising levels of cohabitation and births outside marriage, it is likely that a higher proportion of individuals in the EU will live outside traditional 'family households' in favour of one-person and multi-person households. Lone mothers accounted for 82.5 per cent of all lone-parent households in 1990/91 (Eurostat 1996a).

The trend towards childlessness can be discerned in countries such as Sweden and Finland, in which 32.2 and 30.6 per cent of all private households respectively were composed of couples without children in 1990/91. Such family forms were least common in Ireland (13.7 per cent), Spain (17.9 per cent) and Italy (19.4 per cent) (Eurostat 1996a). Countries with the highest proportion of 'traditional' nuclear families, consisting of couples with children, were: Spain (55.8 per cent), Portugal (49.9 per cent), Ireland (47.9 per cent) and Italy (46.7 per cent) (Eurostat 1996a).

Female-headed one-person households accounted for 16.9 per cent of all private households in 1990/91, compared with 9.8 per cent of male-headed one-person households (Eurostat 1995a). The gender difference holds in all member states, but the gap is widest in the southern countries where it is a less common pattern: in Portugal 4.2 per cent of all households were headed by a man living on his own, compared with 9.7 per cent of households in which a woman lived alone. The gap was also wide in Germany where 21.2 per cent of all households consisted of a woman living alone, compared with 12.4 per cent which had a solitary man. In Sweden and Denmark, the level is closer for men (17.9 and 14.4 per cent respectively) and women (21.7 and 19.9 per cent respectively) (Eurostat 1995a). Part of the divergence between countries may be attributable to the 'choice' factors (e.g. separation/divorce) already mentioned, operating in the northern countries, as distinct from the patterns of widowhood which may account for a more involuntary pattern of lone-person households in the southern countries.

Conclusion

In considering the complexities of demographic change it is important to note that trends have not always been consistent, with the possible exception of a steady decline in mortality rates. Some, like marriage rates, have risen to fall with the same degree of intensity. While it is not possible to extrapolate from current trends, there are some indications that the Nordic countries have tended to be the precursors of more European-wide patterns. Hirdman reminds us (in Chapter 3) that patterns of divergence in family forms emerged in the Nordic countries in the 1960s and 1970s. These were to become familiar in other parts of Europe, though the southern countries have been slowest to shift towards less 'orthodox' family forms. As Papadopoulos shows (in Chapter 4) Greece still maintains a strong adherence to the traditional extended/nuclear and patriarchal family forms. Demographic trends have brought about a degree of convergence to smaller families in all member states, particularly in southern countries such as Italy and Spain, where fertility is declining faster than in the northern countries of Europe.

Household structures are becoming increasingly diverse, in all countries, reflecting the greater degree of choice in lifestyle: to live alone, with a partner or with other individuals; to stay single or marry; to remain in/terminate relationships and subsequently divorce/remarry/cohabit; to forgo/postpone childbearing or have children within/outside marriage or other consensual unions. The consequences of these trends are developed further in Chapter 2 which relates family forms to the allocation of caring responsibilities.

Altered family forms can sometimes exacerbate levels of poverty, particularly for lone parents; individuals who live outside consensual unions and 'no-earner families', and where the state, as in the UK, expects individual 'breadwinners' to provide. This situation is clearly illustrated in Chapter 7. Even within two-parent families, Folbre (1994) has noted that mothers are more likely to be disadvantaged, since they tend to spend a higher percentage of their income on their children. Gains in individual rights, particularly for women to bear children outside wedlock, or having preferential rights in child custody, have to be counterbalanced against the 'growing costs of motherhood' (Folbre 1994: 112). These costs are not purely financial and extend beyond obligations for childcare to elderly and other adult dependants. As Chapter 2 illustrates 'new terms of endearment reproduce, even intensify, some gender inequalities' (Folbre 1994: 113).

Notes

1 Life expectancy is defined as 'the average number of additional years a person would live if current mortality trends were to continue. The expectation of life at birth represents the mean length of life of individuals who are subjected since birth to current mortality trends' (Council of Europe 1996).

2 While the total fertility rate for the former West Germany (FRG) was 1.35 in 1994, the equivalent rate in the former East (GDR) was 0.77.

3 The total fertility rate is 'the average number of children that would be born alive to a woman during her lifetime if she were to pass through her childbearing years conforming to the age-specific fertility rates of a given year' (Council of Europe 1996).

4 The abortion rate represents the number of abortion rate expressed as a percentage of live births.

5 The crude divorce rate represents the number of divorces per 1,000 population.

6 A lone-parent family comprises at least one child resident with one parent only (either father or mother). International comparison is not facilitated by the differing criteria – age limits and marital status – used to define a 'child' (Eurostat 1996a).

7 Family households are defined as households with one family or two or more families; non-family households are defined as one-person or multi-person households.

2

CHANGING FAMILY FORMS AND THE ALLOCATION OF CARING

Eileen Drew

Introduction

As Chapter 1 of this book shows, Europe is facing a wide range of demographic changes which will affect individuals, communities and nations. The shift towards delaying or abandoning marriage, choosing one or no children and living longer all point towards population decline and possible labour shortages in the future. They also raise the issue of dependency aside from the traditional association with child dependants, including a broader mix of children, elderly, incapacitated and disabled dependants. Of major policy concern is that these trends point to a contraction of the financial and physical base which is needed to support dependent groups. However, counter-forces also operate – the increasing labour participation rates of women (which in some Nordic countries are close to those held by men), the desire for a more flexible retirement age to take account of new generations of 'young' elderly, hence active, people and new waves of migrant workers who, in past decades, met the labour shortages in western Europe.

In the debates around falling fertility rates it is often forgotten, or ignored, that women have sought to control their fertility (through infanticide and abortion) long before technology could provide a safe and practical means of avoiding unwanted pregnancies. It is therefore unlikely that fertility rates will rise again appreciably. The consequence of this trend is that more women are available for work, either before and/or after the birth and rearing of their (average) 1–2 children. In previous generations women's working lives had been prescribed by their more demanding reproductive role. This has become increasingly irrelevant with lower rates of fertility, which are decreasing fastest in precisely those countries in which female labour participation rates have been lowest: Italy, Ireland, Spain and Greece.

However, fertility decline does not in itself promote gender equality, within the family or labour market, since for women the ability to participate in the labour market, and as full citizens, depends upon the distribution of home-based and community-based, mainly unpaid caring work (Drew 1995b). According to

Humphries and Rubery (1995: 22) 'Men and women will never be able to compete on equal terms in the labour market so long as women continue to bear most of the responsibilities for childcare, housework and other caring work within the family.' The arena of the uneven playing field which persists throughout European labour markets is explored further in Chapter 8.

The lag between fertility decline and equal opportunity in employment may be attributable to the different 'gender contracts' (see Chapter 3) operating in different member states which influence state policies on taxation, childcare and equal opportunities. 'Familistic' gender regimes presuppose the existence of a home-based dependent wife who is responsible for home-making, childrearing and care of other family members. State intervention is minimal, 'the family will provide' and men's role is one of providing financial support in 'caring for' family members. This 'familistic' model, as exemplified by Ireland and Greece but also prevalent in Sweden up to the 1970s, is one in which the breadwinner/housewife nuclear family form is dominant. Such a 'familistic' gender regime clearly restricts women's ability to compete on equal terms with men in the labour market.

In contrast, other states such as Sweden and Denmark have evolved gender regimes in which individuals are treated equally. In those countries exhibiting 'individualistic' gender regimes, women are not assumed to be financially dependent upon men, and the state reinforces this in its taxation policy, parental leave and provision of child/eldercare. In gender contract terms these would be viewed as supporting 'dual-income families' and an 'equality contract'.

This chapter explores the fundamental division of labour within the household in terms of women's responsibility for childcare and elder/adult care. The term 'household' is used in Walby's (1990) sense, as a site of production relations, a patriarchal structure in which women's labour is appropriated. The chapter illustrates that though demographic change has extended women's lives (more so than men's) and reduced the period of time for childrearing, care of the aged and infirm could become a more extensive part of the familial productive processes (Drew 1995a). Changes in fertility and life expectancy do not lead automatically to altered divisions of labour. According to Frankenberg (1991: 119), 'the nature of social interaction changes when individuals or groups decide to change it, and set about doing so, overcoming the opposition of other individuals and groups'. Experience in the Nordic countries, particularly as Hirdman (Chapter 3) shows in Sweden, bears this out, and illustrates that changes in the prevailing 'gender contract' are unlikely to occur without the support of women as agents of change, working with other groups to secure equality for women and men.

The allocation of caring responsibilities

While referring directly to the historical contribution of women's labour, Gittins makes a key point relevant to patriarchal relations today:

Work did not bring women independence from patriarchal authority, even if in some circumstances it brought them relative economic independence. Whatever the individual circumstances . . . [women] never had access to the equivalent 'work identity' as men. They were always expected to provide services for men.

(Gittins 1993: 38)

The current delivery of such 'services' extends beyond male recipients to an array of domestic and caring responsibilities. Jensen illustrates, from a Norwegian perspective, her hypothesis that:

we have experienced a strengthening of *female* responsibility for childcare even though that of *mothers* has waned. Moreover it is argued that partly because childcare *has* remained a female responsibility, there has been a slow societal response to the new demographic and social situation.

(Jensen 1989: 112)

At a more theoretical level Tronto (1993) has identified the four analytically separate, but interconnected, phases of caring which are important in seeing 'caring' as a gendered process:

Caring About involves the recognition in the first place that care is necessary;
Taking Care Of means assuming some responsibility for the identified need, determining how to respond to it;
Caregiving involves the direct meeting of needs for care;
Care-receiving provides the only way to know that caring needs have actually been met.

Ungerson (1983) distinguishes between 'caring *about*' and 'caring *for*' as having very different meanings, in terms of their basis and the implications for the caregiver and cared-for. Caring *about* someone in the sense of feeling affection for them is based on spontaneous feelings of affinity, and as an emotion *per se* it has little implication for how people spend their time, except that they might want to spend it together. On the other hand, caring *for* someone, in the sense of servicing their needs, may have little or nothing to do with caring about someone, i.e. it may be paid for or given due to compassion or because it is expected due to kinship links. Caring *for* 'comprises such things as feeding, washing, lifting, protecting, representing and comforting' (Ungerson 1983: 31) and equates with Tronto's sense of caregiving.

Taking care of is, in contrast, more associated with public roles and with men rather than women, usually inferring the notion that by 'working at his job, a man is taking care of his family' (Tronto 1993: 115). This association with masculinity reinforces the gender, race and class associations of care. 'Women and people of

29

colour have very little to take care of, they care about private and local concerns' (Tronto 1993: 115). To recognise the value of care calls into question the structure of values in our society.

Tronto shows that care was mainly the work of slaves, servants and women throughout Western history, with the largest tasks of caring for children, the infirm and elderly almost exclusively relegated to women (Tronto 1993). Ironically, when care is so crucial to the functioning of society, a vicious circle operates in which care is devalued and the people who do caring work are devalued. Caring about, and taking care of, are the duties of the powerful while care-giving and care-receiving are left to the less powerful (Tronto 1993).

Eldercare

Caring for the elderly (and people with a disability) is associated with the home and family, in contrast to the social relations which operate in the labour market, which all too frequently engender a degree of social distance incompatible with the giving of care. The exceptions are in occupations with a 'woman's touch' built into the 'caring professions', which are largely female, and an extension of women's housekeeping function to society at large (Graham 1983: 16). The testimony of caregivers further illustrates that 'caring is experienced as a labour of love in which the labour must continue even where the love falters' (Graham 1983: 16). All too readily 'Caring . . . tends to be defined as an act of female sacrifice and supreme selflessness' (Graham 1983: 17). Not surprisingly then:

> woman's paid work is often the market equivalent of her unpaid work at home. The growth of services sector employment has involved the transfer of many of the more highly specialised aspects of caring from the home, with the result that in secretarial and clerical work, in nursing, teaching and social work, the woman finds again herself always in response to others – an unending unspecific task of helping, nurturing, educating, supporting.
>
> (Graham 1983: 27)

Ungerson (1983: 35) states that in relation to women's labour market behaviour 'the limit to the *hours* they actually work is imposed by a set of beliefs that they have about what they really *ought* to be doing for the good of their families back home'. She points to the continuing fact that since opportunity costs are lower for women than men to stay at home, the breadwinner/housewife model predominates and women's labour market activity is more likely to be in low-waged part-time employment. Hence women's role is reinforced by powerful material (opportunity cost) and ideological (women's place) forces.

Altered demographic conditions will inevitably have a political dimension as well as socio-economic consequences, not least in state responses to the allocation of responsibility for caring. Waerness (1989: 217) has noted that 'as a consequence of the division of labour between the sexes, the expectations of care and service and the responsibility for the physical and emotional well-being of the family members, are laid mainly on the female members of the family'. Caring has frequently been seen as an extension of a woman's 'domestic' responsibilities, even when the person in need of care is not a direct blood relative (e.g. in the case of a step-child, parent-in-law, partner's sibling).

The exception to this gendered pattern of eldercare occurs when women are cared for by a male spouse. Even then, inequalities exist since women live longer than men, and tend to marry partners who are some years older. Men have higher rates of remarriage, usually to even younger female partners. As a result, nearly three-quarters of elderly men in the UK, but only two-fifths of elderly women, were married in 1985 (Arber and Ginn 1992). Furthermore, disability is strongly gender differentiated, due to the greater longevity of women and the fact that women are not only more likely to become disabled than men, but the gender differential increases with age (Arber and Ginn 1992). Commenting on men's advantage in terms of health and caring resources, compared with women, Arber and Ginn noted that disabled elderly women were more likely than men to be perceived, and to perceive themselves, 'as a burden simply because they are more likely to live alone or in the home of an adult child . . . . The limited access of older women to both financial and caring resources is a poor deal for the "carer sex" after a lifetime of unpaid work looking after children, husband and others, often in addition to waged work' (Arber and Ginn 1992: 105).

Childcare

'The issue of whether women work because they have few children, or the inverse, remains unresolved . . . most research indicates there is a conflict for women between their paid labour force participation and having more children' (Jensen 1989: 115). In Norway it has been demonstrated that among women who have been economically active without interruption for the birth of their first child, the probability of giving birth to a second child is reduced by 40 per cent, compared with women who interrupted their employment. Jensen expresses concern about the strengthening of women's relationships with their children since:

> almost without exception, [the child(ren)] will be taken care of by women, either their own mothers or women who get paid for the work. Due to the feminisation of public sector healthcare, children will come across female dentists, doctors and social workers. Importantly, the teaching during a child's first years at school has increasingly become a *female* profession.
>
> (Jensen 1989: 119)

Even the availability of state supports such as family allowances and maternity leave provide 'benefits to mothers who refrain from paid employment in order to care for children, but not to fathers' (Folbre 1994: 161). The financial costs to women who make such choices are considerable. Folbre (1994) claims that a West German mother sacrificed 49 per cent of her lifetime earnings, through embarking upon the employment and earnings path (lost years of employment, lower hours on return to labour market and lower rates of pay) typically associated with caring in a two-child family. A British mother was likely to sacrifice 57 per cent. In France and Sweden, due to public investments in childcare facilities, the estimates were 12 per cent and 6 per cent respectively (Folbre 1994).

However even in the state subsidised childcare system of France, virtually all its employees are women, and men are not encouraged to take a more active role in childcare. As Fagnani shows in Chapter 5, recent changes in French law, will further discourage mothers from remaining in employment after the birth of a second child.

Even in households where both parents are employed full time, Brannen (1991) demonstrates that this does not necessarily lead to greater equality in employment or domestic life. Reasons for this are: women's earnings are used for immediate or secondary priorities, unlike men's; expectations in marriage are based on ideas of romantic love, togetherness and emotional sharing rather than material equality and due to the 'gendered construction of parenthood and the powerful influences upon the construction of parenthood' (Brannen 1991: 59). The behavioural and ideological practices of individual parents reflect a wider arena than the immediate household and are affected by what Hirdman (Chapter 3) refers to as the prevailing 'gender contract'. In the UK, the gender contract was influenced strongly by the Bowlby discourse which required mothers to devote themselves to their child(ren)'s development. This is formulated on the concepts of a male breadwinner and the centrality and exclusivity of the mother/child relationship (Brannen 1991).

Caring for young children in modern industrialised societies is demonstrably a woman's role and for some researchers this has created an 'image in the minds of both men and women of "mothers" as immensely powerful, able to give and able to withdraw warmth and closeness and food' (Ve 1989: 254). This is purported to have negative consequences for male and female offspring and implies that fathers should share more in the nurture of small children. For this to occur there need to be changes in parental rights, a trend which is only beginning to emerge in European member states, though better established in Nordic countries.

Hopflinger (1991: 310) has claimed that within European families 'there are two main obstacles to an egalitarian division of domestic labour: children and attitudes toward man's role as breadwinner'. This asymmetry in personal relations underpins Waerness's (1989: 244) claim that:

> to put it in a somewhat exaggerated form: the public care system in most European societies has *mainly* been designed supposing the male worker in his best years with no responsibility for household work and caring for dependent members in the family. It has also presumed a

female service provider, a person both able to provide family care and services and to relate to the services provided by the state and the market.

Jensen (1989: 120) refers to 'new roles for men' to facilitate the emotional strengthening of ties between fathers and their children. Empirical time budget study results suggest that fathers have increased their participation in childcare and that a higher percentage of fathers overall participate in such activities (a rise from 51 per cent to 70 per cent). Chapters 18 and 19 of this book pursue this theme to establish the degree to which men have adopted more active and positive roles in parenting. Folbre (1994: 119) states that: 'As long as male individualism is counterbalanced by female altruism, as long as rational economic man is taken care of by irrational altruistic woman, families play a particularly important (and unfair) role.'

Yet these imbalances may not be sustainable, given the rate of demographic change and the emergence of more complex and inherently less stable family forms than the classic 'nuclear family'. The reliance on women's unpaid labour will also be undermined by initiatives to promote women's advancement by positive actions and the enforcement of equal opportunities policies. As women's earning power increases and sex-roles are further questioned, women may no longer be willing to waive these opportunities and take on their traditional 'caring role' within the family. Another factor which influences female labour force participation is that of education. As Callan and Farrell (1991) have shown, the greater the investment in education by women the stronger their attachment to the labour force will be. It has been demonstrated within the EU that 'the better educated women are, the more they are economically active', and this has contributed to the breakthroughs made by women in the labour markets of Europe (Maruani 1992). The finding is reinforced by Brannen in relation to the UK, as seen in Chapter 7.

As European data show, there is a class dimension to women's labour market participation. Highly educated women have continuous careers, not interrupted by the births of their children, whereas women with few educational advantages are forced off the labour market by the 'poverty trap' in which the individual sees no pecuniary advantage to (re)enter the labour market or extend their working hours since net income would remain the same or, in some instances, decline. This situation most commonly arises when women are faced with caring responsibilities and is addressed in Chapter 7.

EU policy welcomes initiatives to create new employment opportunities, such as in 'domestic work or the caring industry' (Commission of the European Communities 1993a: 29), without referring to the already sex-segregated nature of domestic and cleaning work and caring work in health and social care, education and catering. Yet whether 'caring' occurs within the labour market for remuneration, or unpaid within the home, it is work which, to date, remains ascribed on the basis of sex. Consequently it is women who experience most acutely the conflicting demands from paid employment and caring activities which may extend beyond children to other family members. Hence the need, in the interests of society as a whole, for working life and family life to be more mutually reinforcing, a theme which is examined in Part III of this book.

The issue of 'sharing the caring' must be addressed, since as Briggs and Oliver have commented:

> If the situation seems bleak now, how much more so will it be when the full effects of changing policies and a diminishing ratio of carers to dependants are felt? At the turn of the century, there were seventeen women relatives to every person over the age of sixty five. There are now fewer than three to every elderly person . . . Caring is now out of the closet. Let us give it a good airing, shake it around a little and see if the garment can be adapted so that it actually fits those who take it on or have it thrust upon their shoulders.
>
> (Briggs and Oliver 1985: 121)

Hopflinger (1991: 310) has observed that:

> while the development towards greater equality is a slow process, there are some indications that role sharing will become more widespread in the future. Younger Swedish couples are markedly more egalitarian than older ones, even when education and family life-cycle were controlled for.

It will be important to observe whether this tendency (a) is a long-term trend, (b) extends to all forms of caring and (c) is being adopted in other European states. A less optimistic picture is painted by Davidoff:

> Despite some public shifts in attitudes, it is still women who are seen today as basically responsible for servicing members of the family, protecting them from the pollution of dirt, waste products and untidiness, for transforming the raw into the cooked; and for transforming 'little savages' into civilised adults. In the vast majority of cases it is women (particularly mothers, but also the women responsible for the elderly and chronic sick) who peel the potatoes, wash, sort and put away the socks, mop up the vomit, change the nappies and the sheets. These activities are still performed for love (and support).
>
> (Davidoff 1991: 91)

Two alternative scenarios are outlined by Folbre (1994). In the first, women have the same rights as men, but class and race inequalities remain. In the second, men have the same responsibilities as women, across class and race lines. In the first scenario, women's full-time labour force participation rates reach those of men.

Former 'women's work', such as teaching and childcare, is performed by men and women from disadvantaged groups who would work for a minimal wage to provide institutional and home-based care of children, the sick and elderly. In Folbre's second scenario:

> men would substantially increase their hours of unpaid work, devoting more time to home, children, and community. Their formal labour force participation rate would decline to levels more typical of women today. Forms of work that women once specialized in, such as child care and teaching, would be re-valued.
>
> (Folbre 1994)

Only the second scenario assigns responsibility for family and household-based work equally to men and women. Folbre recognises that the latter scenario would be more difficult to achieve 'because it would require more sustained collective effort and coordination' (Folbre 1994: 103).

3

STATE POLICY AND GENDER CONTRACTS

The Swedish experience

Yvonne Hirdman

Introduction

In this chapter a gender analysis is used to illustrate the history of the Swedish welfare state.[1] The use of the concept 'gender', as in 'gender system', helps us to examine the relations between the welfare state and women; relations hidden behind concepts of 'social policy', 'family', 'population question' and even behind the word 'women' itself. In contrast to 'women', 'gender' implies power and the relations between the sexes, and helps us to reformulate the so called problem of women and society. It is a reformulation that enables us, for example, to put on the agenda and into the spotlight the second gender, man, and turn him into the problem.

The gender conflict

A gender system should not be read as if it is a functional, deterministic box operating in society, but rather as two consistent patterns, clearly distinguishable historically as well as geographically. Looked upon from above, as if society were a map, these patterns can easily be followed: one is that of the segregation of the sexes, the other, just as clear, is the male norm. The interdependence of the two patterns acts as the motor for the gender system, although its form and content varies.

These patterns, although historically changeable and different in content, were threatened in a fundamental way by modernisation. A structural disharmony, a *de facto* gender conflict, became the unintended result of the operation of the main modern 'institutions', democracy and capitalism. These contained the one ingredient that would develop the conflict: namely, a potential for integration which challenged the gender order built upon gender segregation. By threatening or questioning segregation, they also undermined the male norm of society: democracy by stating the irrevocable notion of 'equal value' of human beings, regardless of race, colour and sex; and capitalism by its greedy logic of choosing the cheapest labour force, women. The potential for integration as well as its achievement in politics or the labour market, were what created and expanded the gender conflict as it clashed against a segregating gender order/regime. The more women are integrated into society, the more conflict-ridden the relationship between the sexes becomes, as this relationship *de facto* is built upon the primacy of man. This conflict was and is accepted as a social dilemma when described as the 'Woman Question'; that is when looked upon from the male position.

From this androcentric level, women seemed to be a problem either as 'similar' and hence equals or as 'different', either in the field of production or reproduction. The conflict of similarities occurs whenever women enter (or there is a threat of them entering) male-dominated areas, like parts of the labour market and the sphere of politics. The conflict of similarities rapidly entered the agenda in modern states, as early as the last century and forced politicians to deal with delicate questions such as: should women have the vote? Which areas of work were 'proper' for women? Should women, especially married women, be permitted to work at all? Should the education system be open to girls as well? and so on. Who were they to claim these rights – equals?

The conflict of dissimilarities had another form in which women's sexuality and procreative ability, the real sex difference, created its *raison d'être*. The 'dysfunctional' effects of modern society on sexual mores, family life and work and fertility rates were not, in the beginning, supposed to be political questions at all. Yet, it is in this area that the rationale of modern welfare states operates. Slowly the question of state responsibility for the inhabitants of the country began to form a political demand within liberal and socialist parties until it became the core of a welfare state.[2]

The gender contract

The questions which became more and more demanding as a symptom of the expanding gender conflict, thus had to be dealt with. One way to discuss the solutions at a theoretical level is to speak in terms of 'gender contracts', to focus on the very concrete, and often very explicit aspects of the human drama in the gender-creating process, which might otherwise be viewed as something too impersonally structural. The objective is also to highlight the explicit negotiations that were being conducted about the place of women in modern society, and implicitly also those of men. It will help to 'deconstruct' the subtext of gender within various political reforms, norms, statements and not only those about women, but also the so-called gender-neutral laws and reforms where 'man' is the self-evident leading character.

Women as agents seldom took part in these negotiations. The conductors of a new gender contract on this level were men: representing the state and the labour market.[3] Thus the main character of the partners in the modern gender contracts could be said to be the state on the one hand and the abstract collective 'women' on the other. What happened, and what will be made more explicit in the discussion below, was that 'men' disappeared as the counterpart of women in the contract.

Another important point is that the various solutions to the conflict had a dramatic impact on the shaping of modern society. In a schematic way we can say that the solutions take two forms. The first could be called limited integration, i.e. a certain degree of space was made for certain women, preferably unmarried women (the 'little men'). The second was a modernised form of segregation, which could take many forms: either that of a modernised private sphere or that of a newly founded female social or political public sphere.

Whether the solution involved limited integration or a new kind of segregation, both attempts to allow women's entry into society clearly led to society's expansion and political growth. Above all, modern segregation was a means of creating new social 'rooms', public space and political avenues. If we look at it from this perspective we can see that the gender conflict actively contributed not only to the shaping of a new, more legitimate gender system, but also to the formation of the welfare state.

The Swedish Social Democratic state and the gender conflict

Applying this set of concepts to the historical development of the Swedish welfare state facilitates a new content of history, with a new chronology. Two kinds of gender contracts can be distinguished, one between the years of 1930–60 and one from the 1960s.

The household contract: Sweden 1930–60

In 1932 the Social Democratic Party won the election and the long era of social democracy started. Within the labour movement, a strong traditional gender ideology operated, creating tensions for example in the labour market, where many 'radical' socialists demanded a prohibition on married women working.

The ideology of 'man the breadwinner' and 'woman the housewife and mother' was strong, especially within trade unions. Against this conservative, bourgeoisie-imitating gender contract ideology however, a forceful, and partly successful, counter-ideology operated. It consisted of two groups: radical theoretical Marxists, for whom the questions of 'reproduction' were to be solved within the framework of production. Household and childcare were to be socialised in some form. More pragmatic politicians sought a solution in the same area but from a more scientific position and with more political will. They could be labelled 'social engineers' who came mostly from the new strata of intellectuals, architects, social researchers and economists, who joined the Social Democratic Party in the early 1930s. The ideal-types were Gunnar and Alva Myrdal, economist and sociologist.[4]

The social engineers looked upon society as a well-oiled machine which should be governed by the principles of rational positivism, science, technology and that indefinable something which was called 'the modern'. In my opinion, their intellectual heritage was more utopian than Marxist, which meant that the strong, separating dichotomies of production and reproduction did not have a powerful hold over their minds. Like the utopian philosophers, they tended to treat the two as a package. By doing this they re-formulated the political agenda in Sweden and gave the new social policy a huge place on it.

They articulated the gender conflict as a question of de-population. Shortage of people, and the fear of under-population, cleverly used by Alva and Gunnar Myrdal, created a new climate for modern social policy and broadened the arena of state intervention. As part of a radical 'prophylactic social policy' the solution was to persuade people to legalise their sexual relations within the framework of marriage and to have at least four children. The family as a unit would then receive economic and practical assistance in the form of housing, rent subsidies and child allowances. However, the family unit was then subdivided and the woman was earmarked for special social aid, not only as 'different', in the form of paediatric centres, ante-natal clinics, assistance in delivery and maternity compensation, but also as 'similar' in the form of day-care centres, large nurseries and other social services designed to make it possible for a mother to work outside the home, despite the fact that she had children.

The feminism within social engineering was quite noticeable as the objective was to speed up and facilitate the process of women's social integration and, with the help of an active governmental policy, to remove the obstacles in its way. Social policies, according to their conception, meant an imaginative way of solving not only the 'problem with women' but also the economic problem, thus by an expansion of social reforms and a 'prophylactic social policy', the stagnant economy would start to work again, and on a higher level. The satisfaction of so called 'social needs' (defined and cultivated by experts) was the formula for this Keynesian New Economy.

With this new formulation of the problem women certainly came to the centre of the political stage: as producers of children (who were in short supply in the nation); as consumers of the various utilities that a modern life and a new economic policy required; and finally as foster mothers of new human beings in line with a modern, socially developed and technically adjusted society.

The new articulation: the family policy issue

Even though the whole concept, including the full integration of women in society, was not adopted in the actual social politics that followed, important reforms inspired by social engineering were introduced: free school lunches for children, newly built apartments designed for the rationalisation of housework and reforms that made a working mother's everyday life more manageable.

The old household gender contract survived though in a modern, rationalised *form*, which meant that the welfare policies of Sweden, in the period between 1940 and 1960 were still modelled around a housewife – modern, professionalised, educated in rational housework – and a man – the breadwinner. By taking this new form, old meanings of gender were able to survive through a radical socio-political programme aimed at resolving the 'issue', now defined as the family policy. It was in this political context that women could now take part, to a larger extent, as participants. And it was at this point that a 'semi-integrative' solution to the problem of women's proper place in society was formulated – by women.

Women's dual role

During the late 1940s and 1950s the formula of 'women's dual role' was presented as a solution to the gender conflict.[5] Women were to play a similar human role as workers – before marriage and after the first years of childbirth and childcare – and the different female role at home in between. At the level of political reforms, the conflict of dissimilarities dominated both the articulations of, and the solutions to, the gender conflict. The child allowances that mothers began to receive in 1948 could be seen as a modern form of 'pin money' (still of great importance to women, as pin money often is), paid out by a signatory of the gender contract that was becoming increasingly more important, the state. Joint taxation drove home the message that women were part of households and that work outside the home was undesirable though not prohibited by law. Employment was also made difficult for mothers with small children as childcare was non-existent. In Sweden the total number of places in various institutions (many of them remnants of poverty assistance for single mothers) was about 20,000 in the 1950s.

Not much, however, was said about the conflict of similarity. None the less, there was an increase in the number of women working outside the home. From 1950 to 1965 the number of married working women increased from 15.6 per cent to 36.7 per cent[6] and the demand for a female workforce was intense as the Swedish economy was growing. Women were thus in a good negotiating position as the state wanted children and industry wanted labour. The obvious demands put forward by women should have been for day-care centres and for conditions at work to make the situation of a 'working mother' possible. Research has yet to be done to determine how women attempted to exploit this situation.[7] The result, however, corresponded well with the explicit divisions of the dual-role theory giving women a kind of half-person status both in the labour market and in the political life.[8] This 'half' status (which also created a widening gap between housewives and 'working housewives') illustrates the strenuous tension between integration and segregation in the gender conflict during the 1950s.

The individualistic gender contract 1960–90

The equality contract 1960–75

In the 1960s, dramatic changes took place in Sweden. A new normative, gender contract was formulated stating the individuality of men and women, in the family as well as in society, followed by an expanded state policy to make it possible. The radical ideas of the 1930s thus returned. In 1969 a labour movement committee on equality issues adopted the following important statement of principle: 'Thus there are strong reasons for making the two-income family the standard in the planning of long-term changes in social insurance.'

A bustling decade lay behind this statement during which the growing gender conflict had begun to be politically exploited by both Liberals and Social Demo-crats. This political exploitation can be seen as an expression of the gender conflict's expanding character. Democratic logic was playing an increasing role, leading to the post-war developments within the education system, which was reorganised and improved, based on the concept of a gender-neutral person. Economic integration of women continued, in spite of the difficulties for 'working mothers' in making ends meet in private life.

In 1972 the new articulation of the gender conflict reached its peak when the Social Democratic women published their new platform: 'The Family in the Future, a Socialist Family Policy', containing the plan for a completely new society which would be based on a 6-hour work day and which would give men and women equal rights and obligations in the areas of paid work, housework and childcare. The Social Democratic women now dissociated themselves from the 'freedom of choice' (for women only) doctrine which was built on the imperative of women's dual role.[9]

The Social Democratic Party Congress was held in the same year, with equality for women as an item on the agenda. Olof Palme vigorously argued that equality between the sexes had to be grounded in the labour market and that women's right to employment had to be underscored. Society would have to be shaped by this concept of equality. This would require more day-care facilities, an expansion of social services, a broader plan for solidarity between the sexes in the building of society and the introduction of a 6-hour work day.[10]

This truly dramatic change in gender ideology (if problematised at all) has in later analysis been elucidated through a perspective of historical materialism in which ideologies and ideas are reflections of economic need: the economic boom created the need for a female workforce, and consequently a change in ideology took place. This kind of explanation effectively diminishes the political will and logic behind these gender-events. It also neglects the fact that the societal change, which had begun, was instead shaping the new needs. The 'dissatisfaction of raised expectations', referred to by Prime Minister Tage Erlander in the 1950s was now beginning to satisfy itself and it provided the engine which powered the development of the second phase of the welfare state.

Women as political possibilities

There is reason to believe that the new articulation of the gender conflict was an important factor in the change in Social Democratic ideology during the 1960s in the development of a larger, more powerful state where the explicit gratification of needs was the *raison d'être* of policy. Taking seriously the idea of women as members of society on the same level as men, expanded the need-structure enormously, creating new possibilities. Society which had seemed to be all fixed and ready built (a metaphor in line with Social Democratic thinking) now had to be reorganised and rebuilt.

In the formulation and articulation of these needs, which undoubtedly legitimised the further development of the strong state, women once again played a significant role. What had formerly been, for the most part, a conflict of 'dissimilarities' (placed within a segregated gender context) was now a conflict of both 'similarities' and 'dissimilarities' (placed within an integrated gender context) which created political needs and new possibilities. We can see this politicisation of the conflict in the shift from a Liberal gender discourse, wherein the relationship between man and woman was the dominating factor, to a Social Democratic gender discourse in which the man virtually disappeared, and once again the woman and the state were the new principals of the gender contract.

One reason for the strong political articulation of the gender conflict was that this conflict was written into the era's heated discourse on equality. In this way the equality discourse, whose principals were really labour and capital, received a new player as women became a part of the labour category.

The new social gender contract which was drafted during this period was therefore based on two primary participants: the woman, who was released to do work outside the home, and the state, which provided aid, mainly in the form of day-care centres; a tax reform which did away with joint taxation in 1971; and a parental leave insurance in 1974, based on the model of male insurance in the labour market, which meant receiving 90 per cent of usual income for the first 6 months, later 12 months, to be at home with a child and a guarantee of being able to return to employment. Women's link with the employment market, by this gender-neutral reform, was not only threatened by childbearing, rather it was reinforced by this legislation.

Consequences

The number of women participating in the labour market increased from 1.6 million in 1970 to 2.1 million in 1990, or from 53 per cent in 1963 to 86 per cent in 1990, indicating that these political reforms played a major role. Behind the proportionally high figures lay however a new, modern form of segregation. The labour market had become stratified so that women's new right to employment in practice meant that a special place had to be created for women to occupy. A new form of female subordination had been formed whereby over 1 million women are engaged in part-time employment working in low-paid occupations within the public sector. The new order had brought about the creation of new strata in the labour market, not only between men and women, but also between women. Still women reacted positively to the new gender contract which allowed them the possibility to have both children (not necessarily within wedlock any longer) and a job. As Chapter 1 shows, Sweden's fertility rate has become one of the highest in Europe.

Entering the labour market, albeit a segmented one, also meant becoming citizens. Female representation in parliament, as well as in local and regional government, increased at a rate proportional to that of women's labour market participation. From roughly 10 per cent in 1950, female representation in national, regional and local elected bodies is now around 40 per cent. At the same time, politics too is becoming stratified and hierarchical with female politicians mainly responsible for the 'soft,' 'reparative' areas of policy.[11]

Thus, from the experiences of the past two decades, we can seriously begin to study how the gender logic or pattern of segregation is constructed in modern democratic societies. There seems to be an almost structural way of avoiding the gender conflict exploding, by opening up new areas.

The 'equal status contract'

One way of illustrating this process, is to point to the shift from 'equal' to equal status which makes it reasonable to call the period since the late 1970s the era of the equal status contract.[12] Behind that label we can distinguish how the gender conflict has been institutionalised, given its own political territory consisting of a normative as well as a legislative level, mainly conducted by women. The gender contract is now negotiated by people, mostly women, who are in some way responsible for creating 'equal status' within companies, trade unions, political parties, even within government. This way of dealing with the conflict sets the agenda and governs the solutions and the rhetoric.

The rationale of 'equal status' rests upon an equal opportunity ideology openly stating that men and women should share not only the same opportunities but also the same responsibilities and duties. Here, the conflict of similarities is stressed as if it is a simple matter of dividing and sharing equally. The false simplicity of this rhetoric is however revealed when women, usually, in unions, political parties, companies, etc. are trying to implement the agreed programmes of equal status. Sharing equality often means conflict and one way of avoiding conflict is to stress the supplementary, and hence difference. The term 'equal status' has this potential as the very image embodied by the term, of standing beside, 'the other', the 'different', signifies a harmonious complement. The corporate character that the institutionalisation of the equal status territory brought with it has also directed both talk and actions toward an emphasis of dissimilarity and difference, since it has been regarded as an area of special interest to women. Thus the implicit meaning of the concept, as well as its institutionalised form, turned the articulation of the gender conflict into that of dissimilarities within a segregating context. This is a concrete way of showing just how a segregating process is put into action. The danger with this second interpretation of equal status for the emancipation of women lies in the new legitimation that will be given for a 'post modern' gender segregation as many women are the architects behind new meanings of gender differences.

The paradox

The politically useful solutions to the gender conflict have made a powerful contribution both to the expansion of the Swedish welfare state and to the conflict itself. The very mechanisms within the solutions have undeniably emerged from masculine norms which were based on the assumption that women would never actually demand real social and economic justice, while the solutions themselves provided women with the incentive to make just these demands, by granting them more social and economic equity.

One way of solving this paradox has been to create new 'rooms', new 'space', through expansion. This solution fitted very well the expansive welfare ideology of the labour movement, reformulated in the 1960s. Thus it is true to talk about women as means in the creation of the 'strong society', as the integration of women into society was achieved within the expanding public sector. The gender conflict in the Swedish context was thus built into the political welfare system in a symbiotic way. The political response has transformed it into a fundamental self-propelling logic within the welfare system, a logic threatened by the dramatic events of the 1990s.

From political possibilities to economic problems?

In 1991 the Social Democrats lost electoral power and a bourgeois coalition, led by the right-wing party-leader Carl Bild, governed the country until the 1994 elections. Over these three years, when female participation in the parliament shrank from 38 per cent to 31 per cent, when economic policy halted expanding social democratic policies, when the Swedish crown was defended beyond reason in 1991 and the state deficit grew to unforeseen highs and unemployment also became a Swedish problem, ideological attempts were made to re-negotiate the gender contract of the previous thirty years.

In political praxis, the demand for a two-income norm was no longer unyielding. On the contrary, in some political circles, it was looked upon as both expensive and ideologically questionable. Thus the Christian Democratic Party and the Centre Party did succeed in bringing forward a reform, a so-called childcare allowance which is both 'equal', i.e. equally (low) for everyone, in accordance with the old charity model and completely separated from the labour market. The ideological attacks on the public sector, portrayed as the sick man in the Swedish economy and the scapegoat for worsening economic conditions, were easily read as attacks on millions of women's jobs. In that articulation of the gender conflict women lost their bargaining position as agents of potential, even as agents of utility, and ended up in a defensive position.

Female discontent very clearly lay behind the election in 1994 when the Social Democrats regained power. Threats from a feminist network named the Supportive Stockings (Stöd Strumporna) to create a Women's Party helped to re-fuel the equal status debate. The feminist analysis of power and subordination moved into the political discourse. Of those elected, 41 per cent were women and the government provided a good example in practising equal status by allocating an almost equal distribution of governmental positions between the sexes.

Still, female discontent has not ended. The policies of the new government were and continue to be directed towards the EU and after a referendum when the Swedes voted 'Yes' (many women belonged to the no-voters) with a very weak majority, the Swedish government is working hard to fulfil the Maastricht conditions for full EMU membership. The hostility towards the public sector from the Bild government years has diminished, but demands for policies to cut public sector costs have heightened, as in the rest of Europe. Unemployment amongst women is now higher than for men and opportunities for women's employment in other sectors are not promising.

The situation today from a gender contract point of view is a split one. On the one hand, the equal status contract is reinforced. For example, the childcare allowance, with its implicit inducement to create new housewives in Sweden, has been annulled. Women's lower wages have begun to be seriously questioned. On the other hand, there is a rather dark economic situation with unemployment and low or no growth, in a political situation where an autonomous political economy may not be possible any more.

Returning to the theoretical framework, the gender conflict is more explicitly articulated than ever, and certainly is on the agenda. The simplistic stress, however, on the conflict of similarities, embedded in a discourse of equality, has vanished. Tendencies to articulate the gender conflict as a conflict of dissimilarities within a segregating context are quite common, as there seems to be a need for a more conservative gender system in a society with a rather uncertain future.

In between we have Swedish women who, in spite of the segregating tendencies, are integrated in society in various ways and in their new positions are becoming increasingly legitimated as problematists, coming forward with new demands and even defining the social problems, instead of simply being defined as the 'social problem'[13] themselves.

To end optimistically then, at present the most powerful integration rationale appears to exist in the everyday actions of individuals, each of which is a consequence of solutions to the gender conflict that have arisen in recent decades. These solutions have shaped both theories and practice, which together have engendered a new and natural willingness among women (and men?) to be participants in society. Thus, it could well be said that we are witness to an historic situation; never before in Swedish history have the actions of women been as decisive as they are now.

Notes

1 For a more detailed version see Hirdman (1990a, 1994b).
2 In the early utopian thinking the everyday, or intimate aspects of life were active parts in the planning of a new society, see Hirdman (1992).
3 To be able to discuss their own position was of course the main question in the feminist movement(s).
4 For the history of the 1930s, see Hirdman (1992, 1994a)
5 See Myrdal and Klein (1956).
6 These figures should be taken with considerable scepticism as they are constructed by taking the male worker as the norm. Other forms of counting women in the labour market in those days show that women, including married women, did various kinds of paid work to a larger extent, some mention the figure of 30 per cent participation already in the 1930s, see Nyberg (1989).
7 A research project on 'The Trade Union (LO) and Women 1945–1980' is currently being undertaken at Stockholm University, Department of History under Yvonne Hirdman.
8 In the 1920s and 1930s the number of female representatives in the government was about 2–3 per cent, in the 1950s it was about 7–10 per cent.
9 For the post-war history of the Social Democratic Women's League, see Karlsson (1996).
10 A splendid interpreter of the *Zeitgeist* was Olof Palme at the SAP congress in 1972: 'In this society it is self-evident that man and woman should take the same responsibility for the care of the home and the children, and that they both have an equal opportunity to take an active part in both the work and the cultural activities of the community', *Social Democratic Party Congress report*, p. 759.
11 Or this was the picture when women entered the political areas. See Hernes (1987) in *Welfare State and Woman Power: Essays in State Feminism*, where she defines this trend. The picture is more blurred now.
12 'Equal' is the translation of the Swedish word 'jämlik'/'jämlikhet', as in the revolutionary slogans of the French Revolution: Freedom, Equality and Brotherhood. 'Equal Status' is the literal translation of the word 'jämställdhet', which has a slightly different connotation of standing equal – beside. Terms like 'equivalence', 'equality' and 'equal status' had been used synonymously in the gender rhetoric of earlier times, but it was the term 'equal status' that won out. Another translation of the official word 'jämstalldhet' is that of 'equal opportunities'.
13 See Myrdal (1941) *Nation and Family. The Swedish Experiment in Democratic Family and Population Policy*, where she wrote 'Women – A Social Problem', a sentence which should be read as a radical way of putting 'women's issues' on the agenda.

4

GREEK FAMILY POLICY FROM A COMPARATIVE PERSPECTIVE[1]

Theodoros N. Papadopoulos

In Greece, as in most southern European countries, the key welfare provider is the 'family'.[2] This chapter explores the role of Greek family policy in sustaining this welfare arrangement. The policy components under investigation include arrangements for childcare provision; arrangements for maternity, paternity and parental leave; and the value of the total 'package' of transfers to families with children in the form of benefits, tax allowances and various subsidies. The results point to the rudimentary character of the Greek family policy as one of the major factors in reproducing the primacy of the 'family' in welfare provision in Greece. Furthermore, they raise questions about the type of gender relationships within and outside the household that the Greek family policy sustains and, eventually, legitimises.

The predominance of the nuclear family in Greece

A comparison of family composition in the European Union countries reveals the strong attachment of Greeks to the nuclear family form (Papadopoulos 1996). Greece has the highest percentages of couples with children (89.1 per cent) and married couples with two children (42.3 per cent) in Europe. Not surprisingly, it has also the lowest percentage of lone-parent families (10.9 per cent) and one of the lowest percentages of lone mothers with one child (5.4 per cent). However, Greece appears closer to the European average for larger families. Couples with three children constitute 10.7 per cent of the total number of families with children, a percentage close to those of Belgium (10.6), Italy (10.9) and the UK (10.9). In addition, Greece is amongst the countries with the lowest percentages of families consisting of couples with four or more children.

The centrality of family as a social institution in Greece is clearly manifested in ideological and symbolic terms in the social values and attitudes held by Greek men and women. In comparison to other Europeans, Greeks appear as the most strongly attached to, and supportive of, the institution of the family (Commission for European Communities 1993a). An overwhelming 99.4 per cent of the Greek respondents placed the family as their top priority on the value scale – the highest percentage in the European Union. However, despite the strong ideological attachment to the institution of the family, a series of ideological changes have taken place in respect of the social roles within families. They relate to a series of socio-political and economic changes, often defined as 'modernisation'[3] that have occurred in Greece since the early 1960s. Directly or indirectly these changes have influenced the structure of families in Greece, especially their size and the gender roles within and outside the household. During the late 1970s and through the 1980s what has been clearly observed was a transition from an extended family system to a nuclear family system. This transition was accompanied by a shift from traditional to more egalitarian gender roles within the household, a modest but steady increase in women's participation in the labour market and a gradual adoption of individualist values (Lambiri-Dimaki 1983; Doumanis 1983; Kouvertaris and Dobratz 1987; Georgas 1989).

Current demographic trends (see Chapter 1) provide further evidence of the strong attachment to the 'family' and the shift towards smaller family sizes. Greece continues to have one of the lowest divorce rates and the lowest percentage of births outside marriage in Europe, 0.7 and 2.7 per cent respectively (Eurostat 1994c), despite the fact that the Greek Orthodox church exerts far less moral pressure on issues like divorce and abortion compared to the Roman Catholic church. Low levels of lone parenthood are attributed to the stigma attached to it, access to private, and relatively unrestricted, abortion and the limited welfare support for lone parents. This lack of support reflects and reproduces certain attitudes and social practices with regard to the institution of marriage and the nuclear family.

The shift towards smaller families is evident in the trend towards lower fertility rates. In the period 1977–93 the total fertility rate has fallen from 2.27 to 1.38 children per woman, one of the lowest in Europe (Papadopoulos 1996). The decrease was more dramatic during the 1980s which registered the largest single decrease in Europe during this period (Commission of the European Communities 1994). However, the causes behind this spectacular fall cannot be solely attributed to changes in social values. Dretakis (1994) investigated the changes in the levels of income of couples with and without children during the period 1981–91, and associated them with behavioural changes in regard to having children. He found that Greek couples without children, whose income lost 16.4 per cent of its purchasing power during the period, increasingly tended to delay having their first child. Further, couples with one child, whose income lost 7 per cent of its purchasing power, either postponed having subsequent children or stopped having children altogether. Dretakis concluded that there was an urgent need to take serious measures to alleviate economic inequalities amongst Greek families and most importantly to increase the level of child allowance.

Greek family policy in a comparative perspective

In this section, the Greek family policy is compared to the policies of other European Union countries. The aim is to seek patterns of similarity and difference, especially among the countries that constitute the periphery of the European Union. In particular, the aim is to examine the extent to which the latter countries go in helping parents to reconcile work and family life and, in the case of the Greek family policy, how this policy sustains the predominant role of the nuclear family in welfare provision in Greece.

Childcare

Table 4.1 presents a comparison of the regulations and levels of childcare provision in the EU member states. Ten countries have the sixth year as the age of compulsory schooling, a clear case of convergence. However, in childcare provision for children up to 3 years of age a clear case of divergence emerges. Two clusters of countries are evident: Austria, FRG (formerly West Germany), Greece, Ireland, Luxembourg, Spain and the UK which have minimum provision, for only 2 to 3 per cent of children in this age group. Italy and the Netherlands offer higher levels of coverage, 6 and 8 per cent respectively, but this is still low in comparison to the rest of the countries. The second cluster consists of countries with levels of childcare provision well above 20 per cent: Finland (21 per cent) and France (23 per cent) are at the margins, followed by Belgium and Sweden with 30 and 33 per

Table 4.1 Regulations and levels of childcare provision in the European Union (15)

Countries	Reference year	Age of compulsory schooling	Child care* for children 0–3 %	Child care* for children 3–6 %
Austria	1994	6	3	75
Belgium	1993	6	30	95
Denmark	1994	7	50	79
Finland	1994	7	21	43
France	1993	6	23	99
Germany (West)	1990	6	2	78
Germany (East)	1993	6	50	100
Greece	1993	6	3	64
Ireland	1993	6	2	58
Italy	1991	6	6	91
Luxembourg	1989	6	2	55–60
the Netherlands	1993	5	8	71
Portugal	1993	6	12	48
Spain	1993	6	(2)	64
Sweden	1994	7	33	72
UK	1993	5	2	60

Sources: Ruxton (1996); data for Luxembourg from Glasner (1992: 83).

Notes:
* Places in childcare or children attending, as a percentage of children in that age group. For information on the method of measurement see Ruxton (1996).

cent respectively. Denmark and the former GDR (East Germany) offer the highest levels of coverage in the EU (50 per cent).

The pattern changes when one examines the childcare provision for children between 3 and 6 years of age, that is pre-primary school care. Provision is significantly higher and, although there is still diversity, a degree of convergence is evident. At the low end of the provision continuum there is Finland (43 per cent) and Portugal (48 per cent) followed by Ireland (58 per cent), Luxembourg (55–60 per cent) and the UK (60 per cent). Spain and Greece (with 64 per cent), are closer to the average. At the high end of the continuum there is the Netherlands (71 per cent), Sweden (72 per cent), Austria (75 per cent), FRG (formerly West Germany) (78 per cent) and Denmark (79 per cent). Italy, Belgium, France and the former GDR (East Germany) are at the top, all providing more than 90 per cent.

Overall, Denmark, Belgium, France and Sweden are the countries that have the most comprehensive childcare provision in the European Union. In the eastern part of Germany the levels of childcare remain high but, due to the economic constraints of unification, it is reasonable to expect a reduction in provision. In the periphery of Europe (Ireland, Spain, Portugal, Italy and Greece) the level of childcare for children up to 3 years of age is very low. In pre-primary school care (3–6 years of age) provision is better – but still at modest levels – with the exceptions of Portugal (low) and Italy (very high).

Leave provisions

Another key element in examining the extent to which the peripheral welfare states support parents in reconciling working and family life, concerns the arrangements for maternity, paternity and parental leave provisions. Table 4.2 provides a summary of these arrangements in the fifteen EU countries.

The arrangements for paid maternity leave in Greece follow the European average, 16 weeks with 100 per cent income replacement. The arrangements in the countries of European periphery vary. In Ireland paid maternity leave is given for 14 weeks on 70 per cent income replacement, in Spain for 16 weeks on 75 per cent, in Portugal for 18 weeks on 100 per cent and in Italy for 22 weeks on 80 per cent replacement rate. However, Greece pays the lowest maternity benefits compared to the other EU countries (Eurostat 1993b) far below Spain, Portugal and Italy which also pay low maternity benefits. Ireland is exceptional in this case having one of the highest maternity benefits in the European Union.

Furthermore, with the exception of Spain, no other country of the European periphery provides a right to paternity leave. As far as parental leave is concerned arrangements vary considerably. While in most of the EU member states there is statutory entitlement to paid parental leave, this is not the case in Greece, Portugal and Spain. Greece offers the shortest period of parental leave in Europe, although there are special provisions for lone parents (six months). However, the fact that parental leave is offered only to those employed by companies with more

Table 4.2 Regulations for maternity, paternity and parental leave provisions in the European Union (15)

Countries	Maternity leave (paid)		Paternity leave (paid)		Parental leave
	Weeks	RR[a]	Days	RR[a]	
Austria	16	100	–	–	2 years
Belgium	15	82–75	3	100	6–12 months
Denmark	18	flat rate	10	flat rate	6–12 months
Finland	17.5	66–45	6–12	66–45	up to 3 years
France	16–26	84	3	–	3 years
Germany	14	100	–	–	3 years
Greece	16	100	–	–	3.5 months[b]
Ireland	14	70	–	–	–
Italy	22	80	–	–	6 months
Luxembourg	16	100	–	–	–
the Netherlands	16	100	–	–	4 years[c]
Portugal	18	100	–	–	6–24 months
Spain	16	75	2	100	12–36 months
Sweden	12–24	90	10	80	18 months
UK	14	flat rate	–	–	–

Sources: Ruxton (1996); Ditch *et al.* (1996).

Notes:
[a] Replacement Rate of normal earnings during the period of leave.
[b] For lone parents the period is six months. It applies only to those employed by companies with more than 50 employees.
[c] Parent entitled to work reduced hours – not transferable.

than 50 employees excludes the largest part of the labour force which is employed in small enterprises. Indeed, it is generally accepted that take up is very low.

The Greek child support package

The third most important element of a family policy is income transfers to families. Table 4.3 sets out a comparative table of the main forms of these transfers, that is family benefits (income and non-income related) and tax allowances, and the criteria used in twelve European Union member states. A method increasingly used in evaluating the resources aspect of family policy is to 'translate' these data into policy outputs and compare them across countries. Thus, in order to evaluate the total Greek child support income package, the results of a series of comparative studies are used. The first of these studies used a standardised methodology in order to simulate the net disposable income that a number of 'model' families would theoretically receive in fifteen countries in 1992 (Bradshaw *et al.* 1993). The net disposable income of different family types was calculated by taking into account: the earnings from employment, family benefits (both non-income and income-related), tax allowances, social security contributions,

Table 4.3 Family policies in the European Union (12)

Countries	Non income-related family benefits	Vary according to	Taxable	Income-related family benefits	Vary according to	Tax allowances	Vary according to
Belgium	yes	number of children age of child employment status	no	no	n/a	yes	number of children age of child some tax relief for children expenditure
Denmark	yes	age of child lone parents	no	no	n/a	no	n/a
France	yes	number of children age of child lone parents mother's employment status (various schemes)	no	yes	number of children age of child lone parents mother's employment status (various schemes)	yes	number of children
Germany	yes	number of children age of child	no	no[...] (means tested benefit)	n/a	yes, fixed accounts for each child special tax allowances for lone parents	age of child
Greece	yes	number of children age of child	yes, some types of benefits	yes	number of children lone parents	yes	number of dependants
Ireland	yes	number of children no additions for lone parents	no	yes	number of children	no tax allowances but tax exemption limit is increased accordingly	marital status number of children

Country						
Italy	no	n/a	yes	number of persons in the household, special allowance for lone parents	yes	number of children, some school costs are deducted from taxable income, marital status
Luxembourg	yes	number of children, age of child	no	n/a	yes	age of child, marital status
the Netherlands	yes	number of children, age of child	no	n/a	no, but lone parents receive a tax free allowance	
Portugal	yes	number of children, age of child	no	(various schemes)	yes, tax deduction	marital status, number of [...], number of dependants
Spain	no	n/a	yes	number of children	yes, tax deduction pre-school care costs can be deducted from taxable income	couples can be taxed separately
UK	yes	number of children, lone parents	no	age of child	no, but lone parents can recieve a personal allowance	n/a

Sources: Compiled from national reports (Bradshaw et al. 1993: 103 30; Eurostat 1993c: 86 212).

health costs, housing costs (rent) and benefits as well as education costs and subsidies.

Overall, southern European countries and Ireland provided the least generous packages across all family types, including lone parents. Greece, in particular, ranks last in the overall evaluation of generosity and, with regard to lone parents, second from the bottom, above Spain. Moreover, further elaboration of the data (Bradshaw *et al.* 1993; Papadopoulos 1996) in terms of the welfare system's vertical and horizontal redistributive efforts – from wealthier households to poorer and from childless couples or individuals to families with children respectively – revealed that the Greek system was among the least redistributive.

When the same methodology was applied again, simulating net disposable income for 1994, researchers arrived at similar conclusions. A comparative study on the impact of tax and benefit systems on the financial incentives facing lone mothers in twenty countries (Bradshaw *et al.* 1996) and the report of the European Observatory on National Family Policies (Ditch *et al.* 1996) have confirmed that in Greece and the rest of the countries in the European periphery the levels of child support are particularly low.

Finally, a recent comparative study of social assistance in the OECD countries (Eardley *et al.* 1996) and a study of support for the unemployed and their families in the European Union (Papadopoulos 1998) re-confirmed the low levels of Greek welfare support not only towards families with children but also towards families at risk of poverty.

To summarize, compared to other European and Western countries Greece ranks very low in terms of childcare provision (especially for children up to the age of 3), parental leave arrangements, levels of maternity benefits and welfare support for families with children. In the light of these findings, increasing public dissatisfaction with the Greek family policy is clearly comprehensible. A Euro-barometer Survey (Commission of the European Communities 1993a) recorded 36.9 per cent of Greek respondents mentioning the level of child allowance as one of the most important issues on which the government should act to make life easier for families. As an indicator of dissatisfaction with the welfare state support for children, this is the highest in the European Union and far beyond the EU average level of dissatisfaction (22.5 per cent).

Family policy and familism in Greece

Despite the strong attachment of Greeks to the 'family', welfare state support for families is almost non-existent. This inconsistency is illustrative of the socio-economic role that the nuclear family performs in Greece in providing welfare for its members, in both affective and material terms. Thus, the Greek family policy, through its inaction, implicitly nurtures and reproduces the ideological assumption that the family is the main provider of welfare in society. This process is defined as 'Greek familism'.

Primarily, the Greek nuclear family unit – similar to other southern European 'families' – is 'still largely operating as a social clearing house, mediating the difficult relationships between a variegated labour market and equally variegated income maintenance systems' (Ferrera 1996: 21). In addition, it is perceived by its members as the main vehicle for social mobility (Tsoukalas 1987). This belief is embodied in the social practices of almost all social classes through a system of attitudes, visions and expectations which produce a special kind of solidarity within the family collective. One could argue that the Greek nuclear family functions internally as a cooperative while competing with other families in a society dominated by the idea of social mobility. Solidarity remains firmly within the private sphere, as an inter-generational responsibility towards the family unit.[4] In this context, the development of notions of social responsibility or social solidarity, essential for the creation and functioning of a civil society, encounter enormous obstacles. Thus, the possibility of creating a sustainable ideological base for expanding the residual welfare state in Greece is limited.

The gender aspects of Greek familism

Greek familism fosters solidarity within the family. However, this is by no means the only social relationship that it reproduces. If Greek familism is analysed in terms of gender, a pattern of dependency and power relationships among the members of Greek families emerges. The lack of a positive Greek family policy results in reinforcing the role of women as the sole carers of children and the elderly by nurturing, reproducing and legitimising their dependency on men (see Chapter 2). Hence, despite the legislative rhetoric, the Greek family remains firmly patriarchal in its structure. None the less, one has to emphasise that patriarchy is still confined to the private domain and a shift towards public patriarchal relationships, as defined by Walby (1990), has not yet occurred. As in Ireland (Mahon 1994) and the rest of the southern European countries, the residual family policy of the Greek welfare state reproduces the structure of private patriarchal relationships.

Since it is assumed that the family – that is primarily women – will bear the burden of childcare, and given the modest arrangements for maternity leave and the low levels of maternity benefits, Greek women find it particularly difficult to re-enter the labour market after the children have grown or to participate in the first place. A comparative examination of the EU female activity rates reveals that Greece continues to have one of the lowest rates as a percentage of the population aged 15–64 – 45.3 per cent compared to an average of 57.3 per cent for the EU (Eurostat 1996a). In addition, the activity rate of married women between 25 and 49 years of age is the lowest in the EU, 40 per cent compared to the EU average of 59.8 per cent (Eurostat 1994a).

Given the semi-peripheral character of the economy in Greece, a large proportion of this employment is in the agricultural sector and services related to tourism. In 1995, 23.9 per cent of Greek female employment was in agriculture, a figure significantly higher than the EU average of 4.4 per cent (European

Commission 1996). However, only 13.9 per cent of female employment was in the industrial sector, compared to an EU average of 16.7 per cent, and 62.2 per cent in the service sector (the EU average is 78.9 per cent). Moreover, if one takes into account that one of the key characteristics of the Greek labour market is the lack of part-time jobs, the difficulties of reconciling work and family life for Greek women become apparent. In 1995, the Greek level of female part-time employment was 8.4 per cent of total female employment, while the EU average was 31.3 per cent. This figure is the lowest in the European Union. In this context, it is not accidental that the Greek female unemployment rate (13.8 per cent) is double the male unemployment rate (6.2 per cent). In comparative terms, female unemployment in Greece is higher than the EU average of 12.5 per cent, while the unemployment rate among men is significantly lower than the EU average of 9.4 per cent (European Commission 1996). Against this backdrop, the Greek welfare system fits all the criteria for qualifying as a strong male breadwinner regime (Lewis 1992).

Conclusion

The differences between national family policies in the European Union are often attributed to the different patterns of welfare state development in member states. National family policies are formulated and implemented within diverse institutional settings which, due to their history, allow for a variety of responses to what appears to be similar sets of challenges. Hence, successful social policy responses to new challenges are directly linked to the flexibility and adaptability of these institutional structures. In this context, developing welfare states, such as those at the periphery of the European Union stand at a crossroads as they face two contradicting sets of priorities. On the one hand, there is the economic dimension: the erosion of the state's economic sovereignty coupled with the priority of meeting the criteria regarding participation in the EMU and the economic restructuring that competition in European and global markets brings about. On the other hand, there is an increasing demand to expand the role of the state in the welfare mix, as the traditional forms of welfare provision find themselves under enormous pressure precisely because the economic restructuring creates new patterns of employment insecurity and social exclusion (Petmezidou 1996). In addition, there is a pressing need to deal with the complex dynamics of women's participation rates, gender equality and fertility. These create a set of dilemmas significantly different from those that more developed welfare states of the European Union face, namely the 'rolling back' of their welfare states. In the majority of countries in the European periphery, and certainly in Greece, there is no dilemma on this issue simply because there is no significant welfare state to 'roll back'. On the contrary, the dilemma is what will be the role of the state, now that traditional forms of welfare provision are severely challenged. Only the future will show if the institutional structures of the countries in the periphery of Europe will provide adequate responses to meet these fundamental challenges.

Notes

1 This chapter is based on empirical evidence collected for an earlier work (Papadopoulos 1996). The author would like to acknowledge the financial support of the Onassis Foundation for this project and the editors of this book for their comments and suggestions. Special thanks go to Emma Carmel for her invaluable help and remarkable patience.

2 In this study the concept of 'family' refers both to a social institution and a social process and includes material and ideological aspects. A fundamental assumption is that family policies affect the extent to which particular notions of the 'family' are reproduced as resources (material and symbolic) and, consequently, certain family types are encouraged or discouraged in a given society.

3 'Modernisation' refers to: the shift from an economy based on agriculture to an economy based on services and (to a lesser extent) industry; the expansion of Greek statism and the intensification of 'intra-middle-class conflicts for access to the state machinery' (Petmezidou 1991: 40); the phenomena of rapid urbanisation and migration; the cultural and economic impact of tourism; the increase in access to higher education; the increase in women's labour force participation (small though it was); and last, but by no means least, changes in family legislation which followed entry into the European Community.

4 According to Commission of the European Communities (1994: 39) 69 per cent of young people in Greece obtain their job through their family – the highest percentage in Europe.

5

RECENT CHANGES IN FAMILY POLICY IN FRANCE

Political trade-offs and economic constraints

Jeanne Fagnani

Since the early 1960s female participation in the labour force has increased significantly in France, making it one of the countries in the European Union with the highest activity rates for mothers, as well as one of the highest birth rates. These trends may be explained, at least in part, by measures introduced by successive French governments to compensate for the cost of raising a family and to help couples combine family life with employment.

However, since the mid-1980s, in the context of an ever increasing unemployment rate, some significant changes have been introduced into French family policy. Among these, measures aimed at reducing the cost of childcare for dual-income families (allowances and tax deductions) have been progressively established in order to encourage job creation; an *'allocation parentale d'éducation'* (APE) has been extended to parents having a second child; and the parental leave scheme was modified. These measures are primarily the expression of the growing impact of employment policies over family policy, in the context of high unemployment, an issue which is high on the political agenda. In fact, to understand the rationale and the conditions underlying the establishment of these measures, it is important to take into account the socio-economic and political background. Basically, caught between the problems of rising unemployment[1] the growth in social security and public spending deficit,[2] the need for job creation, and pressures from pro-natalist and New Right lobbies, successive governments have hedged between ambiguous positions and reacted with piecemeal measures without any coherent strategy, by using family policy as a means of reducing unemployment (Jenson and Sineau 1995; Fagnani 1996a). These tensions and contradictions have led to policy choices, the impacts of which, in terms of social equity, have led to numerous criticisms from the social partners.

Consequently, from which socio-economic groups can mothers take advantage of the measures aimed at reducing the cost of childcare? Do the measures contribute to social inequalities among working women, while also maintaining a gendered division of domestic responsibilities and caring work? On the other hand, are the measures concerning the 'APE' deviating from the principles of a family policy which had integrated the model of the working mother (Fagnani 1996b; Hantrais and Letablier 1996)? To what degree can the measures influence the choices and judgements which women, particularly mothers, make in the spheres of family and professional life? What are the possible adverse effects and consequences on the daily life and career paths of the beneficiaries? Taking into account the reality of relations between the sexes, which manifest themselves particularly in a strong sexual division of work within the family, these questions echo more global concerns on the interaction between women's strategies, sex roles, the functioning of the labour market and the principles of social and family policies.

A family policy for the working mother

French family policy has largely integrated the model of the working mother: the reasons are both historic (a long tradition of female participation in economic activity in France),[3] economic (a need for women in the labour market since the end of the 1960s, until the beginning of the 1980s) (Norvez 1990), social (a constant increase in women's average level of education) and cultural (the diffusion and influence of feminist ideas). This is also consistent with a fairly large social consensus in favour of female employment, even of those with young children, as CREDOC (1995) surveys have shown.

Public childcare facilities

Regarding publicly funded childcare for those aged under 3 years, France is at the forefront, with Sweden and Denmark, in the European Union (European Commision Network on Childcare 1994). In 1995, the 'Caisses d'Allocations Familiales' (CAF, Family Allowance Funds) provided nearly 3.6 billion francs for the development of childcare facilities (out of a total of 8.5 billion francs available from the state, local authorities and the CAF). In ten years, the number of places in public and private 'crèches' rose by 65 per cent to reach, in 1994, a total of 192,200. A quarter of a million children are already attending an 'école maternelle' (publicly funded pre-primary schools) all of which have canteen facilities. In addition, there are many 'halte-garderies' (60,100 places for 300,500 children) which welcome children occasionally or for a few hours each day. In total, of the 2.2 million children aged under 3 years, around 30 per cent are cared for in public facilities during the day.

However, the continued increase in mothers' employment has led to a growing need for dual-earner families to employ outside labour for domestic tasks such as housekeeper, nanny, childminder.

Measures towards the cost of childcare:
creating 'family jobs' for whom?

Two allowances aimed at working parents who have children cared for by a childminder, help to reduce the cost of childcare. These are the 'Allowance to Families for the Employment of a Registered Childminder' (AFEAMA) and 'Allowance for Childcare at Home' (AGED). Officially the aim was a 'diversification' of childcare arrangements. However, these two allowances were also designed to relieve some of the pressure on collective forms of childcare. The amount of these two allowances has been increased in 1995.

Allowance to families for the employment of a registered childminder

The AFEAMA is not means-tested. It was created in 1990, revised in 1991, and is intended for dual-earner parents who employ a registered childminder (who is paying social insurance contributions) to care for their child (or children) aged under 6 outside their home. The AFEAMA corresponds to the social security contributions due when a registered childminder is paid. An additional financial contribution is also given to the family of 800 francs per month for a child under 3 years and 400 francs for a child aged between 3 and 6 years. This allowance can also be coupled with a tax deduction, up to a maximum of 3,750 francs a year. One of the aims of this benefit was also to bring the undeclared work of childminders out of the informal economy.

This measure has been very successful. In June 1997, there were 400,000 recipients (there were about 320,000 registered childminders). However, for many low-income families, this childcare arrangement remains too expensive, since they are not earning enough to be taxed, they cannot take advantage of the tax allowances, and so they most often choose a non registered childminder or a member of their family to care for their child.

Allowance for childcare in the home

The AGED is not means-tested and was introduced in 1986. It is paid to dual-earner families (or to lone parents who are economically active) who employ a person in their home to look after one (or several) child(ren) under 6 years when both of the parents (or the single parent) have outside employment. The amount of the AGED is equal to the social security contributions paid by the employee and employer for the employment of one (or more) childcare workers, up to a maximum of 4,130 francs a month in 1996 (only half of this amount, 2,065 francs is paid if the child is aged between 3 and 6 years).

Moreover, until the end of 1997, recipients of AGED can deduct from their income tax an amount equal to 50 per cent of the actual cost of care, up to a limit of 45,000 francs a year. It should be noted that, in 1994, only half of the households paid income tax but fewer than 10 per cent of these paid 45,000 francs or more annually. In June 1997, there were 76,000 recipients.[4]

AGED benefits mainly better-off families,[5] because only those earning an income high enough to be taxed can benefit from the tax deductions. Professionals and high-level managers (or executives) represent 77 per cent of the families who employ a homeworker to care for their child(ren) (DARES 1995). As a result of this tax deduction and allowance, the net cost of a full-time home-help to care for the child(ren) is higher for a low-income family than for a high-income family. In contrast, public day-care, where fees are calculated according to the income level, is cheaper for low-income families than for high-income families.

In households where the woman is economically active, being able to leave household and caring tasks to a domestic help relieves the pressures involved in combining both professional and family life, and allows considerable flexibility in managing time. But among couples, this depends on the socio-economic position of the wife. One female manager in three employs a housekeeper, compared to only one female manual worker in a hundred (Flipo and Hourriez 1995).

For employees providing childcare under the AGED, 99 per cent of whom were women in 1994, the picture is more mixed:

- this measure has indisputably created jobs, which, taking into the account the small labour pool, increases the possibility of being hired, which until now has been slight for semi-skilled or unskilled women workers;
- domestic helpers, previously working in the black economy, benefit from legal protection and social insurance cover (for retirement in particular). For foreigners, frequently employed in this sector, obtaining the status of a protected worker can also facilitate the process of integration into French society;
- legally, these workers also have the right to continuous training.

However, these jobs are usually precarious, low paid, have a low social status and offer no promotional prospects. Engaged in menial work, which usually entails caring for the child coupled with cleaning, employees are often isolated, they are very rarely unionised, and remain dependent on the whims of their employers regarding hours and timing of work. In addition, how can overtime payments (time and a quarter) and rights to training be claimed with the spectre of unemployment constantly present?

On the other hand, if AGED and AFEAMA facilitate women's access to paid work by helping families (in particular middle-income families) meet the costs of childcare, they have the effect of being anti-redistributory measures in contrast to public childcare where fees are calculated according to the level of income.

These diverse policies could explain in part why French mothers are more frequently employed than, for example, West German women (Fagnani 1996b). They also illustrate how strongly policies have integrated the underlying values of the 'working mother' model. However, the law on family policy passed by the

French Parliament in July 1994 and the government measures to reinforce parental leave in 1995 and, in particular, the APE (Childrearing Benefit) raise doubts concerning whether there is a return to the traditional model of the 'mother at home'?

APE and parental leave: strengthening the 'male breadwinner model'?

The 'family' remains an important political issue in French society. Everything concerning this institution – intimately or tenuously – arouses passionate debate in political circles and gains media attention. Thus while the draft family law was being prepared in spring 1994, much debate and controversy took place concerning the form of extension of the APE, pitting those advocating a temporary cessation of maternal employment following the birth of a child (family associations, in particular), against those advocating additional financial aids for childcare to help the reconciliation of professional and family life (the socialist party and women's associations).

Contrary to the situation in Scandinavian countries (Sweden and Denmark in particular), the parliamentary debates were not focused on the promotion of equality between the sexes or the struggle against sexual discrimination in the labour market. The implicit foundation of all the proposals made in this area was that mothers must assume responsibility for the bulk of childrearing. It was therefore a matter of justifying, on grounds of ideological criteria and financial limitations (taking into account the growing social security deficit), the institution of measures which in reality are aimed, implicitly and sometimes explicitly, at employed women with young children. The implicit objective of these measures has been to encourage them to retire from the labour market, thereby leaving their jobs open for others (Afsa 1996). Officially, the aim was 'to help couples combine family and professional life'. In fact, as Jenson and Sineau (1995: 258) pointed out 'the goal of promoting equality and democracy in the family was threatened by a programme designed to be, in effect, a 'mother's salary'.

Established in 1985 and modified in 1986, APE was extended to families having a second child in 1994. The flat-rate APE benefit of 2,964 francs per month in 1996 is not taxable nor is it means tested, and is available for up to three years (until the youngest child is 3 years old) to families with at least two children. It had formerly been limited to families with three or more children up to July 1994. A parent (the mother or the father) can only benefit if s/he stops work completely or works on a part-time basis (in which case, the amount of the benefit is reduced). This benefit is intended to provide partial compensation for the loss of income connected with an interruption of paid employment on the part of one of the two-parents. The APE can be paid at a reduced rate if either, or both, parents work part time or enter a course of paid vocational training.[6]

However, parents with a second child under 3 are only eligible if they have worked or have been registered as unemployed for at least two years out of the five preceding the birth of the youngest child (ten years for parents having a third child). This condition of eligibility was implicitly set up to encourage economically active mothers to stop work and to decrease the unemployment rate. Moreover, mothers represent 98 per cent of the recipients. Given the differential between women's and men's salaries, if any parent takes the leave it is likely to be the mother.

The current difficulties faced by young women on the labour market and the degradation of working conditions seem to have had a strong impact on the take-up of APE. The number of recipients has increased regularly, reaching 500,000 by the end of 1997. Not surprisingly, the economic activity rate of mothers with two children, with the youngest aged less than 3, has dramatically decreased from 69 per cent in 1994 to 53 per cent in 1997.

The parental leave scheme '*congé parental d'éducation*', which is unpaid, was set up under the '*Code du travail*' in 1977. Modified in 1984 and 1994 it allows all salaried employees, male or female, who have worked for at least one year in the company before the birth of a child, to cease employment totally or partially, in order to care for that child. This leave can be up to two years duration and must be taken before the child reaches 3 years of age. Since the Family Law of 1994, all companies must provide this leave, no matter how few employees there are. After parental leave, an employee is entitled to reinstatement, without a reduction in pay, in the same position or in a similar one, and is eligible for retraining with pay. It is possible to be on parental leave and also claim APE but only if the mother gives birth to a second or higher-order rank child. Of the parents taking parental leave, 99 per cent are mothers.

Perverse side effects

Gender equality issues are not high on the political agenda in France (Jenson and Sineau 1995) and policy makers are not really concerned with the implementation of measures promoting a more 'gender-neutral approach' by encouraging fathers to take up parental leave and APE. Research conducted in this field demonstrates that all these schemes and arrangements (parental leave, career breaks, part-time jobs and childrearing benefit) have the effect of:

- reinforcing the social construction of fatherhood in terms of the breadwinner role, with involvement in family care as optional;
- maintaining the gender division of domestic tasks (the mother who reduces her working hours feels less justified in asking for her husband's help) and unequal gender power since mothers have to stop work to be eligible for the APE at a full rate;[7]
- contributing, due to a complex number of factors, to the maintenance of gender discrimination in the labour market by establishing asymmetrical professional trajectories within the couple and wage differentials between men and women;

- also contributing to the reinforcement of employers' prejudices towards female workers, i.e. that they would be less committed to their work and less willing to pursue a career.

The ILO itself recently recognised that employment adaptations for women, while easing women's double burden in the short term, would not ultimately create gender equality and would instead reinforce and perpetuate the status quo (ILO 1995).

Allowing mothers to make the choice of spending longer periods out of the labour market can be very detrimental to their career prospects. The results of my research on former recipients of APE returning to work (Fagnani 1996c) show that long periods caring for children are costly, although cash benefits for mothers with low earnings can meet this direct cost. Of greater significance are the missed promotions and the decay of human capital, which often leads to lower earnings among mothers even after they have returned to work. Moreover, mothers working in the private sector may have some difficulties in being re-employed by the same company. Many employers are reluctant to take on someone who has stopped working for such a long time. Parental leave is also sometimes used by the employers of the private sector as a means of reducing the number of staff.

Conclusion

While it cannot be said that French family policy regarding the reconciliation of family and professional life is being reversed, since in 1994/95 the government has reinforced measures relating to childminding in the home and to childminders outside the home. These new measures are above all the expression of the growing hold that employment policies have over family policy. This 'engulfing' tendency has been at work since the institution of benefits linked to childcare (AFEAMA and AGED). The extension of APE to families with a second child has reinforced that tendency.

However the French government has opted for costly measures which benefit mainly the better-off and middle-income families, at the expense of the development of public childcare facilities, taking into account that places are still not available in sufficient numbers to meet demand. Certainly, the measures analysed here have allowed the creation of female jobs, as childminders and homeworkers, and have increased the solvency of households. Thanks to these measures, a significant proportion of middle-class women and men can continue to work full-time. However, the cost is the development of a massive number of precarious and low-paid jobs, occupied principally by women. This does little to question the current sexual division of domestic responsibilities and these political choices may also adversely affect the mechanisms of vertical income distribution in France.

Notes

1 Between July 1990 and July 1994, unemployment increased by some 800,000 to over 3 million, from below 9 per cent of the workforce to 12.5 per cent.

2 From 1990 to 1994, the public sector deficit rose from below 2 per cent of GDP to 6 per cent.

3 On the eve of the First World War, there were 20 active women per 100 inhabitants in France, while there were between 13.5 and 15.5 per 100 inhabitants in England, Italy and Germany (Marchand and Thélot 1991).

4 AFEAMA and AGED accounted for a cost of 7 billion francs in 1995, for the CAF.

5 Well-off and large families also enjoy the tax advantages stemming from the '*quotient familial*' which represented a tax loss for the state in the order of 75 billion francs in 1995.

6 Only one APE, at full rate, can be paid per family or two APE at a reduced rate if the parents work on a part-time basis. Recipients of the APE continue to be entitled to family allowances and can belong at no charge to the old age insurance system when the family's resources are below a certain ceiling.

7 The in-depth interviews I have conducted in my research on recipients of APE have shown that, during this period of leave, there is a reinforcement of the traditional division of work between couples by which the women assume all the domestic and family tasks.

6

PAID WORK AND CARE OF OLDER PEOPLE

A UK perspective

Judith Phillips

Changing economic, social and demographic trends across Europe are significantly influencing the traditional roles women play in relation to the home and the labour market. In northern European countries the demographic shift over the last thirty years with increasing numbers of older people, particularly those over the age of 75 (see Chapter 1), together with the restructuring of many welfare states resulting in a slow-down in the expansion of services, has led to a continuing reliance on the family, particularly middle-aged and older women, as well as increasing numbers of older men to provide care. At the same time labour market changes are pulling women in the opposite direction – toward paid employment. Consequently women face pressures from home and at work as they balance the two roles as carers and employees. Although this is not a new phenomenon for families the issue has grown in importance over the last ten years and is increasingly becoming a concern for all European states as well as employers. In southern European states, where familistic models of care predominate, similar issues are slowly emerging. This chapter outlines these trends, describes the pressures such women face in the workplace, considers work-based options to support them and discusses where responsibility lies to assist working women.

Growing demand for care of older people

As Chapters 1 and 2 have shown, increasing life expectancy and the ageing of the European population have made eldercare an emerging issue. The number of older people is rising across Europe and will continue to rise for the next few decades; the highest rate of growth will occur amongst those over 75. Although people are living longer it is the fall in the birth rate that has been the real cause of an ageing population – the population is ageing as a whole. In the European Union, for example, the ratio of women aged 45–69 to people over the age of 70 fell from 2.26 to 1.53 between 1960 and 1990 (Salvage 1995). Even in families with more than three children, generally there is only one who becomes a carer. There is a concern, therefore, among commentators that a 'crisis' in the care of older people is looming as there will be fewer young people per household to support an increasingly dependent older population. Although such a pessimistic scenario ignores the impact of technological change, advances in medicine and pharmacology as well as changes in economic structure, the impact of this imbalance is currently manifesting itself in spheres of both domestic and work life. This has consequences in particular for women who both receive and provide the bulk of care.

Women predominate in this older population because they still live longer than men. Since the likelihood of functional limitations, chronic diseases and dementia increase with age, many women will require care and support as they grow older. Almost one in three people over the age of 80 need extensive care, most of whom are women (Eurolink Age 1995).

Definitions as to what extensive care consists of vary across Europe; in France, for example, of people aged 85 plus, 6 per cent of men and 9 per cent of women are bedridden. The majority of caregiving is provided by a spouse (for example 75 per cent in Germany) among whom there are many men undertaking care tasks (apart from Spain where male care is rare). This is often ignored in discussions of working carers, since spouses (both men and women) tend to be older and out of the labour market.

'Prevalent social norms, family structure, concepts of life and individual histories influence carers to take on their tasks. Duty is a dominant notion in European countries' (Eurolink Age 1995: 7). Close ties between caregiving, duty, social norms and inheritance have a long tradition in many European states. All European studies illustrate that when eldercare is being provided to a parent it is women who generally provide the personal care (Jani-Le Bris 1994b). Such women tend to be in their 50s and 60s, married, non-resident with the person needing care; potentially caring for children and grandchildren and are likely to be caring for older people at the same time as they are re-entering or wishing to remain in the labour market.

All member states of the European Union have witnessed an increasing feminisation of their workforce. In southern Europe, for example in Spain and Greece, female participation increased by 25 per cent during the 1980s. With population decline, resulting in fewer younger people in the workforce, competitiveness and growth are under threat. In order to avoid this, efforts have been made to attract women back into the labour market. Transitions in labour markets with a shift from heavy industry to servicing and manufacturing and from traditional models of work (forty hours) to more 'atypical' forms of work (job-sharing, flexible working hours) have allowed women to (re)enter as outlined by Drew and Emerek (Chapter 8). As higher educational and occupational qualifications become available to women, their aspirations are changing; they assign greater priority to working life and increasingly want equal opportunities with men in the workplace.

Attitudes and aspirations are also changing in relation to caregiving. Although the family remains the main arena within which care is given and received across Europe (Jani-Le Bris 1993; Stathopoulis and Amera 1992) the changing structure of the family is challenging long-held obligations and duties (Finch and Mason 1993). Fragmentation of families through separation, divorce, geographical distance and mobility is being experienced on a large scale by older people today (Phillips 1995). It could be suggested that divorce and remarriage will confuse the traditional, familistic patterns of caring, leaving uncertainty about who will care for whom in older age. Certainties about caregiving may no longer be available as kinship obligation has to compete with other pressures, such as employment. Older people themselves have changing attitudes – many, even very old people, want to be independent (Parker 1990; Daatland 1990) and not a burden to their children. For some this aim can be realised as they have accumulated financial resources across the life course while in employment, through occupational pensions and home ownership, but large numbers of older people without financial resources will look to their spouses and children to support them in later life. For those without children a move to residential care may be the final outcome, although this is often viewed as the last resort.

Social isolation can be a problem in countries such as Germany, where large numbers of older people live alone as well as in southern states where a 'familistic' model of welfare is applied. One of the distinguishing features of this model is the co-residence of older people with younger generations; in exchange for support older family members have various social roles and status within the family. Geographical mobility among younger generations has altered such solidarity and patterns of caregiving. With younger populations moving in search of employment the distance between family members increases, reducing the availability of younger members of the family to provide personal care especially in rural areas. In Italy, Spain, Portugal, Greece, Ireland and France, older people are left behind on the land while younger people go in search of work in the towns (Eurolink Age 1995); many older people are therefore socially isolated and lack support of any kind. Despite these changes, in Italy, for example, there is still a refusal to abandon elderly relatives and the relative lack of services for older people reinforces this attitude; in Greece, responsibility for older people by family is still rooted in the Constitution (Jani-Le Bris 1993) and everywhere the feeling of duty to older parents is omni-present (see Chapter 4). Caring over distance is becoming an increasing phenomenon with different pressures upon carers whose main function in caring may be to send money home to purchase care.

Political changes, too, have led to caregiving becoming an important issue in the workplace. The last decade has witnessed major changes in the size and focus of the welfare state in most European countries as governments attempt to control public expenditure. Consequently two major shifts are observable, first a more pluralistic form of welfare (for example, the privatisation of services in the UK) and, second, a continuing move in many countries from institutional to community care. Both changes, however, have relied on the family in terms of financial (for example, to top up residential care costs) and practical support. Money from institutional care has not followed people into the community, i.e. 'community care' relies on informal sources – the family and mainly women in the family. This has created a dilemma for many women who want to be in employment or need to work for financial reasons; for example, to contribute to their pension, or in order to spend time away from the stresses of caring. At the same time they meet barriers in achieving this. Women's earning power is lower than men's and many women accept part-time work to fulfil responsibilities at home; many women are in low-paid caring jobs outside the home. Yet most women cannot afford to finance the care of their elderly relative and work in such low-paid positions and therefore become financially dependent on unpaid care at home themselves (Graham 1983). This situation applies equally in EU states such as the UK and Luxembourg which promote equal opportunities for women, particularly in relation to caregiving of children and in employment but where the lack of adequate community support has denied equal opportunities for women becoming a reality. Furthermore, although this has been posed as a women's issue, men too find caring and working a difficult combination, despite studies showing they take on more managerial tasks rather than direct caring (Berry Lound 1994).

In southern states (Spain, Portugal, Greece and Italy) the development of public sector community care is at an embryonic stage; in practice such care is fragmentary, inadequate and restricted to urban areas. As a result, even more than in other countries, the family is primarily responsible for the care of older people. States which have followed an 'individualistic' model of welfare – Denmark, Sweden and the Netherlands, where an extensive range of community care services have been developed to support older people – are potentially better able to support carers in employment. Research by Salvage (1995) shows that the northern countries especially Denmark, the UK, the Netherlands and Germany have high rates of female employment (72, 63, 47 and 55 per cent respectively) (Green 1988).

Profile of working carers

It is difficult to estimate the numbers of working carers for dependent adults. The few representative studies of those combining work with caring for an adult have indicated that a third of employees are caring for an adult, mainly an older person (Whatmore 1989; Berry Lound 1994). This is likely to be an underestimate as workplace-based studies are fraught with difficulties in collecting data since carers do not wish to expose details of their family life. In Greece, France and Germany, where the family is legally responsible for the support of older people (in the latter countries the children's income determines the amount older people have to reimburse the state if they seek 'social assistance') and where the percentage of those balancing work and care is likely to be higher, there are very few studies from which to draw conclusions.

Most carers providing physical and practical care are female, married and aged 40 years or over (Phillips 1995). Daughters, and to a smaller extent daughters-in-law, form the majority of the group providing care. Caring for a dependent adult can range from occasional shopping and assistance with finance (instrumental care) to providing assistance with toiletting, dressing and washing (physical care). Consequently, time spent in caring differs. In a recent German study 20 per cent of caregiving employees claimed they had to be available all the time; 48 per cent were engaged in caregiving for a couple of hours each day (Beck *et al.* 1995).

The motivation to combine work and care differs across Europe. German research highlights material reasons: to acquire pension credits and social insurance as well as income; in contrast, carers in France were not concerned with their future rights to a retirement pension. Across Europe non-material reasons were emphasised, such as personal enhancement and source of satisfaction (Jani-Le Bris 1993).

Although there is increasing documentation of the situation of carers in Europe, there is still little available data, for example, on the different conditions men and women face in the workplace. On the whole male and female carers experience similar effects of caring on employment. Available studies show, however, that although male carers are increasing in number (Whatmore 1989) there are differences, with women providing more personal care, men receiving more professional assistance (Jani-Le Bris 1993) and men more likely to be carrying out caregiving responsibilities jointly (Evandrou 1990) all of which confirms the hypothesis indicating a potentially easier situation for men. Differences in type and status of employment also have an effect on how carers manage at work with those in high-status jobs being better able to balance the two roles.

Balancing employment and care

All the existing European studies on carers in paid employment show that if people attempt to balance caregiving responsibilities, domestic life and paid employment they often suffer psychological, social, interpersonal, practical and health-related stress (Phillips 1995). All of the problems and difficulties working women face are generally intensified when they combine work and eldercare (Jani-Le Bris 1994b). In general the needs and problems of working carers vary depending on the degree of dependence and actual location of the person for whom they care (Pearson 1994). Such problems include tiredness, apathy, worry and lack of concentration. In nearly all studies, half the respondents reported that caring significantly affected their work (Berry Lound 1994; Naegele and Reichert 1995). German data reveal that employed caregivers suffer depression, headaches and exhaustion, particularly when the care recipient becomes more impaired (Naegele and Reichert 1995). Family life is also affected as the stress at work is transferred to home; there is often little time for relaxation and holidays are taken up with caregiving. Isolation from other work colleagues, who do not experience caring, and the fear of sharing problems with management, is commonly reported.

Problems associated with the loss of pension, lack of promotion and training opportunities are often a consequence of such problems for carers. Caring also has a significant effect on work histories. Research shows that the longer the period spent caring, the more carers are disadvantaged. Additionally, caring for long periods of time is associated with markedly lower accumulation of pension rights than caring for short periods (Tinker 1994). As many women will also have taken on childcare earlier in life they are often doubly disadvantaged.

For employers the problems due to combining work and caring have an impact on work productivity and employee-related costs. The existing workplace-based audits describe the negative effects of caring on work performance. Taking time off, arriving late and leaving early, using work resources such as the telephone to arrange care services and making mistakes, are reported. In two UK studies by Help the Aged, 40 per cent of employees (N = 400) took unscheduled time off for caregiving duties resulting in 250 working days being lost in six months (Berry Lound 1994). One of the companies in this study suggests gender distinctions with women taking longer periods off than men (Berry Lound 1994). One of the negative consequences is in the loss of qualified and experienced staff, bringing recruitment and replacement costs for employers.

Caregiving, however, is not always stressful and the combination of work and care can have beneficial effects for both carers and employers. Social and psychological benefits are important; in one study by the Open University, 38 per cent of carers said it helped them put other aspects of their life into perspective (Princess Royal Trust for Carers 1995). The interpersonal, managerial and practical skills carers acquire can also be translated into benefits within the workplace. From an employer's perspective working carers could be more responsible, sympathetic and responsive (Lazcko and Noden 1992).

Workplace options for care providers

Solutions in the workplace to assist both men and women with childcare responsibilities have been widely documented. Unlike childcare, adultcare presents different challenges for carers. Carers are likely to be older, may have less physical strength, face an indeterminate length of caregiving and often face difficult and unpleasant tasks. Caring for someone with mental disability, for example, brings particular stresses, higher burdens and often uncertainties about how to care appropriately and is very different to caring for a physically disabled adult. Employers need to consider these differences if the workplace is to respond effectively.

Some carers are forced to leave work because of their caregiving responsibilities. In one Irish study 13 per cent of family caregivers left work because they were caring for an elderly parent (O'Connor and Ruddle 1988); a survey in Vorarlberg (Austria) also reports that at least one-third of those receiving family care allowances had cited similar reasons, of which 15 per cent said that only this payment had allowed them to leave employment (Leichsenring 1994). According to two French surveys, one in an urban area, the other in a rural area 11 per cent and 4 per cent respectively left work because of eldercare (Jani-Le Bris 1993,

1994a). In Germany a quarter of carers gave up work after becoming carers (Schneekloth and Pothoff 1993). Re-employment is extremely difficult and is likely to be part-time and at a lower income. As a result, many carers have poor contribution records for social insurance and are likely to have insufficient resources for their own old age (Eurolink Age 1995). Returning to work may also incur costs of substitute care (Glendinning 1988): 'we couldn't go on like that so we brought the old lady here to our house although it meant that I had to leave my job so I could look after her' (Jani-Le Bris 1993: 41).

Returning to work may also be constrained by domestic situations, relationship and psychological circumstances:

> Even if I got someone else to care for her I'm sure she wouldn't accept it. If she could only go back to her own home I would go and give her all the necessary help and then I'd have a more independent life. I could then go back to work, but I'm afraid she'll get worse again during the winter. I still think about going back to work but my mother-in-law doesn't want me to go out. When she was very ill she didn't want even her son to go to work.
>
> (Jani-Le Bris 1993: 42)

Support from others in the household and at the workplace is crucial to assist working carers. Another key factor in carers' ability to balance work and care is the corporate culture and attitude of the employer as well as the availability of flexible policies and practices.

One of the important responses to the situation of working carers is to offer them a choice: of leaving employment; managing both care and work roles at the same time; or of ending the care. In the case of leaving employment the carer needs to be adequately compensated. When ceasing employment temporarily, employees need guarantees that they will be able to return to their former, or another, post after a given period. In countries such as Sweden, schemes have been designed to cater for carers' needs in this way. Care allowance schemes in Scandinavia include guarantees for re-employment or provide generous care-givers' leave. In Norway, people who have been caregivers for at least five years and who are unable to find employment again are guaranteed a basic income until they reach pensionable age.

For carers attempting to balance work and eldercare there is an increasing need for workplace support. Evers and Leichsenring (1994: 4) underline the importance of the 'encouragement of more flexible working patterns (paid care relief, guarantees for re-employment, part-time work, possibilities for reducing and increasing working hours in specific life phases)'. Examples of initiatives across Europe to support carers are limited and schemes that exist are often informal and *ad hoc*. Larger companies have commissioned audits to assess the numbers of carers in the workforce and the extent to which their caregiving responsibilities impact on the workplace. On the basis of these, some companies have responded positively and implemented policies, benefits and services to help the workforce. Flexible work patterns have taken the form of flexitime, part-time arrangements or job-sharing, leave policies and home and tele-working (Phillips 1995). Despite the enthusiasm with which these schemes have been implemented in different countries, for example, by Barclays Bank in the UK and Ludwig Beck in Germany, there has been no systematic evaluation of usage and of benefits to the workforce and in particular women carers. Some companies have directed attention to employees who experience emotional difficulties in the workplace through counselling, information and advice services; support groups can be found in some companies, for example, in Luxembourg. Direct service provision for care recipients organised by and through the workplace is also beginning in Europe, for example, at Peugeot Talbot and Radcliffe NHS Trust in the UK. The crucial question is: to what extent do services meet both the needs of the carer and receiver? Most are developed in isolation from mainstream social services and along a model which has seen low utilisation rates in the USA (Wagner and Hunt 1994).

Benefits such as long-term care insurance and compensation for lost income comprise another type of support that some employers in a variety of countries (examples can be found in Ireland, Denmark and Germany as well as Scandinavia) provide for employees.

Developing initiatives at the workplace in isolation from community services may not be of any great benefit to the carer. The lack of support beyond the workplace is crucial but welfare services are often inflexible and do not cater for carers who are in work. Social and health services need to be more accessible to respond to carers' needs if they are to remain in work. In general, public services contribute little specifically to maintaining the carer in employment (Twigg 1994). Carers can benefit indirectly from mainstream services such as respite care, day-care and nursing care where they exist. Such services are often not flexible enough to cater for those in employment and can often disadvantage those in a caregiving situation.

The response from employers is slow. Neither employers nor trade unions are aware of the impending problems. Such a lack of response has conflicted with the aim of equal opportunities for women and men in the workplace. Women not only need carer-friendly schemes but other forms of employer-financed assistance that can be directed to the whole workforce. Yet there is still an assumption that caring is a female responsibility that employers should accommodate. By seeing it as a women's problem there is a tendency to see women as blameworthy. It is not yet seen as warranting more fundamental change in all employees' work patterns.

Employers, by combining conflicting policies – encouraging early retirement but postponing to a later date theoretical retirement ages – have also disguised the speed of population and workforce ageing (Eurolink Age 1995). Such problems have significant consequences for southern European states where the population is ageing and women are entering the workforce at an increasing rate. In countries with predominantly smaller companies, it is more difficult to offer a range of initiatives to cover the diversity of need that may exist. Workplace-based support has been characteristic of larger rather than smaller companies, especially those with high levels of unionisation and in large technological intensive industries, former public utilities and in the public sector rather than in the growth areas of female employment such as retailing and small businesses (May and Brunsdon 1996). Most schemes are also conditional on length of service and are designed for the company's benefit rather than in response to individual needs.

A crucial question is: where does responsibility lie for assisting and supporting working carers? Caregiving is still seen predominantly as a family responsibility throughout Europe. Yet there are differing degrees to which the family is held responsible. In Denmark and the Scandinavian countries where an 'individualistic' model exists the state takes on responsibility for the care of older people whether this is in the community or in institutional care. In Norway and Sweden there are systems of paid 'family home helps' through which family carers can be employed by the municipality to undertake a large amount of direct care work for a relative (Waerness 1990). However the extent to which the state can continue to support older people and indirectly their carers in difficult economic times is increasingly being questioned. Even if the state takes responsibility for supporting paid work and caring there are no guarantees that this will meet the needs of carers, particularly women. In the Norway and Sweden example above, the patriarchal values of welfare and caring are still evident as payment is low, and employment is often part-time and targeted at women. Different procedures and assessments by various people in differing sections of health and social services pose barriers to a consistent and reliable service, particularly for those in rural areas where information is not easily on hand. Eligibility criteria are increasingly being introduced in relation to access to social and health services, often excluding those who live with carers or have a female carer. By offering poor quality services the state ensures that the family takes on the role and duty of carer. In Denmark, for example, social policy does not see the family as a potential source of care for older people yet, in practice, families do provide basic care and support. The key question here is whether the state can persuade employers to work alongside it in supporting carers by offering financial incentives to do so. Such pluralistic forms of support are more likely in countries such as the UK where a determined policy of privatisation has been pursued over the last seventeen years.

On the other hand the 'familistic' model, as adopted in many southern EU states and Germany, firmly places responsibility within the family. Attitudes to workplace-based support will therefore differ with many employers in these states taking the view that such problems and solutions should not become their responsibility. The scope for partnerships to develop between state and employers has potential but would need to overcome attitudinal barriers which prevail in countries like Italy and Spain where older generations expect their families to provide support. Developments outside the family involving church and other non-governmental organisations are so far piecemeal but could provide a starting point for the partnership with employers.

There is an increasing need to address the entrenched assumptions about women and caring across Europe if the policy of community care is to be a success and if men and women are to successfully balance family, domestic and work roles. There is some hope however as these issues appear on the European agenda and 'specific improvements to working conditions and the needs of employees as carers are introduced through the European Union's social policies' (Tester 1996). Yet there are gaps in our knowledge of working carers which need attention. We know little of the situation of different kinds of carers for older people, for example, those in rural areas, minority ethnic carers across Europe; and we know little of the quality of care given at home and the effects of work on caregiving from the older person's perspective. All of these need attention in the literature. Data on carers in general are absent for many countries and there is little evaluation of already existing workplace-based schemes on which to base any conclusions. Research in these areas is necessary if this is to be identified as a priority workplace issue for all employees and employers.

7

EMPLOYMENT AND FAMILY LIVES

Equalities and inequalities

Julia Brannen

Introduction

One of the most significant changes in family life occurring in the UK and in many other Western industrialised countries is the changing structure of the labour market. The growth in female employment, especially during the family formation and early childrearing phases of the life course, is occurring in all European Union countries. This growth in female employment is accompanied in many European countries by a fall in male employment, the diversification of household structures, a fall in fertility and increased longevity (see Chapter 1). My main concern in this chapter is with a number of social processes related to these changing employment patterns. Changes in women's employment have been conceptualised in terms of integration, differentiation and polarisation (Humphries and Rubery 1992). Fine (1992) also outlines these processes thus: integration is the increased participation and greater spread of women across sectors and occupations; differentiation is the gap between male and female pay and conditions; and polarisation signifies greater differentiation within the female labour force. Especially marked are those who are marginalised within the labour market (and who remain segregated from men and face the poorest pay and working conditions) (Fine 1992: 161).

The first two of these three processes – the increasing integration of mothers with young children into the labour market and the differentiated pattern among groups of women – apply particularly to mothers' employment in the UK. The third process – polarisation – is evident at the household level, with a growing division of 'work full' or 'work rich' households and a continuing significant proportion of 'work less' or 'work poor' households, particularly among UK parents with dependent children.

In this chapter I draw upon primary and secondary analyses from national UK data sets (especially for the 1980s from the Labour Force Survey and the General

Household Survey) which constitute an important part of a major review of the relationship between employment and family life carried out by myself and colleagues at Thomas Coram Research Unit for the former UK Employment Department (Brannen *et al.* 1994).

Mothers' integration into the labour market

Over the past two decades there has been a revolution in both male and female employment patterns. Male employment fell by 2 million in the UK between 1977 and 1991, thereby reducing the proportion of men of working age from 91 per cent to 82 per cent (Balls and Gregg 1993). However, this fall in employment is not fully reflected in the rise in unemployment in the same period. The deficit arises in the context not only of early retirement but also in the changes in the UK official statistical definitions and a shift of many unemployed into the category of 'economically inactive'. Rising inactivity was also occurring among young and prime-age men, though less so among fathers with dependent children. Similar effects are to be found in other countries with a notably high increase in economic inactivity (OECD 1992).

At the same time as male employment collapsed, consequent upon the disappearance of jobs in the traditionally male manufacturing sector, a massive growth in female employment occurred – a rise of 22 per cent between 1983 and 1990 in the UK. Much of the growth in female employment is accounted for by mothers with dependent children. Their employment has risen from 49 per cent in 1981 to 59 per cent in 1989, after which it stabilised until 1992 (Bridgwood and Savage 1993; Thomas *et al.* 1994). What is striking about this growth is that half of the increase for mothers with dependent children has been in full-time work, while all of the increase among non-dependent women with children was in part-time work (Bridgwood and Savage 1993; Thomas *et al.* 1994).

Two factors have contributed to this employment increase among mothers. First, more women are resuming employment after maternity leave. There has been a striking increase in mothers returning to the labour market after having a baby, with about two-thirds of mothers economically active and nearly half back at work within nine months of having a baby by the end of the 1980s; a decade earlier the proportion was only a quarter (McRae and Daniel 1991). Moreover, under the maternity leave provision, mothers are expected to return to work full-time which may account, in part at least, for the rise in full-time employment among mothers with dependent children although fear of job loss is a likely contemporary factor. It is also important to note that UK rates with respect to full-time employment among mothers with very young children have risen from a very low base; only 5 per cent of women having their first child returned to full-time work within 6 months in 1945–49 while, in 1975–79, the figure was still only 8 per cent (Martin and Roberts 1984). A second trend is that women who do not return directly to employment following maternity leave increasingly return between births as well as after childbearing is finished (Martin and Roberts 1984).

The growth in the number of jobs which has occurred in the 1980s and 1990s can be accounted for by the rise in part-time work which is largely in the service sector, and is often low paid. Two-thirds of job growth in the UK in the 1980s was in part-time work and nine out of ten part-time jobs were held by women (Balls and Gregg 1993). Men do not take these jobs for a variety of reasons some of which are related, as will be noted later, to the employment patterns of their partners.

Differentiation in mothers' employment

Women's labour market integration is also leading to increased differentiation in their access to labour market opportunities. Employment rates among women with children grew faster during the 1980s than among women without children (more than 26 per cent compared with over 9 per cent) (Brannen et al. 1994). Employment grew fastest among women with fewer and younger children, white mothers, mothers with higher levels of education, mothers living with a partner and those living with employed partners. In contrast, employment grew more slowly or even fell among Afro-Caribbean mothers, women with older children, three or more children, no qualifications, among lone mothers, and mothers living with non-employed partners (Harrop and Moss 1994).

The upward shift in education levels in the 1980s among mothers is particularly striking. In 1981, the proportion of mothers with a qualification equivalent to 'A' level or higher was 20 per cent while 56 per cent of mothers had no qualifications; by 1989, these had changed to 26 per cent and 38 per cent respectively. Employment patterns reflect these changes in educational level. Employment among mothers with a degree rose much more quickly (from 57 per cent to 78 per cent) but much more slowly among mothers with no qualifications (from 44 per cent to 49 per cent). The most striking difference occurred among women with a child under 5 years, where the proportion of graduate women in employment increased from 36 per cent to 63 per cent compared to a modest rise from 18 per cent to 26 per cent for women with no qualifications (Harrop and Moss 1994).

Reflecting mothers' educational level, employment was highest among women with children in highest status occupations (75 per cent), falling to its lowest level for women in semi-skilled jobs (49 per cent) (Thomas et al. 1994). Moreover mothers in high-status jobs, which tend to be concentrated in the public sector, were more likely than those in low-status jobs to remain in the labour market following childbirth (McRae 1991).

In assessing the variation in mothers' employment opportunities, it is important to emphasise the continuing majority of mothers with dependent children who are in part-time work and, moreover, to note that, in the UK context, mothers in part-time jobs work very short hours: 60 per cent of mothers with a child under 10 years worked part-time for less than 20 hours a week (European Commision Network on Childcare 1993). Furthermore, the pattern of working shorter hours by British mothers with young children is accompanied by fathers working very long hours.

Household polarisation

Women's integration into the labour market and the consequent differentiation between groups of women can be analysed at household level. These patterns of integration and differentiation are contributing to growing polarisation between households in terms of their access to economic resources, especially income from employment. Two aspects of the resultant patterns of equality and inequality within and between households are considered: the different patterns of household employment and unemployment and their associated financial implications.

Household employment patterns

During the 1980s dual-earner families were in the ascendant, single-earner breadwinner families were declining, while a significant proportion of unemployed households remained, particularly among lone mothers. Among households with dependent children in 1981, nearly half contained two employed parents (48 per cent). Just over a third had one employed parent (34 per cent), divided between 26 per cent with two parents of whom only one was employed and 8 per cent headed by an employed lone parent. Fewer than a fifth of households (18 per cent) had no employed parents, divided between 7 per cent of households with two parents and 11 per cent headed by one parent (Bridgwood and Savage 1993). Consequently, there is likely to be enormous inequality between the 48 per cent of households with two incomes and the 18 per cent with no income at all.

As noted earlier, employment has grown fastest among women with children who are living with partners, and among those living with employed partners. Employment also rose fast among those who, like their employed partners, have high levels of education (Harrop and Moss 1994). Secondary analysis of the Labour Force Survey has indicated that in 1981 the chance of a mother with an employed partner being in employment herself was twice that of a mother with a non-employed partner, whereas in 1989 a mother with an employed partner was more than three times as likely to have a job (Harrop and Moss 1994).

Other secondary analysis of the Labour Force Survey further emphasises the rise in employment among women with young children in couple relationships during the 1980s. A surprising finding to emerge from the analysis is the extent to which the rise in female labour force participation is concentrated within households in which there is a couple living in a partnership and with very young children. In aggregate the labour force participation of mothers with partners and with young children (under 5 years old) present in the household rose by 2 per centage points per year over the period 1984–91, more than double the rate at

Table 7.1 Combined employment status of mothers and fathers in the UK 1981–89

Employment status	1981	1983	1986	1989
Both employed	44.4	4.8	49.1	57.1
Father only employed	45.5	1.8	36.8	32.4
Mother only employed	3.0	3.3	3.2	2.9
Neither employed	7.1	10.1	10.9	7.6

Source: Harrop and Moss (1994: 437).

which labour force participation rates grew for other women (Elias and Hogarth 1994).

Table 7.1 illustrates the combined employment status of mothers and fathers in two-parent families (Harrop and Moss 1994). It shows that among couple households, dual-earner households became the dominant group (57 per cent) in 1989. The proportion where neither parent worked stayed the same (around 7 per cent). But while the proportion of two-parent employed households has increased and the proportion of non-employed couple households has stayed the same, breadwinner households with one employed, male head of household fell significantly from 48 per cent to 36 per cent (Harrop and Moss 1994).

If we include single-parent households in the analysis of household employment patterns, the picture changes somewhat. Overall, according to the 1989 General Household Survey, single-parent households have increased rapidly in the 1980s, from 13 per cent of all families with dependent children in 1981 to 17 per cent in 1989 (OPCS 1991). Growth is largely accounted for by lone-mother families which increased from 11 per cent to 15 per cent of all families. As secondary analysis of the Labour Force Survey (Harrop and Moss 1994) shows, in the period 1981–9, the economic activity rates of lone-employed-mother households fell while the rate for lone-unemployed-mother households increased, in the latter case at a faster rate than unemployed couple mothers. Moreover the proportion of lone employed mothers in full-time work also fell as the proportion of employed couple mothers increased.

It has frequently been shown that wives of unemployed men are less likely to be employed than wives of employed men (see, for example, Davies *et al.* 1992). Secondary analysis of the Labour Force Survey shows that nearly two-thirds of mothers with an employed partner were also employed (64 per cent), compared to just over a third of those with an economically inactive partner (36 per cent) and only a fifth of those with an unemployed partner (21 per cent). The 1992 General Household Survey suggests similar variations, although working with smaller numbers (Thomas *et al.* 1994).

Yet other secondary analysis of the Labour Force Survey has suggested that the polarisation of 'work rich' and 'work poor' couple households operates in individual households over time. Gregg and Wadsworth (1995) examined the transition rates of individuals into and out of work over time in single-adult and couple households. They found that between 1979 and 1993 the chances of moving into work were much decreased in households where the other adult partner was also not in work, about half that of households where the partner was employed.

A number of reasons have been put forward for the strong association between partners' unemployment status relationship. One explanation relates to common characteristics, notably skill levels, while another reason proposed is that men who tend to experience unemployment (low-skilled, unqualified, etc.) are likely to marry women who have a low level of attachment to the labour market (Davies et al. 1992). A third explanation relates to the operation of the social security system which acts as a disincentive for married women to engage in paid employment, especially part-time employment, when their husbands are unemployed. However the disincentive effect does not appear to explain all the collapse of the workless families' transitions into employment (Gregg and Wadsworth 1995). Gregg and Wadsworth suggest that rather than underclass explanations which emphasise individual characteristics, explanations lie in the changing nature of work on offer in the labour market relative to the particular life course needs of families.

Complex relationships are also to be found between the economic activity and inactivity of other family members, not only partners. With respect to unemployment, we know that unemployment tends to run in families; unemployed young people (16–19-year-olds) are much more likely than employed young people to have another member of their family – either a sibling or parent – out of work (Payne 1987). Unemployment is, moreover, considerably higher among potentially economically active children (aged 16–22) living in a lone-parent household than in a two-parent household, and particularly high where there is a lone mother who is also unemployed (Elias and Hogarth 1994).

Households differ according to other characteristics, not only employment status, including occupations, working hours, contractual status and atypical employment patterns such as shiftwork and teleworking. The way in which each of these characteristics pans out at household level has implications for resource distribution but much of the analysis at household level remains to be done. With respect to working hours, we know that fathers in the UK work very long hours (see also Chapters 18 and 19) and mothers very short hours. More than a third of employed men with younger children work 50 hours a week or more (European Commision Network on Childcare 1993), a figure surpassed only by Ireland and well above the European average (Eurostat 1992). However there appears to be no inverse relationship between men's and women's working hours within individual households. In our own study of dual, full-time employed parents with young children, men who worked longer hours were likely to have partners who also worked longer hours (Brannen and Moss 1991; see also Dex et al. 1993b for a similar conclusion).

Households also differ according to their overall workload. If work is conceptualised more broadly than employment, there are further suggestions of polarisation between households. The 'Matthew effect' according to which 'he who hath more shall be given' (Matt. 25: 29) is evident also in household work strategies (Pahl 1984). Pahl found that two full-time earner households were more likely to engage in a broader range of household work strategies than households with fewer earners and or those working less than full-time. The range of work included employment, self-provisioning, informal work for other house-holds and purchasing household services on the market. However this analysis tends to underplay the significance of women's caring and other unpaid work inside and outside their households. For example, women working full time when they have young children have little time to allocate to caring and kin-keeping work (Brannen and Moss 1991).

Financial equalities and inequalities between families

Despite the rise in the employment of mothers with dependent children, families with children are, on average, worse off financially than households without children. This occurs principally as a result of mothers' employment histories, in particular mothers' absence from the labour market during childbearing and their subsequent return to lower-status, part-time jobs which result in diminished lifetime earnings (Joshi and Davies 1993) and downward occupational mobility (Dex 1987; Martin and Roberts 1984; Brannen 1989). Moreover, while the gap between these families and families without children was fairly stable in the UK throughout the 1960s, the 1970s and much of the 1980s, it widened substantially between 1988 and 1991. Goodman and Webb (1994) suggest that this is because of the growth in the number of childless professional couples in their late 20s and early 30s who have postponed parenthood as they progressed up the career ladder.

Among couples, those who are childless and economically active have the highest incomes while the group with the lowest income consists of couples with children and the mother economically inactive (Central Statistical Office 1991). The income of households with children and both parents economically active was higher than childless households with an economically inactive woman. In accor-dance with their declining numbers, one-earner two-parent households are at an increasing financial disadvantage (Corti and Laurie 1993). Apart from the relative disadvantage of one-earner households over two-earner households, there is a further financial effect. Fathers with an employed wife earn 10 per cent more on average than fathers with an economically inactive partner. This reflects the higher levels of education and higher-status jobs among the rising number of dual-earner households. However, income in dual-earner households with a child under 5 years old was substantially lower than in other dual-earner households, probably reflecting the shorter hours still worked by most employed mothers with young children (albeit the rate of full-timers is increasing).

Overall the least well-off were those families with no earners. Some of these are two-parent households with a large number of children. These families, especially the children, appear to be among the most disadvantaged:

At half average income as the poverty line, in 1979, 73 per cent of children were in poverty in households with an unemployed head, as against 4 per cent where the head was in full-time work . . . [while] the corresponding figure rose to 88 per cent and 15 per cent respectively by 1990/91.

(Kumar 1993: 41)

Goodman and Webb (1994) conclude that, with an eight-fold growth in unemployment from the 1960s to 1980s, families with children now make up more than half the poorest decile group for household income compared with only around a third three decades ago.

Distinguishing between single-parent versus two-parent households, it is notable that the UK, in common with many other countries including Australia, USA, Canada and Italy, has a high rate of young children in single-parent families who are in poverty (Kennedy *et al.* 1996). As noted, a major cause of poverty among lone parents can be attributed to their low level of employment. Data from the BHPS study indicate that lone parent households, most of whom were headed by mothers, had less than half the income of one-earner couple households, but the lowest incomes were for couple households with no earners. Income is, moreover, lower in single employed parent households with younger, rather than older, children (Corti and Laurie 1993).

In addition to the unemployment of fathers and the non-employment of many single mothers, a further explanation for poverty among households with children is low pay:

Corresponding to an increase in the incidence of low pay by over a quarter between 1979–88, the percentage of children living in households with a low paid [full-time employed] worker as head increased from 26 per cent to 33 per cent in the same period, and to 37 per cent by 1990/91 involving three and a half million children – over a quarter of all children in the country. Significantly, two-fifths of children (1.4 million) in low paid families were also living in poverty (defined as half national average income), thereby suggesting a close link between low pay and child poverty.

(Kumar 1993: 60)

The growth of income inequalities in the 1980s owed a considerable amount also to a substantial increase of inequality in self-employment incomes. As the self-employed have become an increasingly significant group in the labour force over the last fifteen years or so, the incomes of this group have become more diverse so that they are over-represented at both ends of the income distribution. However, the main source of income inequality remains inequality in net earnings which also increased during the 1980s (Goodman and Webb 1994).

Conclusion

Concomitant with the consistent growth of female employment in recent decades, a number of social processes – integration, differentiation and polarisation – are at work which involve the creation of greater material equality within some households but exacerbate inequality between groups of households. Mothers, in particular those with young children, have been increasingly integrated into the UK labour market especially those with higher-level educational qualifications and higher-status jobs who also tend to work full time. This increase is reflected in mothers' tendency to defer having children until they are established in their careers and to remain in their jobs following maternity leave. An uninterrupted employment career in which women return to the jobs they held before maternity leave results in women having increased opportunities for job promotion (that is compared with mothers who resign from the labour market at childbirth) (Brannen and Moss 1991).

These advantaged mothers tend to live in partnerships with men of similar educational and occupational levels, resulting in some cases in greater equality in earnings between themselves and their partners. While these women may acquire a greater degree of financial autonomy, that is, particularly in those partnerships where resources are separately managed (Brannen and Moss 1991), mothers do not necessarily define their earnings as having equal status compared with those of their partners; being a main or equal earner may lead to a strategy of under-statement (Brannen and Moss 1991). Moreover the division of childcare and household work may not alter significantly (Brannen and Moss 1991). The assump-tion that the dual-earner lifestyle is an outcome of mutual couple negotiation, especially with respect to family life, is currently unsupported by the evidence.

The chapter has also suggested that women's integration into the labour market has different consequences for different groups of women, with fewer advantages for black mothers, mothers with more and older children, for those with few or no qualifications and in low-status occupations and more advantages for those with the converse characteristics.

These trends are leading to widening differences in economic activity between mothers in different socio-economic groups at household level. They exacerbate existing social class inequalities based upon men's occupations and are clearly apparent among families where there are young children. Household employment patterns or strategies cluster; all possible permutations of employment status and hours are not equally common. Indeed like appears to attract like resulting in a polarisation between households. At one end of the spectrum there is a growing number of full-time, continuously employed women who are in partnerships. They contribute to a growing cadre of high-status, well-qualified and high-income households. These 'work rich' households are likely to resolve the domestic division of labour problem not by increased sharing between parents but by buying services, particularly those which replace 'feminine tasks' such as childcare and particular types of housework chores (Gregson and Lowe 1994). The net result of buying services is to provide jobs mainly for women but also to reinforce differentiation in the labour market, with one group of high-status employed mothers relying on the services of a second group of women in lower-status jobs. At the other end of the socio-economic spectrum, there is a growing proportion of 'work poor' households, mostly headed by single mothers who are dependent on state benefits and bringing up their children on low incomes. The complementary employment strategy, by which one earner (typically male) or two earners including one partner (typically the mother) work shorter hours, though still large in number, is not increasing its share of the distribution.

At present most information we have concerning employment trends and household types focuses upon the distinction between single- and two-parent households. In the UK it has not so far been possible to identify properly step-families, especially the situation in which a father no longer lives with the children of his first or former partnership but lives in a new partnership. The 1989 Child Support Act requires fathers to contribute to the financial support of their biological children with whom they no longer reside. These obligations have important consequences in terms of financial transfers for children of both their first and second families (where they have children with new partners), with the potential for increasing the incomes of the former but at the expense of the latter.

There is at present little data on the rise of atypical and flexible patterns of working and their implications at household level (for an exception, see Dex and McCulloch 1995). Research has concentrated on occupational status within couples (for example the phenomenon of the cross-class family) (McRae 1986). The ways in which parents' employment strategies intersect is clearly relevant to children's access to care and other resources, together with the further issue concerning the ways in which the scheduling of children's lives relates to parents' work schedules. On working hours, the pattern according to which British mothers with young children work short hours does not necessarily mean that, within individual households, this pattern is accompanied by the similarly common pattern of fathers working very long hours.

Of course, in emphasising financial inequalities between households which arise from household employment trends, I do not mean to suggest that the advantaged, i.e. employed households, do not exhibit other types of inequality. While women's employment may have some effect on what happens to income when it enters the household, it cannot be assumed that income is necessarily distributed in equitable ways to household members (Brannen and Wilson 1987; Pahl 1989). The issue is how far individual desires and priorities conflict with, and take precedence over the interests of the collectivity (Morris 1989). Indeed there is considerable evidence that the distribution of different types of household resources, especially between men and women, is far from equitable (Brannen and Wilson 1987).

The extent to which these processes are reflected in consciousness at the household level is a matter for investigation. As more mothers in the UK question

Part II

RESTRUCTURING
LABOUR MARKETS

8

EMPLOYMENT, FLEXIBILITY AND GENDER

Eileen Drew and Ruth Emerek

Introduction

This chapter introduces Part II on Restructuring Labour Markets in which women are adopting an ever increasing role, with thousands of women joining the workforce in different EU states. It shows how women's activity rate has increased in all countries in the European Union, at the same time as men's activity rate has declined in most countries. As a result, women form an increasing part of the labour force in all countries – on average 42 per cent for all member states in 1995, ranging from 36 per cent in Luxembourg to 48 per cent in Sweden (Eurostat 1996c). The chapter goes on to outline how the flexibility requirements of employers have led to gendered forms of 'atypical' working in which women predominate in part-time employment[1] while men are more heavily represented in shift working, night/evening and weekend forms of 'atypical' working. These employment patterns have had a differential impact on segregation, pay and conditions and the career prospects of women and men in EU labour markets.

The major impetus for labour market change has been the shift from agricultural- and/or manufacturing-based economies to service-based economies, in which service occupations now predominate. One of the consequent manifestations of this shift is in relation to quality and customer orientation, suggesting that quite different norms and values are emerging within enterprises. Another important implication, linked closely to flexibility, is that working conditions are no longer bound by 24-hour production cycles, usually in 8-hour shifts, as exemplified in the manufacturing enterprises. Indeed, with the growth in the service sectors, there has been a growing demand for uneven, extended hours that may vary throughout the week. Finally, under increased competition, enterprises are demanding changes in the way work is performed, which is undermining the 'male model' of work: the 40-hour week, in full-time, permanent employment throughout a continuous and unbroken working life, which necessitated a cleavage from any home-based activities and family connections. This pattern is being eroded by employers' need to cover uneven hours in the workplace giving rise to different balances of working time and workplace practices, and the simultaneous use of full-time plus part-time arrangements.

The connection between an increase in women's activity rate and an increase in 'atypical' working time, and the need of flexibility in new as well as in old sectors is thus obvious, though the pattern is different in the various EU countries. This chapter shows and discusses the development in women's labour market participation and outlines and elaborates on 'flexibility', in some of its many forms, within the context of EU labour market trends.

Labour market participation and 'atypical' work forms

With an increasing activity rate for women and a decreasing activity rate for men, experienced at different speeds in EU countries, we are seeing the emergence of a dual breadwinner model whereby both women and men take responsibility for supporting the family. The activity rate for women of working age (15–64 years) has increased by nearly 10 per cent in most countries within the last ten years (see Figure 8.1). At the same time most countries have experienced a similar growth in the most typical form of 'atypical' working: part-time employment (see Figure 8.2).

France, the UK, Belgium and the Netherlands have an increasing and relatively high female activity rate of c. 60 per cent in 1995, coinciding with rising levels and a high proportion of part-time working (c. 30 per cent in 1995). Only Portugal has, over the same time period, experienced a high female activity rate of c. 60 per cent in 1995 with a low or static proportion of part-time employment (c. 10 per cent in 1995). Countries where women's activity rate (according to official statistics) is increasing and still lower than 50 per cent in 1995 are: Spain, Greece, Italy, Luxembourg and Ireland, in which low levels of part-time work (10–20 per cent in 1995) are the norm. These data do not capture unregistered homework (Chapter 10) or those engaged in the informal economy (Chapter 11).

Exceptions to this general pattern are Germany, where the proportion of part-time work is static at around 45 per cent and the female activity rate is increasing to c. 65 per cent in 1995, and Denmark where the proportion of part-time working is declining (c. 35 per cent in 1995) at the same time as the activity rate is still increasing, if slightly, to almost 80 per cent in 1995 (Eurostat 1996c).

The connection between growing activity rates and the ratio of part-time to full-time employment is not as simple as the overall picture shows. It suggests that there is a difference due to the level in women's activity rates. The figures illustrate that women's increasing participation in the labour market proceeds in different ways, at different levels and at different speeds in various countries. In some countries it is still possible for women's participation to rise in an extensive way, by including more women in the labour market – primarily as part-timers, as in the Netherlands, but also as full-time employees, as in Portugal. Other countries, with already high female activity rates, like Denmark, women's increased

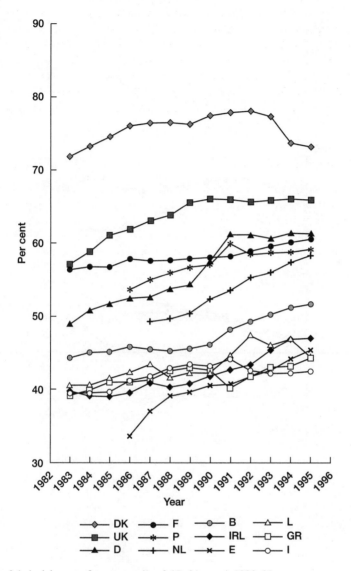

Figure 8.1 Activity rate for women (aged 15–64 years) 1983–95.
Sources: Eurostat (1995b, 1995c, 1996c).
Note: The decline in activity rate in Denmark may be due to new sampling methods being used from
1994 (see Eurostat 1996b).

participation has occurred through more intensive use of women's labour (from
part time to full time). In Germany, women's increased participation has been
achieved through extensive and intensive use of women's labour.

This indicates that the development in women's employment is connected to

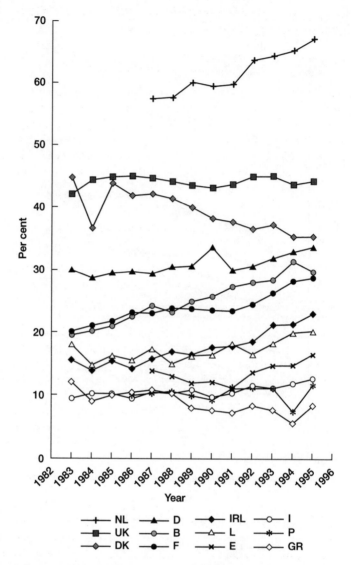

Figure 8.2 Part-time workers as a proportion of all employed women 1983–95.
Sources: Eurostat (1995b, 1995c, 1996c).

factors other than the availability of part-time jobs and the need for flexible working time, and that the strategy used to attract women's labour is constrained by traditions, norms and culture as well as the distribution of sectors and labour market regulations in different countries (Chapter 10). The question is how this can be applied to the pattern of growing demand for flexibility. Part-time working forms only one strategy for providing flexibility in the workplace. Other 'atypical' work forms are outlined below.

Temporary working

Unlike part-time employment, in which there is a consistent divergence in men's and women's rates, the levels of temporary, shift and weekend and homeworking tend to be similar for women and men within the EU (15). In 1995, temporary working was slightly more common among men accounting for 7.3 million male jobs and 6.6 million female jobs (Eurostat 1996c). Temporary employment is most common in Germany, Spain and France which together accounted for 58.9 per cent of all temporary workers within the EU (15).

Weekend and homeworking

'Atypical' working can take the form of non-standard full-time hours as well as alternative arrangements of weekly hours as in Saturday/Sunday working and alternative locations such as working from home (Chapter 9). Regular or occasional working on Saturdays affected 46.5 million male workers and 28.0 million female workers; regular or occasional working on Sundays affected 25.7 million male workers and 14.5 million female workers in 1995, throughout the EU (15). Similar proportions of women and men usually worked on Saturdays (28.3 per cent) while more men (25.2 per cent) than women (17.2 per cent) sometimes worked on Saturdays. Sunday working was also performed by almost equal proportions of women and men at 11.4 per cent and 11.9 per cent respectively, but it was more common for men to sometimes work on Saturday (17.7 per cent) compared with women (12.2 per cent). Homeworking was performed by 6.8 million workers who usually worked from home and a further 10.9 million who sometimes worked from home. It was marginally less important for female workers, with women accounting for 47 per cent of those who usually work at home and 35 per cent of those who sometimes work from home (Eurostat 1996c).

As a proportion of total employment, Saturday working as the usual pattern was most common for men in Greece (46.5 per cent), Italy (40.5 per cent) and Spain (38.2 per cent) compared to the average EU (15) level of 28.3 per cent of all male workers usually working on Saturdays. Among women the proportion was similar, with Saturday working most important in Italy (43.8 per cent), Spain (41.5 per cent) and Greece (40.2 per cent) compared the average EU (15) female rate of 28.3 per cent. The countries in which usually working on Sunday was commonest for men were Finland (22.2 per cent) and Ireland (21.8 per cent) compared with 11.9 per cent in the EU (15). Among women the proportion usually working on Sunday was highest in Denmark (21.9 per cent), Finland (19.5 per cent), Sweden (18.7 per cent).

Homeworking (as the usual pattern), as a proportion of total employment, was highest among men in Ireland (24.1 per cent), Denmark (11.9 per cent) and

Belgium (10.3 per cent), while the EU (15) average for men was 4.2 per cent. Among women, the highest proportions usually working from home were found in Belgium (11.6 per cent), Austria (11.4 per cent), Denmark (10 per cent) compared with the EU (15) average of 5.2 per cent.

Shift work

Shift working was more important for male than female workers in 1995, with men accounting for 64.6 per cent of the 18 million workers who were usually or some-times engaged in shift work. Evening shifts were worked, usually or occasionally, by 31.9 million men in the EU (15), and 16.6 million women workers. Night-shift working was even more likely to be associated with men, with 16.5 million men working usually or sometimes at night compared with 5.7 million women (Eurostat 1996c).

Gender and 'atypical' work forms

If examined as a whole it is clear that 'atypical' working takes on complex and varied forms, and these tend to be gendered. Women workers are most heavily involved in part-time working patterns, compared with male workers. Although, numerically, fewer women are working in a non-permanent capacity, the pro-portion of temporary workers among women is higher than for men. Weekend working is more common and important among male workers and the gender difference is even more pronounced among shift workers. Men are much more likely than women to work evening and night shifts. Home working is more evenly distributed among men and women and accounted for a slightly higher proportion of women's jobs.

Overall this gendered pattern of 'atypical' working shows that men and women are situated in very different forms of alternative work patterns. Men are much more likely to be engaged in atypical work to maximise their take-home pay, by working at times and on shifts which attract a premium, bonus or overtime payments (Drew forthcoming). If women's atypical working is examined collec-tively, and part-time and weekend/evening shifts are interwoven, it is more likely that these options will reduce rather than raise their net earnings. A pattern emerges in which men's work, whether in full-time typical employment or atypical shift/weekend working, allows them to best meet the 'male breadwinner' role, while women's working patterns, much of which occur outside 'typical' employ-ment, facilitate their reconciliation of work/household commitments and thereby reduce their earnings and impede their career advancement.

The concept of flexibility and atypical working time

During the 1980s flexibility was heralded with the same awe and suspicion (depending upon who was responding) as the 'demographic time-bomb' has been. At one extreme 'flexibility' can be viewed as: a 'strategy for the intensification of the exploitation of women's labour power' (Cockburn 1991: 35); 'uninterrupted disturbance of all social conditions' and 'not simply a one-off process of removing a set of entrenched rigidities, but also a means of adapting institutions and expectations of uncertainty' (Hyman 1991: 282). A more benign interpretation is adopted by Atkinson who saw flexibility in terms of changes in institutional, cultural and other social or economic regulations and practices which facilitated the capacity to adapt to turbulence and uncertainty (Atkinson 1985).

Under the umbrella of 'atypical working' in the EU, Meulders *et al.* (1994) outlined many forms including: part-time employment, temporary employment, home working and shift working. Their study showed that the major developments at European level were in the use of part-time and temporary employment as methods of reorganising working time. The growing, if uneven, proportion of part-time employment suggested some degree of convergence particularly since the mid-1980s, while, with the exception of Italy, the growth in temporary employment declined from 1985 (Meulders *et al.* 1994).

For many labour market observers, 'atypicality' has become synonymous with women's employment. Such generalisations mask the fact that within atypical work practices, there is a further layer of sex segregation through which men predominate in shift and night working, self-employment and sub-contracting, traditionally associated with tougher working conditions and greater health risks. Women are over-represented among part-time workers, assisting relatives, home-workers and employees on temporary contracts, where the pay and/or social security coverage are lower than in 'typical' occupations. The gender balance is more mixed among seasonal and casual employees throughout the EU (Eurostat 1996c).

The 'reconcilers' and flexibility

The issues of reconciling family and paid work are extremely relevant to the female activity rate for women aged 25 to 49 years. A high proportion of women in this age group have dependent children living at home, or elderly relatives to care for – or both. This age group of women *have not only the highest female activity rates but also the highest increase in activity rates* compared to women aged 15–24 (whose activity rate has declined due to participation in education) and women aged 50–65. The same tendencies occur in all countries so that women aged 25–49 years have an average EU activity rate of more than 50 per cent. In the Nordic countries the activity rate is over 80 per cent (as shown in Figure 8.3).

Figure 8.4 shows that more than 40 per cent of all women aged 25–49 years were working full time, 20 per cent were working part time and nearly 10 per cent were unemployed in 1995. The rest (30 per cent) were not in the labour market and, according to official statistics, were 'economically inactive' in 1995. Though this picture varies between countries, partly due to the (non) availability of unemployment benefit, it shows clearly that more than half the women in the

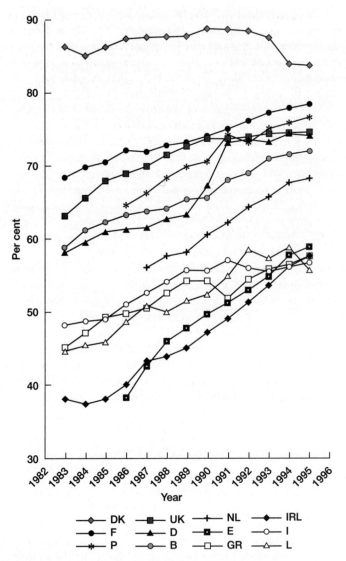

Figure 8.3 Activity rate for women (aged 25–49 years) 1983–95.
Sources: Eurostat (1995b, 1995c, 1996c).

age group 25–49 years are either part-timers, unemployed or not part of the EU labour market. A proportion (difficult to quantify) of these women may hold two part-time jobs, are engaged as homeworkers or are employed in the informal economy.

Working mothers, as parents, need flexibility, which may be achieved by working flexible hours or by working part-time. To a certain degree this appears to be

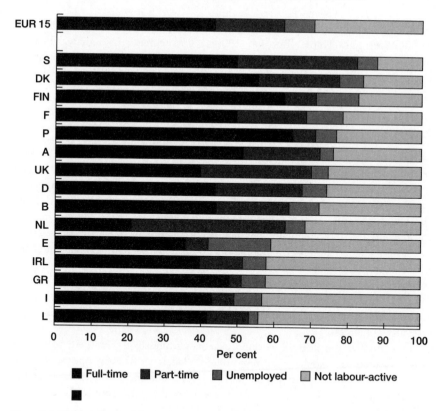

Figure 8.4 Women in the labour force (aged 25–49 years) in the European Union (15)
1995 by full-time, part-time, unemployment and non-labour market activity.
Source: Eurostat (1996c).

true – but it can be difficult to match the flexibility needed for home-based work with the flexibility needed in the workplace. Restrictive service provision schedules, such as those which pertain in Denmark, limited hours of opening (e.g. of crèche facilities and shops), pose further restrictions on women's labour market participation, since it is women who are more directly responsible for the 'time dependent' tasks (e.g. shopping/child collection), than men, who are more likely to be involved in 'time independent' tasks (e.g. house/garden maintenance) (Emerek 1987). Such mothers were traditionally expected to seek employment which matched the scheduled hours when children were in schools and crèches (Chapter 12), or to become homeworkers due to lack of childcare (Chapter 10).

Yet women in the age group 25–49 years have the highest activity rates and have the least flexibility. Compared to younger and old women, those aged 25–49 years have the highest proportion of full-time jobs in most member states and a lower proportion of unemployed in all countries. The only exceptions to this pattern are Austria, Luxembourg, Belgium and Germany, where women aged

25–49 have a higher proportion of part-time employment than women in the labour force as a whole (Eurostat 1996c). The increase in activity rates for women aged 25–49 years also indicates that fewer women leave the labour market even during periods of caring.

Gender segregation and flexibility

Throughout Europe, the 1970s, 1980s and 1990s have been typified by economic turbulence in world trade, economic output and the world of work, characterised by fragmentation and restructuring. Atypical work practices account for an increasing segment of EU labour markets and this process has had important implications for gender relations within the labour market. At a European level, the penetration of an increasing number of women into the labour market, through atypical employment, 'has not been accompanied by any decrease in gender-based segregation' (Meulders *et al.* 1994: 235). Gender segregation of the labour market has been maintained, even recreated, in new forms, and the highest increase in women's activity rates has been found in countries which have experienced the highest expansion in sectors which already employ a high proportion of women (Maruani 1992): in service jobs already marked by low-paid, part-time, irregular contracts.

In examining the flexible working practices which have emerged, there is a strong element of 'old wine in new bottles'. Pollert (1987) was one of the first authors to analyse the concept from a more critical perspective, by challenging the apparent 'newness' of the term and what it implied for different social partners:

> It is precisely the flexibility of human labour which is recalled, before time and task rigidity imposed themselves; the recapturing of this flexibility remains central not just to post-industrialists, but also to socialists and the labour movement in general.
>
> (Pollert 1987: 4)

Other authors noted a similar conclusion to that of Pollert in their comment that 'the forms taken by these types of atypical employment have not necessarily been innovative all the time' (Meulders *et al.* 1994: 233). In reality, part-time employment has been a post-war strategy utilised by some employers, especially in the UK and Denmark, to meet labour shortages and attract married women into the labour market. More recently, part-time employment has been promoted to address the problem of unemployment, most notably in the Netherlands. Italy in the 1950s was typified by a high degree of formal flexibility, especially for employers who could hire and fire at will. This was reversed with the growing power of the trade unions so that by the 1970s and 1980s rigid labour market conditions prevailed at a formal level, supplemented by a burgeoning of informal flexibility through subcontracting, multiple jobbing and informal economy work (Chapter 11).

So flexibility and atypical work can be the answer to different problems and different constituencies seek different things from part-time work:

> governments see it as a solution to rising unemployment; employers see it as a way of securing flexibility, and perhaps cheap labour; and employees see it as a way to combine paid and unpaid work. This pulls part-time work in different directions.
>
> (Humphries and Rubery 1995: 23)

In conclusion, the current state of turbulence can lead society and labour markets in two different directions. If the route to flexibility equates solely with deregulation, it would be flexibility for the firm or the employer only (Chapter 9). In a restructuring process flexibility could lead to the further marginalisation of women workers and result in extended gender segregation within the labour market. Alternatively, flexible work practices could bring joint benefits for employees and employers. This requires a situation where we acknowledge that, while enterprises need different flexible work forms, labour market participants also have different potential contributions to make and varying income needs, throughout their working lives.

Note

1 For more detailed accounts of demand for part-time employment and trends in EU member states, see Drew (1990 and 1992).

9

PART-TIME EMPLOYMENT IN A EUROPEAN PERSPECTIVE

Susan McRae

Introduction

Women's working lives are shaped both by the extent and nature of their other responsibilities and by the job opportunities open to them. Across Europe, part-time work is a common way for women to combine paid work with family responsibilities. It is clear, however, that not all part-time working arrangements suit women's needs and that the conditions within which women work part time can affect their ability to function successfully in both spheres.

Indeed, differing employer strategies regarding the use of part-time labour can often be more important for shaping those workplaces than the gender composition of the workforce. This may mean that women working in establishments with differing part-time strategies have markedly different employment experiences. The evidence presented below suggests that part-timers will be better off in workplaces where part-time employment was introduced initially in response to employee requests. In these workplaces, managers appear *less likely* to offer part-timers lower hourly wages than full-time workers in comparable jobs or fewer fringe benefits, despite believing that part-timers contribute less than full-timers to improving competitiveness or the quality of the goods and services produced.

However, even when part-time working is voluntary, and the expressed preference of women, the question may be raised whether it is to their advantage, or whether it is the case that working part-time reinforces women's generally disadvantaged position at work and perpetuates their economically subordinate status at home. It has been argued, for example, that 'part-time employment . . . is of very little personal value for women, because of job insecurity, awkward working hours, and restrictions on movement to full-time work' (Meulders *et al.* 1991: 156). Those who believe in the social and economic desirability of more part-time jobs would argue, in contrast, that new opportunities for women are created through the provision of part-time working hours, and that women who would not have otherwise sought paid employment are thereby encouraged to enter the labour market.

This chapter examines the advantages and disadvantages of part-time work for women[1] in Europe, according to two different part-time strategies, through the findings of survey research.

A European perspective

A European perspective is adopted for this chapter. That is, information is presented and discussed in relation to eight European countries as a whole, as if there were no important differences between them. But of course that is not really the case. Both women's employment experiences generally and their experiences of part-time work in particular vary from country to country, often quite dramatically. One useful distinction is between the development of part-time work in northern and southern European countries (Blossfeld 1994). In northern Europe, women's participation in part-time employment changed considerably over the post-war period: between the 1950s and 1970s, it grew rapidly and steeply, only to stabilise or grow slowly during the late 1970s and into the 1980s and 1990s. In contrast, the expansion of part-time work among women in southern Europe only began in the 1970s and has reached only comparatively low levels. In Italy, Greece, Portugal and Spain, the large majority of employed women in 1995 worked full time (see Chapter 8).

Of particular interest is the differing impact of the growth in women's employment on employers' use of part-time working hours. In general, part-time employment is highly responsive to the proportion of women in the workforce, and the higher the proportion of women employees, the greater the chances that part-time workers will be employed. However, the relationship between the number of women in paid work and the amount of part-time employment is not always consistent (Chapter 8). None the less, the rate of women's employment is not the *only* influence on the use of part-time workers, and women may be responding to employers' decisions to introduce non-standard working hours as well as purposively seeking ways of working which accommodate their other responsibilities.

Part-time strategies

The reasons why employers introduce part-time work into their establishments may have important consequences for women workers, and provide a useful way of examining the variety of women's experiences. Two contrasting types of part-time work can be found in European workplaces, based on the reasons for the initial introduction of part-time employment. The first of these is found in establishments where management decided initially to use part-time working arrangements in response to economic or organisational need. These workplaces, which we refer to as '*corporate strategy*' workplaces, are characterised by employees who adapt their labour supply to employers' labour demands; and by managers who consider that part-time work yields considerable advantages and few disadvantages to their organisations.

The second type of part-time work develops in establishments where part-time employment was initially introduced in response to the wishes of full-time workers for reduced working hours. These workplaces, which we call '*individual strategy*' workplaces, are characterised by employers who adapt their working practices to fit individual labour supply choices; and by managers who tend to see fewer advantages flowing from part-timers and more disadvantages.

Of course, such categorisations are primarily heuristic; they refer to 'averages' and 'trends', rather than to individual firms or employers. It would be incorrect to assume that within all workplaces categorised in this way, employment decisions always happen on the basis of 'will' or 'strategic thinking'; the suggestion runs against the grain of common sense. None the less, much of our information suggests that strategies do exist, and that they shape the experience of part-time work for women in important ways. The following provides a summary of the main characteristics of 'corporate strategy' and 'individual strategy' workplaces as they affect women employees

Survey of part-time strategies

A survey was carried out on behalf of the European Foundation for the Improvement of Living and Working Conditions in 1989/1990[2] to investigate the experience of new forms of work and activity at establishment level. Management interviews were undertaken in 3,520 private sector establishments with ten or more employees in eight European countries – Belgium, Denmark, West Germany, Ireland, Italy, the Netherlands, Spain and the United Kingdom. Interviews were also carried out with employee representatives in 1,621 establishments. For both management and employee representative interviews, part-time work was defined as all working-time arrangements with a contractual working time below the accepted full-time level in each workplace.[3]

The rate of part-time work in the survey establishments was lower than that reported for national workforces as a whole. One likely explanation is that the sectors which were excluded from the survey were ones with above average part-time rates: agriculture, the public sector, and workplaces with fewer than ten employees; moreover, evidence from European Labour Force Surveys supports this suggestion. Thus lower part-time rates reported by the survey establishments reflect the actual situation in different parts of the economy. None the less, it should be borne in mind that the findings presented here relate only to private sector part-time employment, which, arguably, may provide the fewest advantages for women (Maier 1991).

The focus of the surveys was the establishment rather than the individual employee. Thus, the chapter examines the experience of part-time work for women in an *indirect* way. That is, the experiences of individuals employed in part-time jobs cannot be analysed directly because these were not explored by the surveys; instead, we focus upon establishments *with differing proportions of women employees*. Survey workplaces in each country were divided into groups according to the share of the workforce held by women in each workplace, relative to the share of women in the total workforce of the country. A workplace in any country was considered to be a 'low share' workplace if the proportion of women employees in that workplace was *smaller* than that found nationally; they were designated 'high share' workplaces if they employed *proportionately more* women than found in the country's labour force. The majority of women (62 per cent) worked in 'high share' or mostly women workplaces, while the largest group of men (46 per cent) worked in 'low share' or mostly men workplaces. Twenty-eight per cent of women and 35 per cent of men worked in establishments where the proportion of women matched that found nationally ('medium share'). Ten per cent of women worked mostly with men in 'low share' workplaces; 19 per cent of men worked mostly with women in 'high share' workplaces.

This approach allows us to describe the working environments of women part-time workers who worked mostly with other women, mostly with men, or in establishments that fell somewhere between these two extremes. Not all women (or men) who worked in such establishments would necessarily share the experiences described by our analyses. But it is likely that a great many would, and in this way the paper provides a *broad-brush* view of part-time work in Europe as experienced by women.

Corporate strategy vs. individual strategy workplaces

In the majority of survey workplaces, and particularly in those with a low proportion of women workers, part-time work was initially introduced in order to meet organisational or economic exigencies. In only about 1 in 5 predominantly male workplaces was part-time employment originally introduced to meet staff requests for reduced working hours, while in 61 per cent of 'mostly male' workplaces, it was introduced mainly for reasons of corporate strategy. In 'mostly female' workplaces, 44 per cent of workplaces introduced part-time work for reasons that may be identified as corporate strategy, while 31 per cent originally introduced part-time working hours in response to employee requests.

Part-time workers are more extensively used in establishments which introduced part-time employment for reasons which might be described as being part of a corporate strategy. In 41 per cent of 'corporate strategy' establishments part-timers accounted for at least 12 per cent of the workforce; in over three-quarters of such workplaces, they accounted for 5 per cent or more. This pattern contrasts markedly with the distribution of part-time workers in workplaces that initially introduced part-time employment in order to satisfy employees' wishes for reduced working hours. In these workplaces, part-timers made up only 1 or 2 per cent of the total workforce in 11 per cent of establishments; and no more than 5 per cent of the total in 1 in 3 establishments. In other words, a corporate strategy towards part-time hours results in a greater proportion of workplaces engaged in a high use of part-time workers, particularly in workplaces with a high share of women employees, and a greater proportion of employees working alongside part-time workers. An 'individual part-time strategy' leads to scatterings of part-timers among establishments: that is, to proportionately few part-timers working in many workplaces, with the result that almost two-thirds of the work-force in 'individual strategy' workplaces was accounted for by establishments with no more than 5 per cent part-time staff.

Managers in 'corporate strategy' workplaces are more likely to think that women with young children are inappropriate part-time workers, and to prefer unencumbered, prime-age and healthy workers to fill their part-time positions. They are more likely than managers in 'individual strategy' workplaces to recruit part-timers from the external labour market than from among their own employ-ees; their employees are more likely to experience changes in workload, during the day, from day to day and over the course of the year. Such managers tended to attribute a positive role to part-time workers in improving competitiveness or the quality of the goods or services produced. In contrast, when part-time work was introduced mainly in response to employee requests for reduced working hours, managers were substantially less likely to think that part-timers contributed positively to competitiveness or the quality of goods and services produced. This accords well with the idea of managers' agreeing to accommodate the individual employment preferences of their workers, rather than setting out to construct a labour use strategy which purposively incorporated the use of part-time workers.

Managers' attitudes

Managers' attitudes towards part-time workers have consequences for women's chances to enact employment strategies which allow them to combine paid work with other responsibilities. Managers across workplaces with differing proportions of women employees and differing part-time strategies tended to agree that part-time workers brought advantages in terms of labour turnover and manpower productivity. Their perceptions of other possible advantages of part-time workers were linked to the gender composition of the workforce. The higher the propor-tion of women workers, the more likely managers were to think that advantages derive from part-time employment in relation to improving competitiveness and the quality of the goods and services produced.

It was, however, only a minority of managers who reported that their establish-ments gained cost advantages from part-time employees through the payment of lower hourly wages relative to full-timers in comparable jobs (managers repre-senting 6 per cent of the workforce) or the provision of fewer fringe benefits (managers representing 9 per cent of the workforce). The segregation of part-time and full-time workers into different jobs within the workplace and, in relation to the provision of fewer fringe benefits, the concentration of part-timers in most countries into lower-level manual work, is likely to account for our survey *not* revealing more employers taking similar action, since we asked managers to compare the relative cost advantages of part-timers and full-timers in comparable jobs.

Employee representatives' attitudes

The views of employee representatives can influence part-time working arrangements and, therefore, women's working lives. Our information about employee representatives and part-time work comes from representatives who had responsibility for negotiating working conditions with management, of whom 85 per cent were male.

The most common response to the introduction of part-time working hours found among both men and women employee representatives (speaking for 46 per cent and 47 per cent of the workforce respectively) was to support part-time working hours *only* if it was explicitly requested by employees (conditional support). Employee representatives speaking for about 1 in 5 of the workforce reported that they were against part-time work and *tolerated it* only if it was explicitly requested by employees. A small minority of employee representatives (6 per cent of men, 3 per cent of women) reported that they were against part-time employment *under all circumstances*.

Employee representatives' attitudes towards part-time jobs were affected by the workplace part-time strategy. There was more support for part-time work among representatives in 'individual strategy' workplaces, although mostly conditional support. Representatives in 'individual strategy' workplaces speaking for 56 per cent of the workforce reported that they supported part-time employment when employees requested it. In 'corporate strategy' workplaces, the figure fell to 40 per cent.

Employee representatives were positive about the impact of part-time employment: when asked whether they thought that part-time work helped or harmed women's job opportunities, men and women representatives each speaking for 66 per cent of the workforce considered that part-time employment *helped* women's job opportunities.

Advantages of part-time work

A priori one would expect that the primary advantages of part-time working for women include, first, the existence of job opportunities where none might otherwise exist and, second, flexibility in the labour market of a kind wanted by women at different stages in their lives. Our research suggests that these advantages exist, but that they are more often found in 'individual strategy' workplaces. Generally, opportunities in the labour market are likely to expand for women who want to work fewer than full-time hours: our evidence indicates that women are more likely than men to work in establishments that are growing and less likely to work in establishments experiencing workforce reductions.

Almost half of the employees who worked in 'high share' or mostly women

105

workplaces were in establishments where managers reported increases in the overall size of the workforce during the previous three years, compared with just over one-third of employees who worked in 'low share' or mostly male workplaces. Part-time employment was one of the areas of growth in 'high share' workplaces. Workplaces with a high share of women workers were also more likely to have avoided workforce reductions: managers who reported having fewer workers now than three years previously represented one-fifth of employees in 'high share' workplaces, but almost one-third of employees in 'low share' establishments.

From full-time to part-time hours

In order for part-time employment to be advantageous to women, they must not only have opportunities to move from full-time to part-time jobs when it suits them, but they must also have opportunities to move back into full-time work when the need to work part-time no longer exists. In creating such opportunities, managers' attitudes are decisive: where managers think that women with young children are appropriate part-time workers, movement between full-time and part-time working hours is possible and often happens quickly. But it was also true that the higher the proportion of women in a workplace, the more likely management was to receive requests for reductions from full-time to part-time working hours, and the more likely they were able to grant those requests.

Where workplaces had similar part-time strategies, a high share of women employees led to increased requests for reduced hours. However, a comparison between workplaces with differing strategies showed that managers in 'corporate strategy' workplaces were substantially less likely to receive such requests. This is somewhat surprising, and may indicate something about the differing culture, or atmosphere, of workplaces where part-time employment was introduced mainly in response to employees' requests. That is, it is possible that more full-time workers in 'individual strategy' workplaces *come forward* with requests for reduced working hours because they know from the experience of co-workers that management is open to such requests. Alternatively, it might be that more full-time workers in 'individual strategy' workplaces *want* to work part-time, but this seems less plausible. Certainly, it was not the case that, once asked, management in 'corporate strategy' workplaces were any less likely to grant such requests, given similar proportions of women workers.

Although a few differences in managers' ability to meet requests for part-time work existed between managers in workplaces with different part-time strategies, these tended not to be extreme and, indeed, tended to disappear altogether in workplaces where women represented a high share of the total. It appears, then, that differences in part-time strategies led not so much to variations in the ability of management to meet requests for reduced hours, but to differing workplace cultures which influence the willingness of full-timers to come forward with such requests. This suggestion is given further support by an examination of the links between management's attitude towards the appropriateness of women with responsibility for the care of young children as part-time workers, and employee requests to move from full-time to part-time hours.

Where management believed that women with responsibility for young children were appropriate candidates for part-time employment, requests from full-time workers for reduced working hours were more frequent. In addition, not only were these managers more likely to be asked for part-time working hours, they were more likely to meet such requests favourably. If it can be argued that the views of managers reflect the workplace culture of an organisation,[4] then it seems clear that the *milieu* within which women work has consequences for their opportunities to enact employment strategies which allow them to combine paid work with other responsibilities. Furthermore, where managers were open to the part-time employment of women with small children, they received more requests for reduced working hours, whatever the part-time strategy adopted in the workplace.

Indeed, in those workplaces *least likely* to receive requests from employees for reduced working hours (that is, 'corporate strategy' workplaces), managers who favoured the part-time employment of mothers were much more likely to grant such requests than their colleagues who considered mothers to be inappropriate part-time employees. There appeared, in fact, to be little in their views to distinguish them from managers in 'individual strategy' workplaces.

From part-time to full-time hours

If opportunities to move from full-time to part-time working hours can be seen as advantageous to women wanting to combine paid employment with other activities, then it follows that women also should have opportunities to return to full-time work when they want. To investigate this, managers were asked to describe what happened in their establishments when a part-timer asked to work full-time. Where part-time work was introduced mainly in response to employee requests for reduced hours, workplaces responded more favourably and more rapidly to requests from part-timers to increase their working hours. Managers representing 38 per cent of the workforce employed in 'individual strategy' establishments reported that part-timers could move into full-time work quickly. This contrasts sharply with 'corporate strategy' workplaces, where only 17 per cent of the workforce were in establishments where such a move could happen quickly. Moreover, an inability to move quickly into full-time work was found in workplaces where part-time work was introduced mainly to meet the economic or organisational needs of the establishment, regardless of the proportion of women in the workplace. Further, in 'high share corporate strategy' workplaces, however, managers representing more than one-third of the workforce (36 per cent) reported that movement from part-time to full-time working hours could happen only under special circumstances or not at all. This is likely to be related to the way in which part-timers are used in 'corporate strategy' workplaces. It may be that in these workplaces, as a matter of policy, the bulk of women's jobs are organised on a part-time basis and thus there may be few opportunities to work full-time, much less to move from part-time to full-time working hours.

The pattern changes in 'individual strategy' workplaces. Here the most common pattern among managers receiving requests for a move from part-time to full-time was to respond quickly to the request, whatever the gender composition of the workplace. And in contrast to 'high share corporate strategy' workplaces, part-timers employed in 'high share individual strategy' workplaces were particularly likely to be able to return to full-time employment. Indeed, managers representing only 2 per cent of employees in the latter workplaces reported that there was no chance that such a request would be granted; while managers representing just over 1 in 10 of the workforce reported that a move to full-time work could happen only under special circumstances. Again, the explanation seems likely to be related to the organisation of employment within the establishment. As these workplaces recruit part-time workers largely from among their current full-time staff, and frequently through the request of an employee for reduced working hours, it seems likely that sufficient full-time opportunities exist for management to respond quickly and favourably to a request for extended working hours.

Working hours

The most common arrangement for part-time working hours was 'some fixed hours every morning'. This arrangement was practised by a majority of establishments with part-time work, and was also the most important arrangement in establishments representing more than half of the workforce in establishments with part-time work. However, where part-time had been introduced primarily as part of a 'corporate strategy', a wider range of arrangements existed for part-time working than was the situation in 'individual strategy' workplaces.

Taking the gender composition of the workplace into account confirmed the general pattern, and suggested that, in relation to the main pattern of working hours used in an establishment, the gender composition of the workplace is less important than the part-time strategy adopted.

In 'individual strategy' workplaces, the typical part-time arrangement of 'some fixed hours every morning' stands out as the most favoured option. This arrangement, which was practised in 'individual strategy' workplaces covering about two-thirds of the workforce, is the most likely to fit with the childcare arrangements made by women in a wide variety of countries. In Germany and Italy, for example, kindergartens and public schools are normally open only in the mornings; similarly, childcare arrangements for pre-school age children in the UK often are restricted to mornings. If we assume that many women will want to choose part-time hours that mesh with their childcare arrangements, then 'individual strategy' workplaces appear to give them that freedom, whatever the gender composition of the workplace.

Where part-time employment was introduced mainly as part of corporate strategy, there is increased use of all remaining part-time arrangements, including arrangements whereby working hours are fixed only a few days in advance according to the needs of the establishment ('flexible hours'). Of course, a large number of women workers usually means a large number of part-time workers, which *may* mean many different part-time working arrangements – at least if, as appears to be the case in these workplaces, *management* chooses how and when to deploy part-time labour. None the less, the typical part-time arrangement of 'some fixed hours every morning' remains the most common arrangement, even in 'corporate strategy' workplaces.

Disadvantages of part-time work

The disadvantages of part-time work are likely to lie in reduced income, reduced rates of pay, lack of access to training and poor opportunities for promotion. We asked employee representatives about the disadvantages – if any – faced by part-time workers in their establishments. Their unprompted responses suggested that in relation to wages, fringe benefits and job security, part-time workers were thought to be better off – often markedly so – in establishments where part-time hours were introduced mainly in response to employee requests. For example, employee representatives speaking for 3 per cent of the workforce in 'low share individual strategy' workplaces reported that part-timers in their establishments received fewer fringe benefits than full-timers. The corresponding figure for representatives in 'low share corporate strategy' workplaces was 12 per cent. Similarly, representatives speaking for 5 per cent of the workforce in 'medium share individual strategy' workplaces reported that part-timers in their establishments had poorer job security than full-timers. Among representatives in 'medium share corporate strategy' workplaces the corresponding proportion was 23 per cent.

But employee representatives in 'individual strategy' workplaces expressed strongly negative views about the promotion opportunities open to part-timers. They indicated that in this respect at least, part-timers were worse off than full-timers, and no better off than part-timers in workplaces where corporate strategy dictated the use of part-time working hours. The explanation for this may lie in the different ways part-timers are integrated into organisations with differing labour use strategies. If part-time working arrangements exist largely to satisfy the (possibly time-limited) demands of employees for reduced working hours, there may be little incentive (from the employer's perspective) to create promotion opportunities for part-timers. After all – employers might argue – employees who ask to work part-time most commonly do so in order to balance domestic responsibilities with paid employment and it is unlikely that these responsibilities would fit comfortably with the extra work involved in gaining promotion.

Where part-time employment was introduced initially in response to employee requests, however, managers were less likely to pay part-timers lower hourly wages than full-time workers in comparable jobs or to give them fewer fringe benefits;

and employee representatives were more likely to view reduced working hours as improving job opportunities for women.

When managers thought that women with young children were inappropriate for part-time work, establishments were more likely to offer poorer terms of employment for part-time workers and reduced opportunities for training, regardless of workplace part-time status.

Conclusions

Involuntary part-time employment is one possible result of a clash between the actions of employers who wish to improve their firms' competitiveness, and the decisions of individual women who wish to work full-time. It may also be the result of widespread unemployment. But in addition to involuntary part-time employment, there may be other unfavourable outcomes for women flowing from the drive towards flexibility on the part of employers. The type of part-time employment preferred by employers – in terms of working hours, for example – may not match the type of part-time work wanted by employees. In this way, while a woman may wish to work part-time in order to combine paid work with other activities, the part-time work available to her might not allow her to combine these activities with ease.

Part-time jobs might not, then, always meet the interests of *both* employers and employees. More commonly, it seems likely that part-time work will be *either* to the advantage of the company *or* to the advantage of the woman. This is perhaps most readily illustrated by reference to pay rates. It is clearly an advantage to employers if they are able to pay part-time workers a lower hourly wage than that paid to full-time workers for the same work. And equally clearly, such a situation would not be advantageous to women (or men) employed part-time.

The view adopted here is that fairly paid and non-exploitative part-time employment can be advantageous to women if it is voluntarily taken up. This is not to suggest that women choose to have bad jobs or poorly paid jobs or jobs that are without security or protection. Nor is it to deny the force of gender socialisation which inculcates in many women a deep sense of responsibility for the primary upbringing and care of children. Rather, it is to argue, simply, that women are faced with labour market choices (full-time employment, part-time employment and no employment) which have differing consequences, and that many women see part-time employment as a way of obtaining a desired objective while experiencing the fewest unwanted consequences.

The assessment of part-time work is contradictory. On one hand, part-time work creates employment opportunities for women and is favourable to continuous working during periods of childbearing and childrearing. On the other hand, part-time employment means less income in comparison with full-time employment, and may mean lower hourly wages for the same work. Part-time employment can be incompatible with career advancement, when promotion opportunities are biased towards full-time workers and part-timers are confined to a narrow range of occupations and industries. The reason for the introduction of part-time work into an establishment powerfully conditions the experience and practice of part-time work.

In the past, trade union opposition to part-time employment resulted in its exclusion from collectively bargained rights, and in the creation of a largely peripheral and unprotected workforce. More recently, unions have recognised that part-time work has become a fixed feature of the labour markets and employment structures of most industrialised countries. Accordingly, unions have generally recognised the need to include the working conditions of part-time workers in the collective bargaining process, although only in some countries have union efforts resulted in an equalisation of wages and fringe benefits.

The promotion (or extension) of part-time work by governments (or by employers) does not automatically lead to the creation of good part-time jobs of the kind wanted by employees. The fact that many women want to work part-time for at least some part of their lives does not imply that they wish to work inflexible or awkward hours, in precarious, low-paid jobs that attract few fringe benefits. It should be a matter of importance to ensure that the promotion of part-time employment does not lead to the substitution of normal full-time jobs or good part-time jobs by marginal part-time jobs.

Notes

1 The reasons men and women take up part-time work tend to differ. Although both groups may accept part-time working hours as an alternative to unemployment, male part-time workers tend to be older or younger than the male labour force generally, or suffer from health problems. For Europe as a whole in 1989, about 3 per cent of men and 29 per cent of women worked part-time (Eurostat 1991).

2 The results of these surveys were published in full in January 1992 in a report entitled *New Forms of Work and Activity: A Survey of Experiences at Establishment Level in Eight European Countries* (Bielenski 1992).

3 The universe of the surveys comprised establishments in the non-agricultural private sector with at least ten employees. The distinction between private and public sectors was made identically for all eight countries on the basis of the European classification of economic activities (NACE). The surveys included NACE 1 to 6, NACE 7 (except 71, 72 and 79), NACE 8 and parts of NACE 9. For full technical details see Bielenski (1992).

4 It may not be the decision of the individual manager who was interviewed for the survey to allow employees to move from full-time to part-time jobs (or vice versa). None the less, his or her attitude is likely to reflect those held generally by decision-makers in the organisation.

10

HOMEWORKING

New approaches to an old problem

Sheila Rowbotham and Jane Tate

Homework – the paid employment of women in the home – is often seen as an archaic form of employment associated with Victorian images of sweated labour rather than the economies of modern Europe. Yet recent research has shown that homework has been a resilient survivor right through the twentieth century and is very much alive and well in the 1990s. It is a form of production which can be grafted easily on to flexible manufacturing systems and homeworkers are currently assembling, machining and packing products for some of the biggest companies in the world. They are very much part of the new global economy; integral to the 'flexibilisation' or 'casualisation' which has accompanied new technology and deregulatory policies.

Yet their circumstances remain elusive. Official sources give little information about homeworkers. Their employment is usually unregistered and sometimes illegal. Government surveys which derive their information from official statistics, censuses or from employers' records consequently often omit homeworkers altogether. Few homeworkers are members of trade unions, so they are not usually covered by labour research either. However, the extent of homework in Europe is becoming evident through a growing body of research into the informal sector which is complemented by the findings of grassroots organising groups (Phizacklea 1983; Allen and Wolkowitz 1987; Mitter 1992; West Yorkshire Homeworking Group 1990).

This documentation of homeworking is rooted in a wider understanding of women's work which has implications not simply for women but for employment policy as a whole. Several factors have contributed to this significant shift in perspective. The feminist movement has challenged a narrow definition of work, pointing to the interconnection between the home and employment and this has had repercussions in a growing recognition of the significance of gender in economic development. Over the last decade, women's networks internationally have collected and exchanged information about the conditions of poor women in both the formal and the informal sector (Brett 1991; Boris and Prugl 1996). Moreover as the evidence has come in of the proliferating informal sector globally, terms such as 'atypical' have begun to look increasingly inappropriate. A new paradigm of employment is clearly needed, not only to comprehend the changing realities of the poor, but to develop effective strategies for reform (Holland 1993).

Making homework visible

Uncovering the extent and character of homeworking is not an easy matter. The systems of recording and estimating are extremely diverse and legal definitions vary from country to country (Tate 1995). In some European countries home-workers are registered and can thus be located statistically. Germany, for example, has a law specifically covering homeworkers. As a result thousands are recorded 'on the books' with the highest proportion working for the engineering, optical and chemical industries. In Madeira, the autonomous island region of Portugal, embroidery homeworkers make up about 20 per cent of the total workforce. Here statistical estimates are possible because they won official recognition as a result of their union's twenty-year battle. In Italy and France the law requires registration of homeworkers, but it is widely acknowledged that large numbers work infor-mally and thus remain untraceable.

In most countries official records are problematic sources, covering only a minority of those who are actually working (Chen and Sebstad 1996). This has forced researchers to use a variety of alternative methods of assessment; the consequence has been a patchwork of studies which have complemented the existing statistical material. Investigation has come out of several contexts. For instance, in Britain community groups began to record and organise homeworkers from the early 1980s; in the Netherlands similar projects from the mid-1980s were started by women's groups in connection with the trade unions. Feminist researchers focusing on the growth of an informal sector, particularly in the clothing industry, have contributed information about homework in both these countries, as well as in Italy; while in Greece and Spain material on homework has come to light through research on local economies. For example, a recent survey of the dramatic economic expansion of Thessaloniki in Greece, found many homeworkers through household surveys. It was thus possible to map out sub-contracting chains linking the growth of the informal sector with production for export in a range of industries, including clothing, footwear, electronics and engineering. In Spain, similarly, a regional survey of women's agricultural work in four areas of the country revealed women doing industrial homework in clothing and footwear (Tate 1996).

Characteristics of homework

Though most homeworkers are women there are some broad distinctions which can be made geographically in the structure of the labour force and in the social groups who do homework. In northern Europe homework is common in minority and migrant communities, though it is also to be found among indigenous women in both cities and in the countryside. In southern Europe it is likely to be in both rural and urban areas, can be linked to craft production and is common not only among those who are impoverished but among the better off.

There is great variety in the types of work being done by women at home. At one extreme thousands of women in Madeira do hand embroidery just as their mothers and grandmothers did, often combining it with growing vegetables and fruit on small plots of land. At the other extreme, car wiring systems are being assembled by hand for subcontractors of the giant car companies of Europe. Clothing and textiles are still probably the most likely to be 'put out' to be done in the home, but homework is to be found in almost all types of jobs, including white-collar 'telework', using information technology (Huws 1984).

In such places as Madeira or in the shoe-producing regions of Italy, homework is rooted in an artisanal industrial tradition; skills have been built up over generations and passed down from mother to daughter. In other areas, homework is a new development, part of a restructuring of industry that has taken place as a result of global trends. In rural Spain for example, the widespread nature of garment and shoe production done at home is a recent occurrence. These diverse types of homework mean it is oversimple to interpret homework in terms of theories of one over-arching system of organising production such as post-Fordism simply replacing a 'Fordist' model. Capital's search for means of cutting costs is capable of taking on manifold aspects.

Women's work

One generalisation does, however, hold good; homework is predominantly 'women's work'. A common factor is evident in the surveys conducted both locally and nationally in the United Kingdom and the research which is emerging now from other parts of Europe; women take up homework mainly because of the lack of alternative ways of earning a livelihood (Rowbotham 1993). This is as true for the former textile workers in Holland's urban and industrialised areas where the factories have closed down, as it is for the rural workers of southern Europe who are finding it more and more difficult to make a living in agriculture. While men are sometimes forced to become migrants, the women are left in the villages to care for the children. This has been the basis for the growth of homework in the north of Portugal for instance where shoe factories are putting out the labour-intensive work of sewing the uppers to women in poor villages.

The particular restrictions on women's access to employment outside the home can be seen then to vary even though the results are the same. Similarly it is important to recognise that the *kind* of obstacles faced can differ even within the same region. Two surveys in West Yorkshire for example in the early 1990s showed white homeworkers usually preferring an option of work outside the home but reporting problems with childcare; it was either not available, too expensive on a low wage, or not conveniently geared to school hours for older children. Asian women however stressed their difficulty in getting work outside the home and their fear of racial violence and abuse when going out to work.[1]

Homeworkers are invariably caught in a web of low-paid employment options and are forced to rely on doing several types of work. For example in some rural areas of Spain the regional economic surveys revealed that women are combining agricultural work with seasonal homework. In the very different context of urban England, homework is often combined with part-time work outside the home such as cleaning in offices or serving school dinners.

The lack of alternative jobs, inadequate childcare, bad transport and in some cases a low educational level are important constraints preventing many home-workers from getting better-paid work. There are also strong ideological pressures which, while they vary from country to country are versions of the same refrain; a woman's primary duty is to the family and her place is at home. Cultural attitudes towards gender thus reinforce the invisibility of homework as activity sited within the personal domain. They legitimate the view that homework is not 'real' work, even though in many cases where the man is unemployed it has now become the main source of family income.

There are some examples of men being engaged in homework. In Greece for example, men were found doing homework in industries such as engineering which are regarded as 'male'. In England, homeworking projects are now report-ing more men doing homework in communities with high levels of poverty and unemployment. In general, however, homework is seen as women's work, not least because the terms and conditions under which it is usually done would not be seen as acceptable to men.

Pay and conditions

As information has been gathered both within Britain and internationally, it has become possible to make comparisons which take into account distinctions among homeworkers as a group. A minority, usually highly skilled women with experi-ence of factory work, can be treated equally with their counterparts in factories. In the north of England garment machinists who have been forced to give up their jobs through changes in family circumstance often continue to receive work at home from their employer on similar terms as before. In Germany, the main engineering union, IG Metall, employs one officer specialising in organising homeworkers, many of whom are doing highly skilled component assembly work. The union negotiates rates of pay and conditions for them which are better than those laid down in Germany's homework legislation.

However, for the majority who take up homework, pay rates are well below either legal minimum rates or average earnings in the industry concerned and this low pay is exacerbated by irregular work. Protection through employment laws or trade unions is virtually non-existent. Also homeworkers are rarely compensated for expenses such as heating, lighting, storage space, or the cost of running and maintaining machinery or time taken collecting or delivering goods. They are unlikely to be covered by social security schemes for sickness, maternity or old age or by health and safety protection while working. Nor is there significant protection against dismissal or a right to redundancy payments.

The informality in the arrangements of employment leads to uncertainty and the irregular flow of work can be extremely stressful; homeworkers often report that they have too much work or too little. In Britain, for example, it is common for work to be delivered just before the weekend so it can be ready for Monday morning. Consequently homeworkers can labour through the night to meet deadlines. On the other hand they can wait in the house for an expected delivery which never turns up. Uncertainty and irregularity can easily become downright abuse. Payment can be withheld on a pretext of work done badly and, as homeworkers often know only the delivery man and may not even have the name and address of the employer, there is little they can do about this.

Occasionally the dangers of unregulated homework hit the news. In Italy the glue used in the leather industry was shown to be causing paralysis among local women and girls working at home. In general, however, the injuries remain hidden. Injuries and disablement caused by repetitive actions in unergonomic conditions are common. Hazards include paints, solvents and dust or chemicals in fabrics. Soldering work can produce toxic fumes. Machinery in the home is not always fitted with safety guards and may be lethal on a domestic electricity supply.

Stress, depression and tiredness from long hours of repetitive work also have a predictable effect on health. The stressful nature of homework is intensified when women are juggling their work with childcare, other domestic work and several other paid jobs. Many feel guilty because they cannot meet all the demands upon their time, particularly giving children attention. They are usually isolated from other women doing similar work and have no one with whom they can discuss their problems. Nor is there anywhere that they can go to leave their work behind.

New methods of production

It has always been the case that homeworkers provide a workforce at a low cost to employers, who save on wages, benefits and overheads. Similarly homework has always flourished in industries which employ casual or seasonal workers and have a quick turnover of goods with a variable and changing demand. Homework as a form of production is commonly associated with the kind of fly-by-night manufacturing which operates through cheap labour rather than capital investment or with small firms selling their products on the local market – it is sometimes called a 'cottage' industry with this image in mind. From the 1980s evidence that neither of these tell the whole story has been steadily gathering. Following the closure of well-established large-scale clothing factories and the growth of imports from companies in Asia, a new way of competing with the rates of pay in poor countries developed in Britain. Long subcontracting chains led from homeworkers, often from minority communities, through small companies, who could in turn be linked to giant companies which distributed goods produced through major retailers. This was not production for market stalls; it was not even necessarily just for a national market either (Mitter 1986a, 1986b).

By the 1990s it was becoming evident that subcontracting chains were operating internationally. Pioneering research from homeworkers groups supported by the Dutch trade unions traced goods made in Holland to big British shops. Sectoral and local economic investigations in Spain and Greece provided similar information showing that even where the particular work being done is traditional, the markets and chains of production are increasingly being determined by global patterns. Thus in the San Santiago region of Spain for example, where women have long done hand embroidery for a local market, this has recently been linked to multiple retailers and an export trade. Similarly in parts of Ireland and Scotland, traditional hand-knitting is now produced for export to the USA or Japan.

Not only is craft work becoming globalised, homework has expanded as an alternative to factory production. The study of Thessaloniki revealed subcontracting chains operating in northern Greece with orders from Germany to smaller companies who made use of homeworkers and family enterprises. While the Spanish shoe industry, which had always included some homeworkers, was becoming more dependent on low-paid flexible homeworkers in response to competition from Asia. Factories have been closed down and the production of shoes put out to small workshops in rural areas where it is done by homeworkers.

Tracing the chains

The global subcontracting chains are extremely difficult to trace and have been developing in the obscurity of the undocumented twilight economy. Stimulated by homeworking organisations and the questions raised by sectoral and local economic researchers the European Commission has supported the first attempt to look systematically at the diverse manifestation of these new methods of production and distribution on a European basis. The result is Jane Tate's survey *Every Pair Tells a Story* published in 1995. Since there is no official record of these chains and major companies are usually not forthcoming with information, the starting point was the findings of groups in Greece, Italy, Portugal, Spain, the Netherlands and the United Kingdom, who had already begun to exchange information through homeworking networks. A small number of homeworkers known to be working on products for big companies were selected for in-depth interviews. They ranged from leather footwear workers in Greece, Italy and Portugal, along with embroiderers in Portugal to a wider selection of industries in the United Kingdom and the Netherlands which included clothing and car production. Their evidence was complemented with information from trade unionists, employers and researchers.

Some features of the survey reinforced national and local studies of homework. The majority of homeworkers in all the countries examined were married women between the ages of 20 and 40, with one man in the sample from Greece and one from the UK. Wages and conditions were generally bad. In most places home-workers were working informally, outside the law and thus not covered by employment or social security legislation. Madeira and Italy were the exceptions; there all the homeworkers interviewed were registered.

The innovative aspects were the discoveries of the different patterns of production and employment which have been multiplying and the international context in which they are set. A remarkable number of variations upon the same theme were uncovered. In Italy, a small artisan firm was producing children's shoes for a major retailer in the UK. A number of different subcontractors and self-employed artisans were used in the production process as well as homeworkers, both registered and unregistered. The firm was typical of the region which was known for producing medium- to high-quality footwear for the national market and for export. The response to the crisis in the industry in Italy had been further decentralisation and specialisation within an industry that was already based on small firms.

Greece showed certain similarities, particularly in the skills of the homeworkers, many of whom had years of experience and some of whom had been factory workers. There had been recent expansion because factory closures had resulted in more work being subcontracted to small firms. The industry was less special-ised, however, than Italy and produced lower-quality shoes. Equipment and raw materials came from outside the country.

In Portugal the picture was different again. Here the homeworkers interviewed were working through intermediaries for subsidiaries of big companies based in northern Europe. Work was being put out to remote villages where leather shoe-making had only recently been introduced and even the factory-based workforce was 'green' labour. The homeworkers were hand-sewing the uppers of shoes. Paid extremely low wages and employed on an irregular basis, the women never knew when there would be work. In one case the factory concerned was only producing the uppers of shoes which were then exported to France where the whole shoe was made up.

In Spain a new company of fashion retailers was bringing together two distinct strands of production. Their standard goods were being produced in low-wage areas like Asia, while their more fashionable clothes were produced in Spain near to their headquarters. Key parts of the production process, such as cutting and dyeing, were kept within the company, but the bulk of labour-intensive work was being put out to small workshops, who in turn put out work to homeworkers.

In contrast, most clothing retailers in the UK have moved out of manufactur-ing, becoming removed from the process of producing clothes and from the workers who make the goods they sell. Many have moved into property dealing and banking. Retailers increasingly tend to source all their products from inde-pendent companies. The chains of agents, subcontractors, intermediaries and small companies work for UK companies which are expanding their retailing operations in Europe, as well as for companies based in other parts of Europe. In both cases homeworkers are a crucial element which enables the small companies to keep down their costs and maintain flexibility.

Tate (1995) indicates also that homework can be found in industries that are generally assumed to be based on factory production alone. One trade unionist in a major supplier of electrical equipment for cars reported that his company had recently started putting out work. This supports other evidence collected by local homeworking groups of components in the car industry being assembled at home.

Interviews with employers, researchers, subcontractors and homeworkers showed that the adoption of putting out methods was in response to the pressure on companies to compete, with big companies having the capacity to move production around the world to suit their needs. In the clothing and footwear industries, for example, many big companies have sourced their goods outside Europe in Asia. European producers, however, still have the advantage in being able to respond more quickly to changes in orders with shorter lead times. They are, however, under intense pressure to keep down costs. Subcontractors and employers pointed out the low cost of producing clothes and shoes in countries such as China and Vietnam. Other production sites mentioned were North Africa and Turkey. The most recent openings are in eastern and central Europe and the Baltic states.

Individuals felt trapped by global forces over which they had no control. One of the homeworkers interviewed in the Netherlands for instance was making samples for a Dutch clothing company. The work which was originally all done in the Netherlands had moved first to Turkey and then to Lithuania, leaving only the sample making. She anticipated, however, that her job too would be shifted to Lithuania as soon as someone was trained. A subcontractor from Italy was pessimistic about the future of his company which faced further cuts in profits in the face of foreign competition. In this situation the modest gains made by Italy's legislative regulation of the informal sector since the 1970s were under threat. Even the registered homeworkers there complained of long hours and low pay. As one said:

> Should I calculate the years that I have worked since I was eight years old then I could say that I have worked as a man of eighty years old, instead of a woman of fifty years. And this has not been my personal fate but the fate of hundreds of women of my age living in this area.
>
> (Tate 1995: 17)

Along with the homeworkers of Greece, the embroiderers of Madeira and women in the UK who were making up whole garments, the Italians were not lacking in skills. These were not the most vulnerable groups of homeworkers. Yet they had a grim and accurate apprehension of the odds against them. On the one hand were giant, highly concentrated companies, operating on a world scale in terms of both their marketing and sourcing of goods. At the other extreme there were women who lacked mobility or flexibility in terms of employment options, had families that they cared for and communities in which they were embedded. Tate's work echoes a question posed by Huws *et al.* (1989) 'What price flexibility?'

It also shows that the process of 'flexibilisation' is calling into question a clear distinction between an 'informal' and a 'formal' sector. While unregistered home-workers can be said to be working in the informal sector, this is closely linked to formal production and to major companies. The marked trend in Europe has been to meet growing competition by decentralising and moving production from the large workplace with a unionised and legally protected labour force to the informal sector where labour is flexible and low paid. Chen and Sebstad (1996) who come to similar conclusions, observe that homework does not 'emerge simply because workers prefer to work at home but because employers prefer workers to work at home.'

An international response

The 1990s have seen mounting unease about the economic, social and political consequences of the unfettered market-led policies of the 1980s. Awareness of the importance and size of the informal economy and the realisation that those working for it are outside all forms of employment or social protection and regulation have reached official circles. There is concern in the European Union about 'social exclusion' and the development of a dual labour market in Europe, with a flexible workforce, the majority of whom are women, migrant and immi-grant workers, confined in an employment ghetto. Homework was on the agenda of the International Labour Conference in 1995; an indication of the need to adapt how 'labour' is defined and categorised to changing realities. A significant breakthrough came at the ILO's second discussion of the topic in 1996, when it adopted a Convention supplemented by a 'Recommendation on Homework'. This was achieved despite opposition from the employers' lobby in the ILO and presents an interesting example of an alliance between women researchers and campaigners with trade unions and some states' representatives.[2] Policy demands which had been developed through grassroots groups with homeworkers have thus over the last decade made their way through to the international institutions (Rowbotham 1993; Huws 1995). Now the question is how to make sure that recommendations are implemented.

Trade unions in the older industrialised countries faced with dwindling mem-bership numbers, are being forced to recognise the importance of developing new ways of reaching unorganised sections of the workforce. Not only has there been sustained pressure within their ranks, especially from women, but the problem of a flexible low-paid workforce has landed on their doorsteps. The recent history of attempts to organise among homeworkers has thus assumed a new relevance not only for small grassroots organisations but for trade unions internationally.

Several examples exist within Europe which suggest alternative tactics and strategies towards the informal sector could be possible. On the island of Madeira, for example, the Union of Embroiderers has been led since the early 1970s by women determined to organise not only in the factories but in villages and rural areas where all the embroidery is done by women at home. Years of dedicated work have gone into building up the membership among homeworkers and winning reforms, step by step. As a result, homeworkers in this industry in Madeira have won recognition, social security protection and the right to old age pensions, even though the rates are low. Italy presents a somewhat different example. Here in the 1970s the unions and the women's movement successfully campaigned for a law protecting homeworkers. After this was introduced, redefining homeworkers as legitimate workers, some unions have shown a commitment to the difficult task of recruiting and maintaining a membership among homeworkers. In Britain, the scattered local projects set up from the early 1980s to advise and support homeworkers have recently come together with researchers and trade unionists to form the National Group on Homeworking, an independent organisation which gives homeworkers a national voice.

Outside Europe, the extent of the informal sector and the need to develop new methods of organising in order to bring social protection to the informal sector has long been the subject of debate and campaigns. The depth of understanding and the range of grass roots projects which make up these new social movements have thus grown apace in the last two decades (Wignaraja 1992, Rowbotham 1993, Marten and Mitter 1994). A notable example is the Self-Employed Women's Association (SEWA) in India which has been working in the informal sector since the 1970s. It began in Ahmedabad, Gujerat, among women who carried cloth in the markets and expanded to other regions reaching many thousands of workers outside the existing trade union movement, including home-based workers. SEWA is a poor women's trade union which has developed a bold and creative approach towards organising, incorporating strategies from the trade union and women's movement as well as from cooperatives and development bodies. They combine resistance with cooperative economic initiatives and services for practical survival such as training; they also pay careful attention to the specific and varied needs of the home-based workers who are members, whether they are making *bidis* (cigarettes), *agabatti* (incense), garments or quilts. SEWA helps them not only with finance and production methods but in finding markets and in improving products. Nationally and internationally SEWA has also campaigned through the trade union movement and international institutions like the ILO for the recognition of homeworkers in employment law (Rose 1992; Jhabvala and SEWA 1994; Jhabvala and Tate 1996). The ILO itself has adapted SEWA's innovatory work in India to other countries through programmes in South East Asia. In the Philippines, Indonesia and Thailand there are ILO-backed projects helping homeworkers to help themselves.

The 1990s have seen the development of international communication networks among the groups working with homeworkers; these include those linked with trade unions and non-governmental organisations, usually consisting of women. Their central concerns have been to find ways of making homework visible and to organise homeworkers so they can improve their conditions of work.

These networks were formalised in 1994 when the international network, Home-Net was set up to exchange information between homeworkers' organisations and coordinate work at the international level.

In 1995 and 1996, HomeNet concentrated on campaigning for the adoption of the Convention on Homework by the ILO. It also started a newsletter and has published a series of bulletins, which, through case studies and interviews spread information about organising with homeworkers at the grassroots. Within Home-Net a European Homeworking Group has coordinated work in Europe, supplementing the written accounts of organising by exchanging experience through meetings and visits. These developments have all helped to raise the visibility of homeworkers. They have created a space for debate about the role of homework in the production process, about new ways of organising homeworkers and other informal sector workers and about how to develop legislation and policy informed by the circumstances and needs of homeworkers themselves.

The adoption of the ILO Convention in June 1996 marks a new phase by laying the basis for further work around a campaign for ratification and implementation. It has set an important precedent by establishing standards for workers in the informal sector. A key point is that it went beyond formal legal protection for homeworkers and made recommendations for a developmental approach which involves the active participation of homeworkers themselves in making social and economic alternatives. Such a creative approach to organising and protecting homeworkers owes much to the model established by SEWA and could contribute a great deal to the whole European debate on social exclusion and to the relationship between the state and the market. It has broken with two opposing perspectives; the idea that economic and social policy is to be imposed from the top down, an approach that characterised much state welfare legislation from the early twentieth century, and with the myth of the inviolability of market forces.

By bringing together a new combination of forces the ILO Convention has also demonstrated that it is possible for trade unions, NGOs and researchers working closely with the grassroots to exercise influence upon state policies and international bodies. Just as giant companies move their production around the world, it is possible for groups with much more slender resources to pass ideas across international boundaries and develop new methods of organising and new means of connecting.

The complex and varied forms taken by flexible production have resulted in new problems of inequality and injustice. Women, already concentrated in low-paid work, have taken the brunt of the harsh economic paradigm of 'let alone' which acquired a fatalistic authority during the 1980s. It was initially poor women's groups scattered around the globe which stubbornly resisted the elevation of brutal indifference into an economic doctrine of freedom, for they were living amidst the consequences of selfishness and greed. In denying the lie that there are no alternatives, they have begun to make their own. The lessons learned have a wider significance. As the SEWA organiser Jetun Pathan said at a conference on homework in Bradford organised by the West Yorkshire Home-working Group: 'The future is international.'

Notes

1 See *A Survey of Homeworking in Calderdale*, Yorkshire and Humberside Low Pay Unit (1991) and *Outwork in Leeds*, a report by West Yorkshire Homeworking Unit for Leeds County Council (1992).

2 See *Meeting of Experts on the Social Protection of Homeworkers* (1–5 October 1990), ILO Office, Geneva; Self-Employed Women's Association and HomeNet, *Recognition of Home-based Workers at the International Labour Organisation* (1996); Special Issue on the ILO Convention, *HomeNet Bulletin*, no. 4 (July 1996) (24 Harlech Terrace, Leeds L51 17X).

11

LABOUR POLICIES, ECONOMIC FLEXIBILITY AND WOMEN'S WORK

The Italian experience

Daniela Del Boca

Introduction

Most studies have viewed over-regulation of the labour markets as one of the major causes of high unemployment rates that characterise Italy as well as many EU countries in the 1980s (Freeman 1994). More recently technological change, competition, privatisation processes and migration are having a significant impact on European labour markets, pushing towards more flexible systems. In Italy, however, the process has been much slower and more contradictory than in other EU countries. This chapter describes how the regulations have contributed to shaping the structure of the Italian labour market and in particular female participation and relative wages levels. While no specific labour policies have been directed towards women, female participation and relative wages have been significantly affected by labour market regulations. First the regulations of the Italian industrial relations system are examined. Second the effect of these regulations on important indicators of the labour market and especially women's participation and earnings are considered. Third we analyse some of the recent changes and possible effects on women's work.

Regulation of industrial relations in Italy

In order to understand future directions of the Italian labour market, it is useful to examine past trends. A comparison between the employment patterns in Italy and in several other countries during the period 1950–65, shows that Italy was one of the most flexible labour markets: employers were able to vary the number of employees with a very high degree of freedom (Brechling and O'Brien 1967). These conditions reflected excess supply in the labour market and the weakness of the unions. During this period, the unemployment rate in Italy as well as other

124

European countries was about 2–3 per cent of the labour force. As in other EU countries, economic growth during the second part of the 1950s and the beginning of the 1960s led to the achievement of virtually full employment and then increasing pressure of excessive wage demands. Unions gained strength and successfully bargained for large wage concessions as well as a greater control of the hiring and firing process. This new climate, created by the laws contained in the *Statuto dei lavoratori* (1970), established many regulations on recruitment and dismissal and placed restrictions on employers' autonomy in the field of redundancies. The Italian legislation has instituted many rules for the hiring of workers. Employers were to hire the first workers on a list drawn up by the public Employment Agency, independent of its own preferences for individual workers. The ranking imposed by the public agency and controlled by the unions was defined on the basis of social criteria (essentially the length of unemployment and family size).

The other major objective of the unions during the 1970s was to equalise wages: the majority of waged workers in the private sectors and government have been covered by a formal sliding scale agreement (the *scala mobile*), which at the end of the 1970 was extended to cover pension schemes and severance payments as well. The Italian job security system became, during the 1970s, the most comprehensive relative to those available to European workers and reflects relatively stronger unions, and the influence of traditionally closer relationships between business, government and the unions. One important characteristic of Italian industrial relations is the unions' declared aim of representing class interests rather than their membership. This reflects the heritage of their political origins in the post-war period as private associations promoted by workers with similar political or religious background. The Italian unions have gained most of their bargaining power through workers' unity rather than the number of their members. In this light it is understandable why unions have always opposed part-time work, fearing the potential division of the working force. Given the difficulties of dismissals and layoffs for employers the *Cassa Integrazione Guadagni* (CIG) was instituted to serve the function of maintaining a high degree of flexibility at least in terms of hours worked in the case of economic slowdown: it enables employers to reduce hours of work of workers (to zero) while formally retaining them as employees. The CIG copes with cases of sectoral economic crisis as well as with a firm's restructuring and reorganisation. The wage supplement provided by the CIG is equal to 80 per cent of previous earnings and is almost completely financed by the state and extendable indefinitely by the Ministry of Labour. Since the CIG is mostly financed by the state, firms receive indirect subsidies to compensate employers for the difficulties of reducing number of workers when they decide to reduce hours of work.

Recent research has compared the functioning of the European labour market using empirical estimates of the speed of labour adjustment for the period 1970–90. This shows that Italy has become the most rigid labour market in the EU (Del Boca 1987).

The effect of regulations on the labour market

As a consequence of labour market regulations in Italy, employment rates are lower on average than other countries, while unemployment rates are relatively higher. Italy records the lowest dismissal figure in the composition of unemployment and the highest percentage of first-job seekers. The share of layoffs as a percentage of total unemployment is 29 per cent compared to 65 per cent in France and 50 per cent in the UK. The share of first-job seekers is the highest in Italy (63 per cent), while it is 10 per cent in France, 7 per cent in Germany and 8 per cent in the UK (OECD 1995). First-job seekers tend to comprise a high percentage of women and youths and these groups experience very long unemployment spells: 70 per cent are unemployed for over a year and 80 per cent are unemployed for over six months. Long-term joblessness clogs the market-clearing system: the longer a worker is unemployed, the less attractive he/she becomes to employers. When the demand for labour begins to grow again, it tends to be the short-term unemployed who find work first, the long-term unemployed have become discouraged and have stopped searching or begun working in the underground economy.

During the 1970s, in fact, employers responded to the tighter labour legislation by turning to the unprotected sector of the labour market. They began subcontracting with small firms that could evade union control and/or payment of social security contributions. Employment growth in the 1970s was mostly in firms with fewer than 50 employees. The average size of Italian firms is far smaller than in the rest of the European countries. Italy's smaller companies, with fewer than 100 employees, and mostly family-owned, provide more than two-thirds of private sector industrial employment. Small firms provide the flexibility often convenient to employers as well as to employees (women who cannot find flexible conditions that allow them to reconcile employment and family activities). The success of small firms in Italy might be considered a re-emergence of the tradition pattern of Italian economic development during the 1950s based on labour-intensive products. Among the developed countries, Italy has one of the greatest levels of self-employment and the lowest levels of part-time and temporary workers (see Table 11.1).

Table 11.1 Self-employment, part-time and temporary employment 1994 (% of total workforce)

	Self-employment	Part-time	Temporary employment
Italy	24.1	6.2	5.2
Denmark	8.4	21.2	10.2
Germany	22.3	10.8	7.2
UK	11.2	14.9	9.4
Ireland	12.9	23.8	5.4
France	9.3	15.8	9.1

Source: European Commission (1995).

According to previous studies, Italy has the largest black economy in the industrial world, which accounts for 20–30 per cent of the GDP, while in most other countries it is 6–15 per cent. This shows another way in which employers have avoided strict hiring and firing laws as well as how people have survived in a country with such a large unemployment rate (Dallago 1990).

Women's participation and earnings

While no specific labour policies were specifically directed at women, female participation and relative wage levels were significantly affected. On the one hand the employment rate of Italian women is lower than other countries, on the other hand, wage levels and unemployment rates are relatively higher. The distribution of participation rates by age group in Italy is very similar to that of more advanced countries France, Germany, the UK, Denmark. However, female participation rates are lower than in almost every other advanced country, only about 40 per cent (in 1995) of the working population (aged 15–64 years) (see Chapter 8, Figure 8.1).

Table 11.2 shows that women's unemployment rates are higher than men's unemployment rates and have the same patterns as men's with regard to fluctuations in unemployment rates as well as long-term unemployment rates.

One explanation for the lower female employment rates is the scarcity of part-time jobs: about 10 per cent of jobs in Italy, one of the lowest proportions in all EU countries (see Chapter 8, Figure 8.2). Another explanation is related to the lower proportion of jobs in the service sector, where traditionally women are more likely to be employed. The service sector is only 20–22 per cent of the total economy, while in other countries it is around 30–40 per cent. Finally, the social service system is still inadequate. Childcare and school schedules are not well synchronised with full-time working hours, nor with the opening times of stores and public offices. Recent research shows that most services are still provided by the family. The family unit in Italy still plays a key role in supplying services with

Table 11.2 Unemployment and long-term unemployment rates in 5 European Union countries 1985 and 1995

	Unemployment rate				Long-term unemployment rate			
	Men		Women		Men		Women	
	1985	1995	1985	1995	1985	1995	1985	1995
Italy	5.5	8.7	13	15.7	61	59	66	63
Germany	4.6	7.1	7	10.1	37	41	31	47
France	8.3	10.8	12.6	14.7	39	37	46	38
Ireland	16.1	14.8	18.5	15.8	66	62	52	51
UK	11.8	10.9	11	7.1	48	51	28	33

Source: Eurostat (1996c).

flexible and adequate characteristics unavailable in the market. Around 40 per cent of couples still rely on their parents or other relatives to take care of their children. Relevant findings have emerged from an analysis of childcare use and female labour supply in Italy. The first is that the elasticity of women's labour supply in relation to childcare costs is greater in other countries, but most of this increased demand is for part-time work. Another finding concerns the use of public versus private childcare. The probability of using public childcare instead of private childcare depends on a significant degree on the presence of other adults in the family. This result is strongly related to the characteristics of rigidity of the public childcare (limited hours, frequent interruptions) which need the support of other family members (Del Boca 1996).

In spite of the fact that no specific policies were directed towards women, Italian women have been influenced by the unions' policies of the 1970s and 1980s. Unions have been committed to equality in general, but not to specific policies regarding women. The egalitarian orientation of trade union policies resulted in across the board increases in basic wages, simplification of the job classification ladder based on skill differentials, and flat rate indexing agreements to protect against inflation. These policies indirectly favour the earnings of women. The wage gap between men and women in Italy is one of the smallest of all EU countries.

To analyse the relationship between unions' egalitarian policies and women's earnings, we have followed an approach used by Blau and Kahn (1992) and analysed wage differentials according to factors related to differences in observable characteristics of men and women and characteristics of the wage determination system. In Italy, unlike other advanced countries, the low wage differential is explained by the high level of wage equality rather than the difference in male–female qualifications. In other countries, such as the USA and the UK, the high wage differential is mostly explained by the high level of wage inequality (Del Boca 1993).

In Italy the 'conditional' wage differentials (which take into account differences in experience and education) are actually no smaller than the unconditional one (which does not take into account female/male differences). This counter-intuitive result can be explained by the fact in Italy, more than in other countries, only relatively better-qualified women participate in the labour market (Del Boca 1987). Recent survey data (Bank of Italy Survey of Households' Income and Wealth 1993) show that the advantages of Italian women are limited to lower qualification levels. Italian women have in fact steeper earnings profiles and greater earnings at the lowest educational category compared to other advanced countries. While wage differentials are lower than elsewhere for women at low qualification levels because of the wage equality for all workers, the wage differentials are much higher for the better qualified. At the lower level of education (primary and compulsory education) the earnings differentials are about 17 per cent, while at the highest 28 per cent.

Changes in labour legislation in the 1990s

Until the 1980s unions did not worry about the consequences of imposing many constraints on firms: they believed that economic growth would take care of the negative consequences of the rigidities imposed on labour demand. Their leadership was weakened by industrial reorganisation throughout the 1980s: as companies reorganised their plants, invested in new technologies and reduced labour, national unions found themselves crowded out. Union membership decreased from 200,000 workers in 1975 to 40,000 in 1990, and the average number of hours lost by strikes per month declined from 6,500 to 1,900. With each company embarking on a different adjustment strategy it became increasingly difficult for national unions to negotiate in relation to the process of reorganisation. In spite of important changes in the 1990s, dismissal legislation is still dominated by high procedural costs and restrictive attitudes that deter firms from reducing their payrolls. When a reduction is proposed it still depends on a judge to approve the company decision. The government has also recommended that all possible alternatives to permanent layoffs should be tried: transfers, part-time work, sharing of the reduction in working hours between employees, providing reduction in payroll taxes to companies which sign contracts involving a reduction in 30 per cent of working time (Del Boca and Rota 1995). In July 1993 an agreement signed by employers, unions and the government ensured that the wage escalator be abolished and that collective bargaining take place every two years.

In terms of hiring, regulations changed in several steps: the importance of rank ordering had been progressively reduced since 1984. In 1984 with fixed-term apprenticeships, workers aged between 15 and 29 years old could be hired for a period of up to 24 months on apprenticeship contracts without references to any ranking. This legislation was introduced to try to reduce the unemployment rate of job seekers. The complete elimination of rank ordering was finally ratified in 1991, but the Public Employment Agency's monopoly on recruitment still remains unaltered, making private employment agencies illegal (except for hiring managerial staff). Temporary contracts have been introduced and the minimum wage is reduced in these contracts. New regulations were introduced by revising the old ones. In order to give effect to their employment plans or to come to terms with the official bureaucracy, companies devise methods for circumventing the rules, which may explain the still very high percentage of job seekers despite some success obtained by the introduction of apprenticeship contracts. In comparison with other European countries the expenditure on labour policies, especially for active policies, have been the lowest, even though the unemployment rate is the highest.

All the empirical evidence reported as well as more detailed studies of employment patterns and the effect of job security regulations have not shown that changes in the law have changed the speed of employment adjustment, or the unemployment rate (Blank and Freeman 1993). One possible explanation could be that the constraints imposed by collective bargaining agreements are more important than those imposed by the law, so that legal changes have modest effects. Another possible explanation could be that employers have adapted to a strong job security regime by using alternate adjustment mechanisms (adjustment through hours subsidised by the state), as well as decentralisation of production, and so they feel no compulsion to change. Most of the restrictions imposed by the labour regulations have in fact coexisted with forms of contracts and practices designed to circumvent these rules. In Italy, on the one hand, institutional mechanisms like *Cassa Integrazione* have made discharges of workers less necessary; on the other hand a larger share of the economy, dominated by market laws, has developed, characterised by small firms, more flexible work-rules and lower costs of adjustment and for the most part protected by the constraints imposed by the laws.

Another reason may concern the scale of the change compared with that of the social programmes, which could not reduce unemployment, and the possibility that some programmes may work against each other. This explanation could be relevant for the Italian context in the following sense. Italian unions have obtained most of their goals dealing with a non-supportive government coalition, who, given their weakness, have had to please different and often opposite groups of interests. Because of the conflicting interests actual changes may be minimal.

Conclusions

In the next few years, Italian workers will have to face several important changes, in the form of a more intense competition from other European workers, as well as competition from workers of developing countries where labour costs are much lower and a process of privatisation of the firms which will reduce the size of the public sector.

This chapter has analysed the implications of the rigidities of the Italian labour market for women's participation and earnings. The rigidity of the labour market in the 1970s and 1980s has had the effect of reducing wage dispersion (and male/ female wage differentials) at the cost of reducing working opportunities for full-time employment with negative implications for women's participation. Flexibilisation is likely to increase part-time opportunities and temporary work with a positive impact on women's employment opportunities, but at the costs of increasing wage dispersion and wage differentials. The effects of flexibilisation however are hardly visible, given that the process in Italy has been much slower and more contradictory than in other EU countries.

12

ATYPICAL WORKING TIME

Examples from Denmark

Ruth Emerek

The growth in the labour force in Denmark since the Second World War is primarily the result of women's growing labour market participation. Women's activity rates have increased rapidly as men's have decreased, and as a result women accounted for 46 per cent of the Danish labour force in 1995. At the same time Denmark has experienced a shift between sectors. Employment in the primary sector, mainly agriculture, has been falling rapidly, while employment in the private and the public service sector rose until the early 1980s, only to remain static throughout the late 1980s and 1990s. The service sector accounted for 83 per cent of women's employment in Denmark in 1995 (Eurostat 1996c).

Women in Denmark have higher participation rates compared with women in most EU countries, and only one out of three employed women in Denmark worked part-time in 1995 (Eurostat 1996c; Chapter 8).

This chapter discusses the contradiction between the demand for flexible work and the low proportion of Danish women's, and men's, part-time work, and how official statistics, by the choice of survey methods, contribute to this contradiction.

Women's labour market participation in Denmark

To overcome labour shortages women were persuaded to join the labour force in large numbers in the 1960s. The state partly took over childcare in new institutions, where pedagogical concerns were foremost. The average number of children per family was fast declining, so it was thought to be good for children to spend some hours a day in a kindergarten, to meet new challenges and to play with other children, primarily for pedagogical reasons. Later the 'working mother' was added to those reasons.

Women gradually became more economically independent, and the increase in women's labour market participation was higher than expected in forecasts made by government officials in Denmark, increasing particularly for married women aged 25–44 years. Though women's labour market participation also meant an increasing demand for childcare, government officials believed that, based on a

1970s cost–benefit analysis, despite larger investments in childcare facilities, Danish society would gain overall in the form of higher levels of production (PP II, 1973). Forecasts also showed that the only way of enlarging the labour force was to involve a higher proportion of married women. At that time women's unemployment rate was lower than men's, both were less than 3 per cent. In the middle 1970s (for the first time since the Second World War) women's unemployment rate registered as higher than men's and, from then onwards, a higher unemployment rate has persisted for women. A growing part of women's unpaid work at home has been taken over by public and private services. Today a very high proportion of women are part of the labour force and the age group 24–49 years have the highest labour market participation (Figure 12.1). Statistics show that 85 per cent of all women between 25 and 49 years are part of the labour force. Younger as well as older women have lower participation caused respectively by education and retirement.

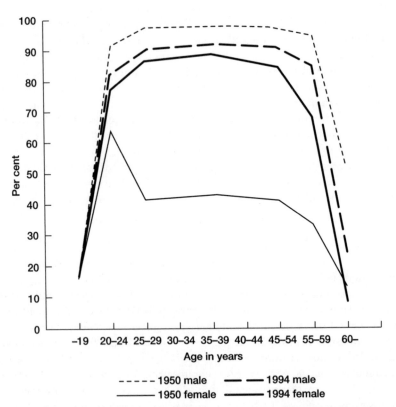

Figure 12.1 Participation rate for women and men in the Danish labour market 1950 and 1994.

Source: Danmarks Statistik (1995).

However, women still bear the main responsibility for the time-dependent work in the family such as taking children to and collecting them from kindergarten, shopping and cooking. Men do the time-independent housework such as cutting the grass and washing the car (Emerek 1987; Mogensen 1990). This gendered labour pattern is very similar to other countries in the Western world.

In undertaking the time-dependent work in the family, women are more affected by and dependent on the time-structuring of everyday life, including closing hours of kindergarten and shops. The narrower the time-structuring, the fewer possibilities arise for planning a life which includes both work and family-life with children. The time-structuring of everyday life in Denmark is very narrow compared to other member states in EU, making it very difficult for women with small children to reconcile family and working life (Bjerring and Emerek 1990). On the other hand, most families with small children need two salaries to survive. This is a dilemma which Danish women have tried to solve by working part-time, night-shifts or by 'running fast' while their children are small. Research on working time also indicates that a proportion of women (trained in the service sector) solve the dilemma by having unskilled work with fixed working time in manufacturing industries while their children are small (Ipsen 1993).

Danish legislation in relation to unemployment benefits also contributes to the explanation for relatively high and stable rates of part-time work in Denmark. This legislation supports part-time work by allowing a person to receive supplementary unemployment benefits if he/she is full-time insured even if he/she is permanently part-time employed. The legislation has been amended to gradually reduce the possibilities of receiving supplementary benefit. However the decline in women's part-time work started before this legislation was enacted in 1991. This indicates that employment patterns of women are shifting from part-time to full-time jobs, partly due to generational shifts.

Labour market statistics

Different statistics have been provided on women's, and men's, labour market participation in EU countries. An official statistical portrait has been drawn of 'Women in the European Community' (Eurostat 1992b). This portrait includes: employment status, sectors of activity, hours worked, and unemployment. It provides a context in which to examine patterns of women's work, and though the figures date back to 1987, gives an idea of the cross-national variation.

The statistics used in the 'portrait' (like statistics provided in other Eurostat publications) are based on the ILO labour force concept, which gives a cross-section – a snapshot – of a person's economic status in a single week. The ILO concept distinguishes between persons who are economically active (persons in employment as well as unemployed persons) and persons who are not economically active. Surveys based on the ILO definition also distinguish between temporary and permanent jobs, and between full-time and part-time jobs, where the number of hours a week is given in grouped categories. However, these surveys provide no information on the duration for which a person is permanently or temporarily employed.

Unemployment

Data for the length of women's and men's unemployment indicate considerable variations in the flow in, and out of, employment among the member states (Eurostat 1992, 1996c). The duration of unemployment is very differently distributed. The figures show that a high proportion of unemployed women in Denmark and Sweden have a very short period of unemployment. About 60 per cent have experienced a period of unemployment of *less than six months* in these countries, whereas the EU average shows that a half of the unemployed women had been unemployed for *one year or more in 1995* (Eurostat 1996c). This may indicate that the concept of flexibility and the concept of a permanent job and long-term unemployment could be different in various member states.

Statistics from other sources in Denmark make it possible to discuss the concepts which underlie the measures used. Special statistics on unemployment show that even though the average number of unemployed persons in the labour force was 10 per cent for women and 8 per cent for men in 1995, a much higher percentage of both women and men was affected by unemployment for a longer or shorter period within the year: 27 per cent of the female labour force, and 22 per cent of the male part of the labour force, were unemployed for longer or shorter period of the year (Danmarks Statistik 1996). The average unemployment figures have varied over the years, but the percentage of persons having one or more period of unemployment within the year has been relatively stable at around 25 per cent for women and around 20 per cent for men – or one quarter and one fifth of the labour force! This indicates that permanent jobs in Denmark are not necessarily as permanent as international statistics seem to show. The figures depend on the methods of measuring and counting.

This brings into question comparisons of unemployment between various countries, in that the unemployment rate may be an insufficient measure, requiring the median duration or variation of unemployment, to give an adequate representation of patterns of employment and unemployment in a country. It is also questionable as to whether it is appropriate to use cross-sectional data to describe unemployment, when a high percentage of employees have an unstable or fluctuating attachment to the labour market.

Full-time versus part-time jobs

The discussion of the increasing need for flexibility in the labour market, particularly internal flexibility, pinpoints another serious problem associated with surveys based on cross-sectional data. Such surveys do not allow analysis which would distinguish between persons who have many short periods of unemployment and persons who sustain numerical flexibility in continuous temporary jobs and part-time jobs over a longer period. To examine these kinds of questions longitudinal data are needed.

The Danish Integrated Database for Labour Market Research (IDA)

The Danish Integrated Database for Labour Market Research (IDA) enables further analysis of categories of working-time. The IDA provides another picture of the labour market activities of both women and men. It contains information on every person and every workplace in Denmark and, in addition, of the most and second most important appointment for every person in each year. The database contains annual data from 1980 onwards. The creation of the database produced a new dataset for participation in the labour market, making it possible to follow a person through the years to see, for instance, if the same person has had series of temporary jobs, or if a person is continuously employed from one year to another (Emerek *et al.* 1990). This gives rise to new indicators to meet the need for a more differentiated view on wage-earners' participation in the labour market and on the employers' use of workers.

To meet the need for an empirical base for discussion of internal flexibility, at least three new indicators are necessary:

- the *duration* of employment which is the length of time the person has been employed at the workplace, including periods of unemployment or employment at other workplaces,
- the *intensity* of employment measured by hours per week in employment,
- the *continuity* of employment capturing whether the person is continuously employed, or has experienced one or more periods of unemployment.

Shift work, in the evenings or at night, is not registered in the IDA, hence persons working in such jobs, characterised by this dimension of flexibility, cannot be recorded as such in the empirical base.

The problem is how to define and measure the indicators, knowing that any definition and measurement will cause problems.[1] In this context, duration and continuity are defined as dummy variables, and intensity is grouped into five categories. The only two values of *duration* considered are 'less than one year' and 'at least one year'. As IDA is a longitudinal database, it gives the opportunity of adding up the duration over years. *Intensity* is measured as the average number of hours per week during weeks in employment at the workplace. The person is only considered full-time employed, if he/she is full-time employed for all working weeks.[2] *Continuity* is measured as 'serial', if a person's appointment is registered as several periods a year, or if the person has had at least one break in employment with unemployment of one per week or more. If not, it is measured as 'continuous'.

Figure 12.2 is based on a sample from the IDA database.[3] The figure shows the distribution of appointments in relation to duration, continuity and intensity for female and male employees in 1980, 1983, 1987 and 1992.

The picture for male wage-earners in 1992 was:

- 54 per cent were continuously employed full-time for a minimum of one year;
- 22 per cent were continuously employed part-time for a minimum of one year, most of them working for more than 30 hours a week;
- 6 per cent were serially employed for a minimum of one year;
- 13 per cent were continuously employed for less than one year – mostly part-time with more than 30 hours a week;
- 5 per cent were serially employed for less than one year.

The picture for female wage-earners was different in 1992:

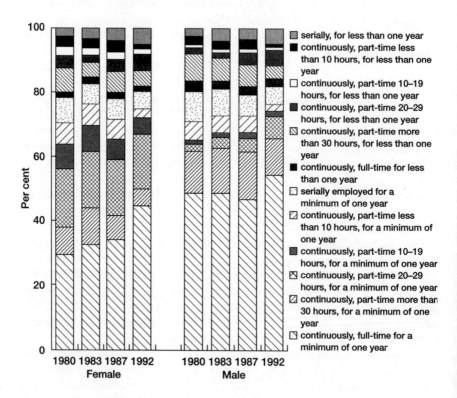

Figure 12.2 Employment for women and men in relation to duration, continuity and intensity in 1980, 1983, 1987 and 1992.

- 45 per cent were continuously employed full-time for a minimum of one year;
- 28 per cent were continuously employed part-time for a minimum of one year, most for more than 20 hours per week;
- 6 per cent were serially employed for a minimum of one year;
- 15 per cent were continuously employed for less than one year, most in part-time jobs with more than 30 hours a week;
- 5 per cent were serially employed for less than one year.

The major difference between female and male wage-earners is in relation to continuous full-time and part-time work, and the much higher percentage of women working part-time for 20–30 hours per week. This pattern, and the figures in the distribution, are relatively constant over the years, despite fluctuation in market trends over the period. The figure shows a tendency for female wage-earners to increase their proportion of continuous full-time employment with a reduction in continuous part-time employment. A similar tendency is found among men.

The figures based on the longitudinal study show first, that permanent part-time work (here counted as continuously employed part-time for at least one year) is gradually being replaced by permanent full-time work (here counted as continuously employed full-time for at least one year). Second, part-time work is more widespread in Denmark than statistics based on the ILO concept normally show.

Statistics and contradictions

The IDA-based figures suggest that the number of part-timers among employed women in Denmark is much higher than the figures normally show.[4] The typical working contract for women in Denmark is not a full-time permanent contract but rather some form of part-time contract. So, in fact, while there is a shift from permanent part-time to permanent full-time work for both women and men, only 54 per cent of male wage-earners and 45 per cent of female wage-earners in Denmark held a full-time job for a minimum of one year at the same workplace, without periods of full-time or part-time unemployment in 1992. Despite official statistics suggesting low unemployment and high proportion of full-time employment in Denmark, there is still a high proportion of employees, together with unemployed persons, who meet the need for a fluctuating flexible Danish labour market. Longitudinal studies based on the IDA database also show that it is the same group of persons who respond to the demand for numerical flexibility (Emerek 1995).

Measuring working time in future labour markets

Even though the labour market has changed and greater flexibility is demanded from a higher proportion of the labour force, labour market statistics have not changed their methods of measuring labour market activity. The ILO survey concept from 1982 of 'snapshots' of the labour market is still in use, though some methods have been changed (Eurostat 1996b).

However, the changes in working time and work patterns, caused by new technology and a growing service sector, make a revision of measurement of working time and contracts essential. If society wants to take an active rather than a passive role in determining changes in patterns of work and working time, it should necessarily be in possession of new methods of measuring and analysing the development of the labour market. This should also make it possible for employees and women to act as 'change agents' in bringing about a better balance in the use of time.

The investigations based on the new Danish data (IDA) show that it is fruitful to examine at least three dimensions of employment: the duration, the intensity and the continuity to understand the difference between women's and men's labour market activity. Future statistical portraits of the variation in the labour market participation of women and men will have to include these three dimensions to be sufficient, adequate and diverse. Furthermore the new measures will have to include more comprehensive information about the location of the hours of work. This information about a work contract may not mean very much (possibly just fluctuations), when one wants to estimate cross-section measures as: the activity rate, the employment rate, the proportion of part-timers, etc. The extent and continuity of employment, and the placing of working hours do, however, mean a lot to the person employed, to her/his family and to their everyday life, and to the possibilities of reconciling family life and working life.

To create and design new ways of measuring is of course difficult. Different traditions within various member states further complicate this process. The Danish case, however, shows the importance of looking behind the figures, and brings into consideration factors such as labour market legislation and time-structuring of everyday life, in discussing various patterns of labour market activity. Designing new measures of the work contract and working time is a small, but important, step in understanding the development of the labour market. This step should be followed by another important step – a description of the story behind the figures, such as the structuring of everyday life, legislation and the family concept – to make it possible to discuss the assumptions in making comparisons between the various member states.

Notes

1 A discussion of definition and measurement is part of the description of how wage per hour and workload is estimated in IDA (Emerek 1991).
2 If the number of working weeks is registered too high (typically as a whole year), the estimate of intensity will be too low. This means that full-time work, part of the year, may be estimated as part-time work all year. And subsequently the person's work might change category from one type of 'part-time work' to another.

3 The sample is part of a representative sample of about 3 per cent of the Danish population for 1992 (the figures from 1980, 1983 and 1987 are based on a sample of about 0.3 per cent), selected by the Danish Central Bureau of Statistics. It consists only of employees.

4 These figures are also different from the figures given by the Central Bureau of Statistics in Denmark in the Labour Force Survey, because the definitions used in this chapter include more dimensions. In the Labour Force Survey, a person is considered full-time employed if he/she was employed full time in the job he/she held the last week before the survey. The figures however are still compatible, remembering that full-time employment, in the definition used in official statistics, may turn up here in many categories: as continuous full-time employment for a minimum of one year, as continuous full-time employment for less than one year, as serial full-time employment for a minimum of one year, as serial full-time employment for less than one year, and as various kinds of part-time employment.

13

WORKPLACE CULTURE, FAMILY-SUPPORTIVE POLICIES AND GENDER DIFFERENCES

Lis Højgaard

The purpose of this chapter is to discuss the options for reconciling family and working life that are offered by Danish employers, and to analyse the consequences these possibilities may have for women and men in different workplace cultures. The discussion is based on case studies of eight public and private corporations and it is my intention to illustrate how different family-friendly practices work in different workplace cultures.

The increase in family working time

Within the last thirty years in Denmark, the working week has decreased from 45 hours in the 1960s to 37 hours in 1996. This, however, is individual working time; the picture is quite different from the point of view of the family. The decrease in individual working time conceals the substantial increase in the paid work that goes into reproducing a family now compared to, say, thirty years ago. Or, to be more accurate, what was formerly true for working-class families is now true for almost all families. It takes two incomes to support a family with children.

The increase in family working time is of course due to the increase in the activity rate of women over the last twenty years – both in terms of the number of women working and in terms of the amount of time they spend in paid work. After Sweden, Danish women have the highest activity rate in the EU, in 1995 it was nearly 80 per cent (Chapter 8, Figure 8.1). Only 6 per cent of Danish women are full-time housewives and most of these are older women (Danmarks Statistik 1992). The high activity rate has traditionally been accompanied by a high rate of part-time employment. This rate is decreasing substantially in Denmark (Chapter 8, Figure 8.2).

It might be expected that the activity rate among women with small children would be lower than average, and that a substantial amount of part-time work would be found among this group of women. A recent study however (Stenvig *et al.* 1993) shows that the participation rate is higher among men and women with small children than among both single men and women and couples without children, and that the weekly working time among women with small children is relatively high, only 3 hours less than full-time. The weekly working hours for men with small children are 5 hours above the full-time working week.

No matter how the working hours are distributed among the sexes, it seems, on average, to take no less than 76 hours of paid work to support a family with small children. This high rate of paid work delivered by the family intensifies the contradictory demands of work life and family life – family life with small children being especially vulnerable to the demands, created by limited time, of the structuring of time.

Family strategies

How do families cope with this situation? A precondition is the availability of sufficient childcare facilities. Denmark has a fairly high rate of public and private day-care. Even with available day-care, families with small children and two-parents working nearly full time are pressed for time. In the Danish context, where privately hired help in the home is very rare, there seem to be a number of different possible strategies, all of which are more or less voluntary and dependent on an employee's position:

- *Part-time work* This long-standing and traditional strategy is decreasing among mothers. The lowest rate of part-time work is found among women in the age groups between 25 and 34 years of age. This strategy may be dying out with the new generation of women seeking full-time employment.
- *Shift work or working at odd hours* A growing number of people are working hours outside the regular working day. Some have chosen this on account of the family.
- *Unemployment* This can of course hardly be called a strategy since it is seldom a choice, but statistics show that unemployment among parents with small children is significantly higher than for other groups (Stenvig *et al.* 1993). It could be an option to reduce the conflicts between family and working life.
- *Parental leave* A new law in Denmark (1994) makes it possible for parents to take up to one year of parental leave on 80 per cent of unemployment benefit. This 'pay' can be supplemented in different ways – by an employer, by the municipal authorities or by a trade union.
- *Just live with it* Parents cope in the best possible way with the contradictory demands. This is what you can see from the statistics that most families do, since the above-mentioned strategies cover only a limited proportion of families with children.

In the following discussion I look at the measures and practices to reconcile family and working life that the labour market offers full-time or nearly full-time employed women and men.

Family-friendly employer policies

This concept covers a wide range of corporate-specific agreements on practices that are designed to ease the problems connected with the contradictory demands of family and working life. These agreements comprise measures concerning: working time, working conditions, vacation agreements and leave on behalf of sick children. They can be both formal and informal agreements. Among the informal agreements there are a variety of permissions often negotiated on a daily basis concerning emergency situations mostly connected with children.

How widespread these agreements are in the Danish labour market is not known. Two surveys (Andersen and Holt 1990; Gregersen 1991) conducted in 1990 and 1991 on flexible working time in the public and the private labour market show that access to flexible working time is dependent on the worker's situation in the labour market. Flexible working time means the opportunity for an employee to change the extent and the place of a proportion of their daily working time by formal and informal agreement. The survey that covers both the public and the private labour market showed that 59 per cent of the higher salaried employees had a formal flexibility agreement, while this was true for 30 per cent of the salaried employees and for only 15 per cent of the skilled and unskilled wage-earners. Women and men are distributed in these categories or positions on the labour market in such a way that more men than women have access to flexible working hours and parents with children of pre-school age have a more limited access to flexible working time. The results of the survey can be summed up as follows: it is typically the young families with small children, women and manual workers who do not have the possibility to vary their working time at their own discretion (Gregersen 1991).

My case studies provide a broader range of family-friendly measures than these surveys, and offer the possibility of further investigating the conditions under which these measures are obtainable, and to what extent the use of these measures by employees implies specific consequences.

Corporate case studies

The case studies are based on two research projects investigating the significance of workplace culture for gender differentiation and the possibilities of reconciling family and working life which different work-cultures offer. They explore the consequences that the exploitation of these possibilities have, in terms of position in the labour market and equality between the sexes.

The first project investigated the barriers facing women in obtaining leadership positions in four different companies: the Ministry of Finance, the Customs

Department (both public corporations) and two private companies: a retail-service industry and a research department of a Medical company (Højgaard 1990, 1991).

The second project examined the relationship between workplace culture and gender-specific wage-setting mechanisms in four different private sector companies: a painting company, an electronics manufacturing company, a plastics manufacturing company and a bank (Højgaard 1993, 1994).

In the first study sector-specific and educational criteria are the bases for the selection of companies. Two private firms and two public were chosen and in each of these, one was chosen in which leaders were recruited from professions, and one in which an academic background was not required in leadership positions.

The second study includes only private companies and these were chosen to illuminate the wage-setting practices within different occupational groups: salaried employees and manual workers, i.e. skilled/semi-skilled and unskilled workers. For the salaried worker a large bank was chosen, for the skilled workers a big painting company was selected and with respect to the unskilled group two different branches of industry were included: a major electronic firm and a very large plastics corporation.

Both studies are based on qualitative interviews and documentary material: 57 women and men were interviewed in the first study and 96 in the second – 153 interviews in all. Both studies looked into the relationship between family and working life.

I will discuss the options available to employees in these companies and the consequences of using these options. The results of the survey mentioned above point to the fact that the higher you are in the job hierarchy, the more you are likely to have working conditions favourable towards alleviating the contradictions between family and working life. My cases support these findings, but they also show that the value of these measures for employees is highly dependent on the specific workplace culture.

Flexible work options

Family-friendly measures offered by the companies in the eight case studies are: flexitime (flexibility in working hours), shift working or part-time work, leave on the first day of a child's sickness and a wide range of special arrangements informally negotiated. The measures offered differ slightly among the companies and according to a pattern suggested by the cited survey. If grouped along traditional lines of differentiation of the labour market in terms of work areas: industry, services and the professions, it is manufacturing and professional jobs which offer the most extensive and varied family-friendly measures, whereas the service sector offers fewer and the construction industry none.

Table 13.1 shows which measures are available in the different work areas and denotes the relationship between the measures and the prevailing attitudes towards them in the workplace cultures of the companies.

Table 13.1 Family-supportive measures in the Danish surveyed companies

Work areas	Concrete measures	Attitudes
Manufacturing industries	Flexibility Child sick leave (Part-time work) Special arrangements: work shifts	Positive
Constructive industries	None	Neutral
Service sector: Shop assistants	Attempts at offering special arrangements for working hours	Negative
Finance	Child sick leave Part-time according to special agreements	Very positive High expectations of employee flexibility
Professionals	Flexibility Child sick leave Working at home Telephone contact Visits by children Part-time	Very positive Also towards men's family responsibilities An overtime culture

In the industrial work area the relationship between the measures and the attitudes towards them is fairly straightforward. Where there are no measures the attitude towards the responsibilities of the employees' family obligations is neutral or indifferent in the sense that it is regarded as an aspect of life that belongs to the world outside the workplace. Where a variety of measures are available the attitudes are, as might be expected, positive.

This relationship is more complicated when it comes to the service sector. As shown in Table 13.1 the cases in this sector seem to represent two opposite sets of attitudes. For shop assistants the attitudes towards the measures are negative, in spite of the fact that the workplace does try to accommodate the needs of their, mostly female, workforce, and they are creating family-friendly measures for some categories of employees – though reluctantly.

In finance, the measures are equally few and hard to get. Part-time employment, for instance, is only available for a limited group of employees, and the bank does not offer flexible working time. The attitudes are nevertheless very positive and sympathetic towards employees' problems of reconciling family and working life. But when you look at this attitude in the context of other characteristic traits in this workplace culture a contradiction becomes apparent: on the one hand there is a widespread acceptance and understanding that parents have to rush from work to pick up their children at the day-care centre. On the other hand the bank expects a great deal of flexibility on the part of their employees, and one of the areas that is often explicitly mentioned is flexibility around closing time: employees should not hurry home, they should not be keen on closing time. This is one example among several that illustrates how the positively expressed attitude is modified, maybe even negated, by more general prescriptions in the culture.

The same is true in the cases of professional workplaces. When the many policies and positive attitudes are viewed in the context of the dominant cultural traits another contradiction appears. It is embedded in the fact that this is an overtime culture. There are no distinct behavioural prescriptions, but both work pressure and career structure limit the potential to take advantage of the range of family-supportive policies that workplaces offer.

Manufacturing industries and professional jobs exhibit both the widest range of measures formally and informally and the most positive attitudes towards these measures. However, seen in the cultural context of the various workplaces manufacturing comes out ahead because the culture does not include obstacles that contradict or work against positive attitudes. It is necessary to make a reservation with respect to the extent of this conclusion, because the manufacturing industries included in these case studies are not representative of industry as a whole. These are large, solid, expanding and technologically inventive companies and the fact that they are among the companies that offer flexitime to their skilled and unskilled wage-earners might indicate that their policies differ from industry in general since only 15 per cent of all skilled and unskilled wage earners have access to flexitime according to the survey mentioned above. Keeping this reservation in mind, the cases show that it is advantageous, with respect to the availability of policies that facilitate reconciling family and working life, to be employed in some sectors of manufacturing. This seems to be true if you look at the consequences that exploitation of the policies and the positive attitudes entail for the employees.

The consequences

With one exception my case studies show that in companies that foster a strong gender differentiation, the use of family-supportive policies will reinforce existing gender differences irrespective of whether the attitudes are positive, negative or neutral and irrespective of how many family-supportive policies the company in question has. The opposite is true in companies with weak gender differentiating cultures.

In Table 13.2 characteristic traits of the different workplace cultures are outlined in the second column, and in the third column two types of gender differences are chosen to illustrate the specific gender-differentiating cultures. One is wage differentials and working conditions, chosen for the manufacturing industries, and the other is career advancement and the distribution of leadership positions between the sexes, chosen for the service sector and for the professions.

Table 13.2 Consequences of workplace culture in relation to gender differentials at work

Work areas	Workplace culture	Gender differences
Manufacturing industries	**Obligation to the workforce** Technology innovative New production systems Decentralised wage setting Promoting education of women	Diminishing wage gap Work conditions: changing
	Conflict culture Traditional gender segregation of work	Traditional wage structure and gender segregation of work
	Gender differences A skilled culture– craftsmanship	No wage difference Same working conditions for women and men Few women
Service sector Shop assistants	**The male norm**	Many barriers for the advancement of women
Finance	**Gender differentiating** Gender equality attitudes by management – strong notions of masculinity and femininity	Gender stereotyping as benefit to woman's advancement Wage differences between the sexes
Professionals	**Highly competitive culture** Prestige work areas and work modes Equality orientated	Gender hierarchy
	Result orientated No prestige work areas Outward competitive	Above average proportion of female leaders

I have divided the industrial work areas into three cultures. The first of these fully supports the statement above: the gender differentiation is weak, the wage gap is diminishing and the culture promotes gender equality, not purposely but through specific personnel policies aimed at educating the workforce in order to allow for rapid technological change. Since the majority of the workforce were women, they benefited from this, because education was rewarded in the wage system. In this culture there was no indication that full exploitation of the family-friendly measures affected the gender differentiation – for instance in terms of wage levels or access to education.

The same is true for the other two cultures in the industrial section, but for the second culture it is not connected with weak gender differentiation. This culture was characterised by a fairly traditional gender segregation and a traditional gender wage gap. Both of these cultures had good measures in place and a positive attitude toward solving the contradictions between working life and family life. The third culture in this group showed no gender differentiation in terms of wages and working conditions, but it was characteristic that there were very few women employed in this company. This company offered no family-supportive measures and their attitude was, as stated above, neutral or indifferent. Neutrality in connection with gender has been shown by many feminist researchers (e.g. Acker 1990; Holter 1991) to indicate a predominance of male norms, but this is only partly true in this case. It is true in the sense that female capacities in the craft are seen as different from men's and lacking in some respects (muscular strength for instance), but this difference is not reflected in wages and working conditions.

The relationship between gender differentiation and the consequences of exploiting family-supportive policies is much clearer in the service sector and the professions. In the company that employs shop assistants the workplace culture can be characterised by the concept of the male norm. This can be exemplified in the following way. The standard explanation for treating women differently than men, and for the fact that they occupy different positions and have a harder time advancing, is linked with women's position in the family. The overall message in this culture is that, in order for women to be treated like men, they must behave like men. It is all right for women to have children and family responsibilities but it has consequences for their careers. So whether or not your family life actually interferes with your working life, as a woman you are subject to general suspicion on this account.

In the finance case a similar concept is at work. In the bank there are widespread notions of what men are and how they perform, and of what women are and how they perform, at every step of the career ladder. This culture exhibits very fixed ideas of masculinity and femininity and numerous examples can be summarised to the effect that the way men perform corresponds nicely to the expressed ideal performance of this culture. This means that women who want to advance in the hierarchy have to act against the image of femininity as it is defined by the culture. These images of masculinity and femininity are active and pervasive at the same time as the management are promoting gender equality policies in order to recruit women to leadership positions.

These contradictory signals result in different consequences for different employees. For women to use the existing possibilities offered by the family-friendly measures, there seem to be three sets of consequences. If you are very good and highly estimated by an employer, there are no negative consequences attached to the full use of the measures. This includes temporary part-time employment for women in leadership positions. The other two possibilities seem to be either not to have children, or have children and not to expect to have a career in the bank. An effect of this is that there are several definite barriers to the advancement of women in this culture, such as not having a right to return to one's own job after maternity leave, not being called on to fulfil special assignments, not being asked to apply for vacant prestigious jobs to the same degree as men and so on. For men, exploitation of the formal and informal measures is almost inconceivable – for instance, to take the ten weeks of parental leave that men have a right to is unheard of in this culture. So even though this company has some family-supportive policies and has a generally positive and sympathetic attitude towards the problems of reconciling work and family, the actual use of these policies is assumed to have serious consequences for the career possibilities of most of the employees, namely those who are not already well on their way up the career ladder. Given the fixed notions of masculinity and femininity this also means a reinforcement of the existing gender differences.

The two cases among the professions differ with respect to cultural character-istics and gender differences. As noted in Table 13.2 the first culture is highly competitive internally. Prestige is ascribed to certain tasks and ways of performing, and gendering processes are embedded in the ways that prestige is allocated. This creates a gender hierarchy that is reflected by the few women in leadership positions. This runs contrary to a very outspoken gender equality attitude in the culture with open discussions on how to obtain a degree of equality that make it possible for both men and women to have an acceptable family–work situation. The fight for the 'good' work and the long working hours that signal seriousness and importance limit the use of the relatively numerous possibilities that the family-supportive policies offer. And the use of these measures by women will certainly weaken their participation in the competition, whereas men's use of the measures will weaken their competition relative to other men. The outcome of this is very likely to be a continuation and maybe even a strengthening of the gender hierarchy.

The other professional culture is more team-oriented with the effect that everybody's contribution counts. There are no prestige work areas, the culture is result-orientated. The company is highly competitive on the outside market. This is not reflected in internal competition, but it is noticeable in a high level of work pressure. The culture is less gendered than the previously mentioned case and the proportion of female leaders is above average. High work pressure makes it difficult to utilise the available family-friendly measures, but actual use does not seem to have gender-differentiating effects.

Conclusions

As is shown by the discussion of the eight case studies, family-friendly policies cannot be judged at face value. In order to evaluate the usefulness of a given policy for the employees it is necessary to look into the relationship with the prevailing workplace culture. To what extent do the measures correspond to important features in the culture and to what extent do they contradict them? An insight into these mechanisms is also necessary in order to estimate the progressiveness or family-friendliness of a given company. For companies whose general cultures are opposed to the use of the measures by the employees, it is fairly inconsequential to offer a wide range of family-supportive policies.

These case studies show that there are both sector-specific and cross-sectoral features at work in determining the extent, value and gender differentiation effect of the policies. The discussion of the case studies shows that manufacturing, with the exception of the building industry, and professions offered the widest range of policies, while the service sector offered fewer. It was also shown that the limitations on the utilisation of the measures were greatest in the service sector and among the professions. The contradictions with the workplace cultures were greatest in the companies with the strongest gender differences: in the bank and in the internally competitive culture among the professionals. A cross-sectoral feature appeared here, as it seemed to be the career orientated cultures in the service sector and among the professions that showed the greatest limitations. So the conclusion is that highly gender-differentiated career cultures are the least likely to provide their employees, men and women, with actual access to policies designed to reconcile work and family life, even when their policies are rather extensive and their attitudes are sympathetic towards these problems.

Part III

RECONCILING FAMILY AND WORKING LIFE

14

CHANGING GENDER ROLES, STATE, WORK AND FAMILY LIVES

Evelyn Mahon

Women's participation in the paid labour force is an indicator of women's achieved status in a community (Norris 1987). In Western countries one of the most widespread and significant changes since the 1960s has been a significant increase in the number of married women with children in the labour force. This third section examines the interaction between families and working life with a particular focus on three areas: state policies and their influences on women's participation; mothers' unequal integration into the workplace; and fathers' family roles.

State policies

Feminists have characterized the state as both capitalist and patriarchal (Hernes 1992; Walby 1990). The state, however, is not monolithic and its actions are best viewed as the outcome of competing social pressures (Hartmann 1976; Walby 1986; McBride Stetson and Mazur 1995). Feminist analysis of the state has focused on social welfare policy (Sassoon 1992; Whitting 1992). Feminist analysis of welfare state regimes took Esping-Andersen's three regimes; liberal, conservative and social democratic as their starting point. These clusters were determined according to whether state benefits were provided as citizens' rights or not. This in turn was measured by the level of de-commodification of the labour force, i.e. the degree to which individuals or families 'can uphold a socially aceptable standard of living independently of market participation' (Esping-Andersen 1990: 37). But Esping-Andersen's typology was insensitive to gender differences. De-commodification differs for men and women and a regime can commodify men while de-commodifying women. Borchorst (1994) agued that both liberal and conservative regimes contributed to the de-commodifcation of women in the sense that they actively supported a housewife/breadwinner model. In contrast she argued that the Scandinavian welfare states have commodified women.

Ostner and Lewis (1995) derived a three-fold model based on the balance between market, state and family, with a particular focus on the boundary between the public world of paid work and the private domain of the family. This produced a comparative gendered typology of 'strong', 'modified' or 'weak' male breadwinner states (Lewis 1992), based on the extent to which countries had departed from the male breadwinner model. For instance, in Britain and Ireland the male breadwinner contract remained strong. France, however, had a modified male breadwinner model as women were simultaneously acknowledged as wives, mothers and paid workers. Sweden and Denmark have departed furthest from the male breadwinner model. They introduced separate individualised taxation, parental leave, and increased childcare provision so that the dual breadwinner model was the norm in Denmark and in Sweden.

Orloff (1993) added two new dimensions to the gendered analysis of welfare states: access to paid work and the capacity (of women) to form autonomous households. While her second dimension can be viewed within the traditional welfare context, access to paid work cannot. Her first dimension is an important one akin to that described by Siim (1987) as the 'second stage' of welfare, i.e. the extent to which states promote or discourage women's paid employment.

This can be ascertained by the extent to which the state guarantees access to paid employment and provides services that enable women to balance home and work responsibilities, i.e. facilitate women's participation in the labour market. Siim (1987) has shown that social democratic states, unlike liberal or conservative ones offer childcare services. While both Siim and Orloff extend an analysis of state policies to include female employment, both have neglected the impact of taxation policies. Sainsbury's analysis details the many dimensions of male breadwinner states including taxation policies, and identifies as important whether women's status is based on their status as mothers or as wives. This distinction is a very important one especially as applied to taxation systems in liberal or conservative regimes (Chapter 15).

But while typologies have dominated the classification of welfare systems, comparative research on labour force participation has traditionally explained variations in women's participation in terms of factors of supply and demand (Jenson et al. 1988). A number of comparative studies indicated the importance of state policies in encouraging or discouraging female employment (Dex and Shaw 1986; Dex et al. 1993b, Moss 1988). For instance, while the USA and Britain are classified as liberal regimes and countries with strong breadwinner gender regimes, Dex and Shaw found American women were more likely to be working during their childbearing years and were much less likely to work part time than British women (Dex and Shaw 1986). British women spent more years out of the labour market and were much more likely to take part-time jobs than their American counterparts. In contrast, American women are more likely to work full time for two reasons: the favourable tax provisions for childcare expenses and the payment of health insurance by employers. While neither Britain nor the USA had any uniform government-sponsored childcare schemes, since 1954 working parents in the USA have received some tax concessions for expenses incurred for childcare. A tax credit covered care in day-care centres, nursery schools, day-care homes and care provided by childminders. Those who employ carers in the child's own home must, however, pay social security tax which reduces the net tax credit somewhat.

However such tax credits enable parents to recoup between 20 and 25 per cent of their childcare costs. In addition to this federal tax credit, in 1984 twenty-eight states provided a tax credit or a deduction of childcare expenses from income subject to the state's income tax. British women, with no such tax incentives, were far more likely to have their children looked after by their husbands (Dex and Shaw 1986). Dex and Shaw were of the opinion that women's position in the British labour market would change radically if childcare expenses could be reduced through tax reductions. The significance of taxation policy and the absence of any tax credits for childcare is also important in Ireland which has a strong male breadwinner regime and is discussed in Chapter 16.

In another comparison, this time between France and England, Dex et al. (1993b) reviewed the effect of policies on mothers at work and their impact on the feminisation of the labour force. While 51 per cent of French and British mothers worked in 1980, they constituted two different populations (Dex et al. 1993b). In France, there is a sharp distinction between women who are working and those who are not working at any one time. In Britain, this was not the case. There is far more overlap between working and non-working women. British women have an intermittent pattern of activity over their life cycle. Their continuity of employment is markedly affected by the birth of the first child. This can be attributed to a combination of the small amount of subsidised day-care provision for children under school age, interacting with norms as to maternal responsibilities and the generally low level of women's educational capital.

Mothers' unequal integration in the labour market

As has been demonstrated in Part I, there is considerable variation in women's participation in the labour market between EU countries (Commission of the European Communities 1993). Equal opportunities policies in all EU countries have in general followed a liberal model (Meehan and Sevenhuijsen 1991). The EU directive on equal pay and on equal treatment is consistent with such a model. However, its main deficiency is that it is based on the presumption that men and women are the same. In fact equality in recruitment and promotion insists that women are not discriminated against as *women*. But in the past the life-courses of mothers differed significantly from the life-courses of men (Dex 1987; Martin and Roberts 1984) and different countries, as Lewis has indicated, operate the breadwinner/housewife contract to different degrees. Women's participation has differed from men's because they take responsibility for child-care and eldercare, yet these have remained outside the remit of equal opportunity policies.

France, as Fagnani (Chapter 5) has demonstrated, facilitates mothers who wish to look after their children full time by paying them family allowances. French family allowance policies for three or more children create an unearned income effect which encourages non-working and, to a lesser degree, part-time working among French women. This occurs despite better childcare facilities for full-time care. Generous family allowance policies are very strong in their influence. Once a mother has three or more children the effects of childcare facilities are outweighed by the income effects from family allowances and most of these mothers stay at home; a small percentage work part time (Dex *et al.* 1993b: 160). This reveals class differences in the use of taxation incentives as contrasted with family allowances. It reflects the modified male breadwinner regime operative in France.

Chapters 15 and 16 in this Part, further investigate the relationship between state policy and mothers' employment. Chapter 15 examines the modernisation of motherhood in Norway. While social democratic regimes have often been categorised as homogeneous, Leira shows that there are differences between the Norwegian and Swedish models. Leira argues that there has not been a democratisation of the relationship between the genders in Norway. In its modern form, 'motherhood' has included the notion of women as both providers and nurturers but this was not accommodated by a collectivisation of childcare (as in Sweden), rather she argues that their policies showed a considerable ambivalence towards mothers' employment (Leira 1992). Rather, as in liberal and conservative regimes or male breadwinner typologies, childcare was treated as a private concern and the responsibility of individual families. In a Scandinavian context, Norway has a low proportion of children in publicly funded childcare. Leira claims that women's integration into the labour market is not complete and more women work part time. Fathers' labour force participation has not been challenged, neither has their participation in the home increased. So when examined in terms of childcare provision, Norway has adopted a liberal rather than a social democratic approach.

However, while the proportion of children in publicly funded childcare in Norway is low in Scandinavian terms, it is very high as compared to Irish figures. Ireland does not really offer any state-sponsored childcare or tax allowances for childcare. Further, its taxation arrangements are consistent with a breadwinner/ housewife contract. The result is that low-paid mothers are more likely (as in France) to avail of family-friendly polices such as unpaid career breaks to care for their children or remain as full-time housewives. Ireland's familistic taxation policy promotes the male breadwinner model, in its treatment of women as wives rather than as mothers.

Fathers' family role

Two other aspects of family and working life are reviewed in Part III: the corporate perception of mothers who work part time and the role of fathers in the family. Veenis (Chapter 17) gives us an insight into the way in which a breadwinner/housewife contract is reflected in the labour market, especially among part-time workers. Mothers are tolerated at work but their responsibility for children must not impact on the workplace. Only women are seen as having such responsibilities. Flexible working hours and part-time work, while on offer, are confined to those in the lower-level functions. In addition, those who take them up are unlikely to be promoted. Men are very involved in their work but this affects their time with their children, so gender roles are reproduced both in the home and in the workplace.

While the first three chapters in Part III examine the interface between family and working life, the last two concentrate on the sexual division of labour within the family. Chapters 18 and 19 concentrate on fathers and the domestic division of labour. Much of the research on mothers and work has focused on state assistance or company adaptations to their family roles, to the neglect of fathers' roles and their adaptive strategies. However, the domestic division of labour is an obstacle to women's participation in the labour force. Gender differences are accentuated by fathers' neglect of childcare. There is a realization that if women are to be integrated into the workplace, adaptive strategies are required of men who are expected to play a greater role in childcare. However this is a new area of research and so new approaches to understanding fatherhood in a changing context are required.

These two case studies are located in countries which have different gender contracts: Italy beginning to move away from a strong male breadwinner one while Sweden is reputed to have only a weak one. Not too surprisingly, Italian men have no role models for their new father roles, other than not wishing to be like their own fathers. Giovannini (Chapter 18) offers us a typology of fathers. The involved father is found in families where the mother's career dominates but Giovannini's account reveals that their role is not too extensive. The remainder are categorised along a negative continuum from involved, to involved in theory, to guest, to delegating fatherhood. Italy is usually characterized as having a traditional familistic regime and that accords with this depressing picture. Its significance lies in depicting the missing half of gender equity and the work that is required before an equal status contract evolves.

Bjørnberg's account based on Sweden (Chapter 19) is, as might be expected, somewhat more encouraging. While they too, have no role models as least her typology is one based on involvement. In fact it appears that as fathers become involved in fatherhood, their expectations of themselves increase. Exposure to and time spent with their children increases their need to spend more time with them. In addition, it seems that Swedish individualism means that men have to learn fatherhood by actively caring for their children. Bjørnberg also suggests that being active fathers helps them to develop as persons. She suggests that fatherhood is best understood within the context of changing masculinities. In the past men's orientation to work never conflicted with their breadwinner status within the family, rather it supported and sustained it. However, this breadwinner status is no longer either necessary or central to it. Their roles as fathers must be renegotiated within a new gender order which has often excluded their significance and importance. This suggests that their role and status as fathers has to be earned.

From these case studies, one can argue that a broader view of equal opportunities must include structural factors which facilitate mothers' participation in the labour market: childcare policies, tax and maternity benefits. Participation in the formal paid labour force affords women entitlements to a range of work-related social and welfare benefits not on offer to full time housewives and mothers. EU directives, consistent with the Treaty of Rome, have concentrated on the rights of workers and attempted to secure full social welfare benefits and entitlements for them, while neglecting those not in the labour force. The recent Social Charter seeks to extend such work-related benefits to part-time workers. This is a significant development as it will indirectly benefit many mothers who work part time.

The differences between workers and non-workers are likely to be less significant in countries which have social democratic political systems and offer universalistic social services and benefits to all (Cochrane and Clarke 1993). This situation, however, has to be contrasted with countries which have liberal or conservative typologies of welfare capitalism in which non-workers are entitled to few welfare services or benefits.

This relationship between work and welfare is of special importance to women and more especially to mothers. The latter's low participation in the workforce and their ensuing state dependency has given rise to the problem of the feminisation of poverty. Such poverty and dependency is a direct result of their exclusion from the labour market and its ancillary benefits. This predicament is not peculiar to mothers, as it can also apply to those who, for a variety of reasons (including for instance racial discrimination), fail to obtain employment. It is the problem adressed in the de-commodification and citizenship debate. However, as mentioned earlier for women the issue of commodification still persists. To what extent do policies allowing women to stay at home to be full-time caregivers work at cross purposes to policies that sustain women's paid work? (Hobson 1994: 185–6) Access to paid work and the services that facilitate employment for caregivers are critical aspects of gender contracts. Chapters 16 and 17 show the unequal integration of mothers who engage in caring into the paid labour force and this will continue to be the price paid by them for family care. Apropos this McLaughlin and Glendinning (1994) have suggested that defamilisation rather than decommodification might be a useful concept. This would include an examination of the conditions and terms under which men and women engage in unpaid work.

It is important to emphasise that equal opportunities policies should be interpreted as facilitating an equal chance of securing employment in addition to determining one's equal chances in securing social welfare benefits. Equal opportunities in the workplace, citizenship rights and social welfare policies are all intertwined. It is therefore vital to examine the concept of equal opportunities understood as equality in conditions conducive to access to and participation in the labour force in a comparative perspective. State policy can be more or less mother friendly.

15

THE MODERNISATION OF MOTHERHOOD

Arnlaug Leira

Introduction

What is the welfare state response to new family forms? Apparently, different forms of the welfare state encourage different family forms and motherhood models. In the early 1980s Ruggie (1984) examined differences between 'social democratic' welfare states such as the Scandinavian ones and 'liberal' welfare states such as in Britain and argued that social democratic states are more responsive to the demands of workers, and therefore more supportive of working mothers.[1] Variation in welfare state family policy is noted also by Esping-Andersen (1990) who takes the different arrangements between the welfare state, labour market and family as a basis for distinguishing between three main clusters or 'ideal types' of welfare state regimes: the 'social democratic', among which the Scandinavian states predominate; the 'liberal' cluster exemplified by the UK; and the 'corporatist, conservative' regime within which he places, for example, Germany, Italy and France. Esping-Andersen, however, does not really explore the importance of different family policies for women and men as mothers, fathers and citizens, nor does he elaborate on the importance of unpaid family-related work for welfare production, as observed, for example, in work by Lewis (1992) and Orloff (1993). What different welfare state regimes imply for the political and social definition of motherhood obviously needs further examination.

Scandinavian family policies have had a mixed reception. An American social analyst, Wolfe (1989) finds that the Scandinavian welfare states have created a new family form, 'the public family', in which both parents are in paid work, while the children are cared for in public day-care centres. For him, this family appears as a highly problematic construct. New family forms have also been interpreted as representing a democratisation of the relationship between genders and generations, even as an indication of an emerging 'woman-friendly' welfare state (Hernes 1987). However that may be, both concepts, 'the woman-friendly welfare state' and 'the public family' presume a renegotiation of the boundaries between the

159

public and the private, and a restructuring of both families and labour markets along gender lines.

In this chapter I shall 'deconstruct' the concept of the family and take a closer look at the arrangements between mothers, fathers, state and market in Scandinavia. Obviously, changes in the work/family arrangement have different implications for women and men and should be analysed both gender-specifically and gender-relationally. However, I take the employed mother as my main case, referring only briefly to new forms of fatherhood (see Chapters 18 and 19). In addition to Scandinavian material, data from the EU member states are used to illustrate both similarity and difference in policy approaches to the 'new' labour, that is the employed mothers who combine wage-work and parental responsibility for young children.

Conceptualising motherhood

As an analytical tool I introduce the concept that motherhood (and fatherhood) has both earner and carer aspects.[2] The 'earner' aspect refers to economic activities and material provision, the 'carer' aspect to primary socialisation, nurturing and rearing. By this conceptualisation I emphasise the necessity of breaking down or transcending the models of 'work' and 'family' that ignore or marginalise the interrelationship of production and social reproduction. The concept of the employed mother is of particular interest for social policy and social theory in that it incorporates two essential activities for any society, material provision and human reproduction and care for offspring, and thus transcends the traditional division of labour by gender. Thinking about mothers of young children as both providers and nurturers highlights an empirical fact often neglected in family theories, namely the combination of job and family obligations. Obviously, the responsibility for children, childcare and primary socialisation are essential elements in the definition of motherhood. However, it is important not to underplay the material or economic provider aspects. The increasing labour market participation of mothers shows empirically how the relationship between production and social reproduction is being changed in modern industrialised states. The concept of the employed father does not evoke similar connotations, but is rather interpreted as an unnecessary elaboration of the concept of 'father'.

The concept of the employed mother also provides a perspective on processes of integration and exclusion in modern welfare states and reveals an important premise of welfare state design across western Europe, namely the different citizenship entitlements associated with job and family commitments. Employed mothers are wage-workers, carers for children and citizens of the welfare state. Thus, in my analysis the main questions are: what policies did the welfare states adopt as regards the combination of job and family obligations? How do commitments to employment and childcare respectively influence access to the social rights of citizenship?

In the following, I shall first briefly outline some main characteristics of the Scandinavian welfare states, in order to give an idea of the political culture from which the concepts of a 'public family' and a 'woman-friendly' welfare state emerged. Next, I discuss policies of special importance to employed mothers and I examine the influence of two processes, 'the modernisation of motherhood', which in this context refers primarily to the mothers who joined the labour market, and the 'collectivisation of childcare' which refers to the introduction of state-sponsored day care for children. This data set provides a starting point for discussing different welfare state approaches to employed mothers. In conclusion I examine the differentiation of access to citizens' entitlements. My main concern in this chapter is with the gendering of the social rights of citizens; I do not discuss the differentiation produced by class, race or ethnicity.

The Scandinavian welfare state 'model'

The term 'welfare state' commonly identifies those states in which extensive legislation has been established with regard to the public provision of welfare for citizens, and in which 'welfare', according to specifications, is formulated and interpreted as individual rights. Political sociology often distinguishes between 'institutional' and 'residual' (or 'marginal') welfare states (Wilensky and Lebeaux 1958), or between universal and selective ones (Titmuss 1971). The Scandinavian welfare states are generally classified as institutional, providing a wide range of services and benefits that are commonly universalist in orientation, and regarded as entitlements of citizens. As a social value and political norm equality is still of great importance in Scandinavia and the state is expected to provide a redistribution of economic resources, power and influence between social classes and regions. Traditionally, welfare state policies were aimed not only at providing a safety net for the poorest, but also at creating a more egalitarian society (Allardt 1986; Esping-Andersen 1990; Hernes 1987; Siim 1987). Since the 1970s the egalitarian tradition has been broadened to address also sexual or gender differences.

The gendering of social rights

From the Bismarckian reforms of the last century, the history of the welfare state is commonly analysed as a series of compromises between capital and labour, and between welfare and control. What is less often observed is that welfare states also represent different compromises between women and men, mediated via the state–family–market arrangement.

Following Marshall (1965) modern political theory often conceptualises citizenship as consisting of three elements: civil rights, political rights and social rights. Welfare state entitlements, or social rights, are commonly formulated as rights that in principle are equally available for all citizens. In practice, however, citizenship is differentiated. Mainstream political analysis has been concerned with the effect of social class on citizenship. Feminist research introduces gender as an important, but often neglected dimension to the discussion of social inequality (Hernes 1987; Pateman 1988), and shows how expansion of entitlements, even when formally gender-neutral, has different consequences for women and men.

The social rights of citizenship are differently constructed in different forms of the welfare state and the ways in which women are integrated as citizens also differ. This is not always spelt out clearly. For example, the main concern in Esping-Andersen's much debated analysis is with the wage-workers' welfare state, and his analysis of welfare regimes is closely linked with the analysis of labour market regimes. The social democratic welfare states, he observes, have created a large public sector labour market, which has served to recruit women to formal employment. Though he does comment upon the persistent division of labour by gender within the labour market, he ignores the persistent division of labour by gender in market-external activities. As feminist critique rightly emphasises (see, for example, Lewis 1992; Orloff 1993) the analysis therefore misses the importance of the gendered division of labour to welfare state functioning, and its importance to the gender differentiation of citizens' entitlements (Leira 1993). In a citizenship perspective it is not sufficient to examine the arrangement between state, market and family only; it is important also to consider the impact of the unequal division of unpaid work.

The modernisation of motherhood

The idea of a 'public family' is linked with two processes of comprehensive social change: a rapid increase in mothers' labour market participation, and a comprehensive public investment in the provision of day-care for pre-school children. These processes generate changes in the division of labour both between state and family, and within the family. From the late 1960s Scandinavian women increasingly opted for both paid work and children. The meaning and content of motherhood changed as mothers of pre-school children became one of the fastest growing groups in the labour market. In the early 1990s 70–80 per cent of the Danish, Norwegian and Swedish mothers of children aged 0–10 years were registered as in the labour market compared with 51 per cent of the mothers of children under 10 years in the European Union who were in employment (Table 15.1).

In Scandinavia, the welfare state is usually believed to have promoted the modernisation of motherhood. From the early 1970s legislation that embodied new images of women and motherhood was introduced, such as the legalisation of abortion on demand, the passing of equal status legislation and increased state support for childcare. However, in several fields social change preceded political reforms. In both Norway and Sweden mothers took up formal employment well ahead of large-scale funding of childcare and well before the introduction of generous schemes for parental leave. Smaller families and increased educational attainment facilitated women's employment. Access to oral contraception facilitated

Table 15.1 Employment of mothers with children aged 0–9 years in the European Union (12) 1991

Country	Employment of mothers %
Denmark	75
Belgium, Portugal	60–69
France, Germany, United Kingdom	50–59
the Netherlands, Luxembourg, Italy, Greece	40–49
Spain, Ireland	30–39

Source: Commission of the European Communities (1993: Table 1: 3).

women's reproductive control. Fertility rates declined, but are now higher in Scandinavia than in several EU member states (NOSOSKO 1995). Norms regarding family formation and parenthood changed. Divorce rates increased and cohabitation became popular, particularly among young people. In 1993, approximately every second child was born to unmarried parents. Women in the 1980s commanded a control of their own labour and of their reproductive capacities unparalleled in earlier generations. The comprehensive economic, social and cultural change evidenced in these processes is not special to Scandinavia. Similar developments are witnessed in many countries in Western Europe (see Chapter 1).

Three features of the work/family relationship in Scandinavia are particularly interesting in a discussion concerning processes of integration and exclusion of citizens. First, Scandinavian women's high participation rates have not resulted in integration in the labour market on equal terms. On the contrary, the labour markets of Norway, Sweden and Denmark show a pronounced segregation by sex. In the upper segments of public and private bureaucracies, in finance and banking, in the top levels of trade unions and academic institutions the representation of women is not impressive.

Second, the dual-earner family is not a dual-carer family. In Norway, Sweden and Denmark the dual-earner family emerged as the predominant family form, even among families with very young children. Mothers' labour market participation almost equals that of fathers'. Over the last 20–30 years Scandinavian fathers have become more involved in childcare. However, in no way does this process of change correspond to the massive movement of mothers from full-time housewifery to labour market participation.

Third, gender differences in the mix of paid/unpaid work are decreasing, but are still quite striking. According to time use studies women on average work as long a day as do men, but women get paid for a smaller proportion of their work. Part-time work is important in Norwegian mothers' wage-work, for fathers overtime is important (Ellingsæter 1990). Women's use of part-time work is generally considered as one way of dealing with the incompatible demands of job and family obligations. Among Norwegian employed mothers of young children, part-time work still predominates, though in recent years more have been working full time (Elling-sæter 1987). The prevalence of part-time work is made up of a mixture of supply and demand interests. Some branches and sectors offer mainly part-time or seasonal work. Some employees opt for part-time, as witnessed among nurses and teachers. Among part-time workers in Norway, the majority work more than the number of hours (or income level) required for obtaining access to social insurance and benefits (Bjurstrøm 1993).

In the early 1990s, the integration of mothers in the labour market is not completed. So far, the integrative processes have not, on average, seriously challenged fathers' labour market participation and have not dramatically influenced fathers' participation at home and with childcare. Welfare state childcare policies have not made family care superfluous and have not been sufficient to place mothers on an equal footing with fathers when access to social benefits and entitlements is the issue.

The state and childcare

Since the 1970s the Scandinavian welfare states, acknowledging the parental status of workers – mothers and fathers – have expanded the working parents' rights by legislation concerning entitlements to leave of absence in connection with (i) pregnancy, parturition and the early period of the infant's life, and when a child is sick; and (ii) the provision of high-quality, state-sponsored childcare. By offering parental leave, the state subsidises care by mothers (and fathers); by sponsoring childcare, it subsidises extra-familial care. The right to parental leave is interesting also because fathers as well as mothers are included in legislation that interlinks the concepts of 'worker' and 'carer'. The public provision of high-quality childcare may facilitate mothers' (and fathers') employment and offer children a safe and stimulating environment; it does not necessarily imply a more equal division between parents as regards responsibility for childcare. In terms of the possibilities offered for parental *sharing* of childcare, the schemes for parental leave are the more 'radical'.

Leaves of absence

In the following I examine in some detail the Norwegian legislation concerning maternity, paternity and parental leave and increasing public support for child-care. From 1993 Norway's maternity/parental leave covers 52 weeks at 80 per cent wage compensation, or 42 weeks at 100 per cent, with job security and while retaining social security entitlements. In addition fathers are entitled to two weeks of unpaid paternity leave. Parents can share most of the parental leave period as they wish. Following parturition, six weeks are reserved for the mother. The Norwegian Labour government has recently instituted a 'father's quota', which implies that four weeks of the parental leave are reserved for the father exclusively, and transfer to the mother is generally not permitted. So far, this experiment with 'enforcing fatherhood' is a remarkable success in that the great majority of fathers who are included in the scheme, have taken up their quota. From 1994, a time account scheme has allowed parents to combine part-time work and part-time parental leave without loss of income for up to two years (Leira 1995).

Employed parents have an institutionalised right to paid leave in order to care for a sick child. In 1992, each of the parents was entitled to 10 days' leave and single parents to 20 days per year, in order to care for a sick child aged 0–1 years old (Leira 1995). Generous leaves of absence in connection with giving birth and to care for sick children, with wage compensation and retaining job security, certainly facilitate the combination of employment and childcare. However, in both Norway and Sweden there is concern that if only women make use of these entitlements, their opportunities in the labour market may be impeded (Leira 1992).

Payments for childcare

The institution of a caring wage for those who care for young children at home has been much discussed in Norway, but has not so far been instituted. Alone in Scandinavia, Norway has included benefits for single providers in the National Insurance Scheme, which offers single parents, of whom approximately 90 per cent are women, a chance to opt out of employment while their children are very young. Since 1992 a remarkable change in the National Insurance Act has enabled unpaid carers to earn entitlements to supplementary pension if they care for children under 7, or for old, sick or handicapped people not in institutional care. The reform is interpreted as a recognition of the value of the work performed by informal, unpaid carers, who are most often women; or alternatively as a preference for the traditional gender-differentiated family (Leira 1993).

State-sponsored day-care services for children

In all the Scandinavian countries the provision of high-quality day-care is commonly regarded as a national concern and is incorporated as a part of the welfare state service system. Access to publicly funded day-care is often presented as part of children's democratic rights. The development of national programmes for early childhood education and care with the explicit aim of providing state-funded services for all children whose parents wish for it, represented an intervention by the state in matters that were traditionally considered a family or private concern. Moreover, the provision of extra-familial childcare offered new opportunities for women for involvement outside the home. For both reasons, legislation concerning day-care for children was politically controversial in Norway in the 1970s, although much less so in Sweden and Denmark, where the welfare state from relatively early on supported mothers' economic activity and introduced large-scale public investments in childcare to that end. State-sponsored day-care for children was conceptualized not only as educationally advantageous, but also as a

Table 15.2 Children aged 0–6 years in publicly funded childcare in Denmark, Norway and Sweden 1978 and 1993 (% of age group)

	Age of child	Denmark	Norway	Sweden
1978	0–2	24	4	19
	3–6	40	23	60
1993	0–2	47	20	32
	3–6	74	63	77

Source: *Yearbook of Nordic Statistics*, NORD 1995: 321–2. The figures are not directly comparable because of differences in entitlements to maternity and parental leave, and some differences in registration procedures.

means of meeting the economy's demand for labour. Up to the 1990s Norwegian provision lagged behind, and policies showed considerable ambivalence to mothers' employment (Leira 1992).

As shown in Table 15.2, Sweden and Denmark still have a better supply of day-care services for pre-school children than has Norway, particularly in respect of the under 3-year-olds. When taking the provision of childcare as a main case, the 'collectivisation' of social reproduction, often considered a characteristic of the Scandinavian welfare state, seems to apply more to Sweden and Denmark than to Norway. During the 1970s and 1980s welfare state policies played a more modest part in facilitating the labour market participation of Norwegian mothers. The problems of working mothers, resulting from the structural incompatibility of employment and family organisation, were largely left to be solved on an indivi-dual basis. Up to the late 1980s, informal childminding in Norway provided more services for working mothers than did the state-sponsored system (Leira 1992). Mothers joined the labour market in large numbers, introducing new approaches to motherhood, without waiting for state-sponsored childcare and without ser-iously challenging fathers' work patterns or use of time. Facing a remarkably non-interventionist state Norwegian women enhanced their economic opportunities, acting as change agents in demanding opportunities for part-time labour and in establishing informal labour markets in childcare.

A comparison of publicly funded childcare services across Western Europe also modifies the image of the Scandinavian welfare states as particularly interven-tionist as regards early childhood education and care. Table 15.3 presents an overview of the proportion of children aged 0–3 years who are accommodated in publicly funded day-care in the EU member states.

In the early 1990s Denmark and Sweden provided for a larger share of the under-3s than any other state in this region. However, several EU member states compare favourably with the Scandinavian when it comes to the proportion of children aged from 3 to the beginning of formal schooling accommodated in publicly funded services.

The drawing of boundaries between state (and local authorities) and family responsibility, as regards early childhood education and care, implies not only a

Table 15.3 Children in publicly funded childcare services in the European Union (%)

Country	Percentage of children 0–3 years in publicly funded day-care
Denmark	48
France, Belgium, Iceland	20–29
Portugal, Italy	5–10
Germany (West), the Netherlands, Luxembourg, Ireland, UK, Greece	2–4
Spain	(no information)

Source: Commission of the European Communities (1990: 10). Data refer to different years in the period 1986–9.

re-conceptualisation of childhood, but potentially also of motherhood. Across western Europe policy making as well as public debate, show that the political institutionalisation of the concept of 'the employed mother' is controversial in many countries. Policies towards working mothers, as providers in single-earner or dual-earner families vary. Few countries combine high levels of labour market participation among mothers with generous parental leave schemes and large-scale public funding for childcare provisions for under-3s.

In the late 1980s and early 1990s political conflict over state funding for childcare services is increasing in Sweden and Norway. State support for families with young children is commonly accepted. Political parties disagree, however, over the content of support, whether as cash transfers, or as provision of childcare services. Put differently, the question also concerns whether the public purse should be used to facilitate the wage-work of mothers with young children, or to support the families where the mothers remain at home. A high proportion of women in the national assemblies of the two countries has not produced broad, cross-party agreement on the interpretation of women's best interest when the organisation of childcare is at issue (Leira 1992). Parties to the Centre and Right in Norway and Sweden in the 1990s advocate an increase in economic subsidies to families with young children, in order to promote parental care in the home, and to lessen the demand for public childcare. Although usually formulated in gender-neutral language regarding parental choice as to the form of care, in practice this proposal favours gender-differentiated roles within the family. The Social Democratic parties and other parties to the Left generally have argued more strongly in favour of women's rights to economic independence and in favour of state-funded childcare.

The gendering of citizenship

The post-Second World War welfare state in Scandinavia represents a period of profound change in mothers' relationship to work, family and the state, but also

167

a continuity in the structure of gender relationships. As women increasingly have entered some previously male-dominated arenas such as the labour market and politics, the significance of equality and difference take on new meanings. However, in the 1990s some of the 'old' equal status issues are still important, for example questions concerning the division of time, money, power and care that remain unresolved. Violence by men in the family directed towards women and children persists. The sex of a person still makes a difference to opportunities and therefore to welfare outcomes, for example in regard to citizenship entitlements. The gendered division of labour remains a feature of the Scandinavian societies in the early 1990s, though it appears as less pronounced than in other forms of the welfare state.

This is not to say that the Scandinavian welfare state was not important for women. On the contrary, the welfare state set the general frame within which women developed new approaches to womanhood and motherhood. Welfare state reforms increased women's 'property in their persons', to use Pateman's (1988) formulation, in two fundamental ways: women gained control over fertility and biological reproduction, and women's economic dependence on individual men was substantially decreased. Both as wage-workers in public sector employment, and as pensioners, receiving a state-guaranteed income, women came to depend more on the state for their personal income. Women have strongly opted for this shift in economic dependence.

As my analysis also shows, introducing generous systems of leaves of absence and investing in the funding of extra-familial childcare the social democratic welfare states in Scandinavia represent considerable efforts to bridge the gap between the demands of the market for labour and the demands of children for care. By providing entitlements to maternity, paternity and parental leave, and funding childcare services, welfare state policies improved the situation of working mothers and contributed to an equalisation of the situation of women and men as regards labour market participation.

However, employed mothers who combine work and family obligations give evidence of a contradiction inherent in the welfare state structure: welfare state policies acknowledge the need of citizens for material provision as well as for care, yet more comprehensive and generous benefits are accorded to those who participate in wage-work than to those who engage in vitally necessary but unpaid care and nurturing. The interplay with the gendered division of labour in this differentiation produces an exclusion of carers from some of the social rights of citizenship, and a gendering of citizens' entitlements, available as of right. The social construction of motherhood is set within this framework which clearly expresses a preference for formal employment over informal care and thus for men's traditional activity patterns over women's. The welfare state relationship to employed mothers and fathers, I maintain, has to be analysed within a general context which makes explicit the different approaches of the welfare state to employment and caring respectively.

Welfare state legislation and provisions define a considerable part of vitally necessary care, for example in childcare, as a private concern and as a responsibility of the family. In everyday practice this means that mother most often is the parent to whom the main responsibility for children's upbringing, nurturing and caring is ascribed, even when mother is also employed. The inequalities witnessed in employed mothers' and fathers' parental responsibilities is part of the processes that generate a gendering of access to citizenship entitlements and an exclusion of women from certain kinds of entitlements. This is not particular to Scandinavia. Processes excluding women from some of the social rights of citizenship may well be more characteristic of 'liberal' and 'conservative' welfare states as opposed to the 'social democratic' welfare state.

Notes

1 This chapter draws upon A. Leira (1994). My thanks to the Norwegian Research Council for Applied Social Science (NORAS) for grants that supported the original research.
2 This chapter does not deal with all dimensions of welfare state motherhood, nor with all of the consequences of welfare state policies experienced by mothers across class, ethnic and socio-cultural background. I also do not discuss the different experiences of single and married mothers, and barely touch on the biological aspects or emotional qualities of the motherhood experience. I aim at clarifying the welfare state reconstruction of motherhood as manifested in two basic aspects, economic provision and primary socialisation and care. For a more comprehensive discussion see Leira (1992).

16

CLASS, MOTHERS AND EQUAL
OPPORTUNITIES TO WORK

Evelyn Mahon

As outlined in Chapter 1 this book examines the interrelationships between the triad of the family, labour market and the state. Hirdmann (Chapter 3) conceptualised this relationship in terms of a gender contract. She argued that in Sweden the breadwinner/housewife gender contract was in turn replaced by an equality contract. The as yet unattained ideal is an equal status contract where both men and women share domestic and paid work responsibilities. Within this conceptual framework Ireland has a breadwinner/housewife gender contract.

More specifically, its policies on welfare and taxation support a traditional family with a dominant breadwinner (usually a husband) and a dependent spouse (usually a wife) (see Mahon 1994, 1995). In a country which until the 1990s had high fertility rates, very high rates of unemployment and a low demand for women's labour, this contract reflected the social division of labour and maximised family income. A ban on the employment of married women persisted until 1973 and divorce was not legalised until 1995. Consistent with this contract, deserted wives were entitled to state support and wives were entitled to other forms of welfare as dependents (McDevitt 1987).

From the mid-1970s onwards, married women and mothers entered the labour force, but childcare remained a family's private responsibility. In practice, it was the responsibilty of the mother, who was not granted any state support in the form of publicly funded childcare or tax allowances for childcare costs. The Second Commission on the Status of Women (1993) was critical of this form of gender relations and recommended the provision of publicly funded childcare. But the breadwinner/housewife contract is still dominant in Ireland.[1]

Equal opportunity policies were introduced as part of Ireland's access to the European Community. The national implementation of such policies is likely to reflect the dominant gender contract. This chapter is based on a study of the impact of equal opportunities in the Irish Civil Service. It will describe the interaction between the dominant gender contract and equal opportunity policies and will review the implications of this interaction for gender equity. In the case study of the Irish Civil Service, equal opportunity policies were two-pronged:

170

equal treatment in recruitment and promotion, and the introduction of family-friendly policies, such as career breaks for domestic purposes and job-sharing.

Variation in women's labour force participation in Ireland

The participation rate of Irish women in the labour market was 35 per cent in 1995, the lowest in the EU. This is explained by the low participation rate of married women: 31 per cent in 1995 (Central Statistics Office 1996). Historically, a number of factors militated against women's participation. The Constitution of 1937 enshrined a complementary domestic role for women in the home, and until 1973 legislation prohibited the employment of married women in the Civil Service and in banks (Mahon 1987). Membership of the European Union, and the legal imperatives of Article 119, facilitated the introduction of progressive legal changes. These included the elimination of the marriage bar in 1973; the introduction of the Employment Equality Act in 1977; and the Maternity Protection of Employment Act in 1981. The introduction of this legislation facilitated the greater participation of married women in the labour force. While it initially increased, it then reached a plateau, and the participation rate in Ireland is still below the European average (Callender 1990).

Since the elimination of the marriage bar in 1973, family size, rather than marriage *per se*, and the age of the youngest child, have been the major factors in explaining the variation in married women's participation (Blackwell 1989). However, family size has declined, from an average of 5 children in 1961, to 4.7 children in 1981, to an estimated fertility rate of 1.93 in 1993 (Chapter 1). There has been a corresponding increase in the proportion of married women at work.

These increases, however, do not reveal the variation in participation rates between mothers by occupational sector. Taking mothers with two or more children, only 15 per cent of them worked in the professional/technical area, 15 per cent in industrial employment and 9 per cent in clerical work (McGrath 1990). Yet clerical work has been until very recently the modal category of women's employment (Mahon 1991b) in Ireland.

In the late 1980s a study was undertaken to explore the effectiveness of equal opportunity policies and their impact on the labour force participation of Irish mothers (Mahon 1991b). The Civil Service seemed an excellent organisation in which to investigate this issue, as an equal opportunities policy had been introduced in 1986. This policy included provisions in relation to formal equal opportunity policies with regard to recruitment and promotion. In addition, it simultaneously introduced a series of family-friendly policies: career breaks for domestic purposes; job-sharing; and flexitime. The study explored the impact of these initatives on working mothers. The hierarchical nature of the Civil Service provided a sample of mothers located in different grades within the organisation, extending from the very low-paid clerical assistants to the higher-paid Principal Officers.

While the study examined promotional practices and experiences, and women's satisfaction with equal opportunities in the workplace, this chapter concentrates on one aspect of the study: the interaction between equal opportunity policies and the structural impact of the breadwinner/housewife contract on mothers' relationship to the labour market. It will show that this relationship will vary depending on mothers' occupational status or grade within the organisation.

Gender and location within the bureaucratic structure

The Civil Service occupational structure is a classic example of vertical segregation, with men predominantly occupying the top posts (in this case all the top posts), and women predominantly occupying the bottom posts.

However, an analysis of the recruitment and female promotional patterns, suggests that the organisation is best understood as two pyramids (Table 16.1). The first, or lower pyramid B, extends from Clerical Officer to Higher Executive Officer (equivalent to the Administrative Officer). The second pyramid A extends from the Administrative Officer grade to the Departmental Secretary grade. Administrative Officer is the recruitment grade for honours graduates with 2.1 or First Class Honours degrees. The next grade is that of Assistant Principal, which is considered a policy making grade.

Graduates can take a high-flyer route to this grade, and in fact many recruited

Table 16.1 Women in the Irish Civil Service, general service grades, January 1983 and October 1987 (%)

Grade	January 1983 (a)	October 1987 (b)
Secretary	0	0
Assistant Secretary	1	1
Principal Officer	3	5
Assistant Principal Officer	18	23
Administrative Officer	31	26
Higher Executive Officer	35	34
Executive Officer	40	44
Staff Officer	61	67
Clerical Officer	69	68
Clerical Assistant	84	83

Sources: Tansey (1984: 99), Mahon (1991: 21).

in the 1970s were guaranteed promotion to this grade after six years' work. While promotion from the bottom to the top grades is in theory possible, it is very rare among those recruited as Clerical Officers or Assistants, since Executive Officers or Administrative Officers are more likely to get the higher posts. Women's work, promotional opportunities, childcare and lifestyles differ depending on whether they are located in pyramid A or pyramid B. An analysis of their promotional experiences, and mothers' use of family-friendly policies shows differences by grade.

Equal treatment in recruitment and promotion

Women located in pyramid A work in the higher grades in a predominantly male environment. Those who were recruited as Administrative Officers and who remained in the Civil Service evaluated their career progression in terms of the career achievements of their male colleagues who were recruited at the same time. The result of this male-dominated environment was that women adopted male norms of work practices. They could be characterised in Hakim's (1991) terms as 'committed workers'. The demands of these jobs were such as to often necessitate overtime, working late at meetings or over the weekend to meet deadlines. The Civil Service can be a 'greedy' organisation. Promotion was competitive and the successful made work a central aspect of their lives, and this was the case for women who occupied such posts.

As regards equality in promotion, women as competitive applicants for middle and higher grades were proportionately successful in confined competitions for Assistant Principal Officer posts higher scale, and more successful than men in Assistant Principal and Higher Executive Officer competitions (Mahon 1991b). Given that success, it is not surprising to find that they were more likely to think that women were equally treated in the Civil Service.

For women in pyramid B, the lower grades, promotions are based on open competitions, which in the past meant that established or permanent officers competed with school-leavers in an examination system which favoured school-leavers. Because the lower grades are overwhelmingly female, the effects on women are very negative. For instance, in 1987, in a competition for Clerical Officer, women had a success rate of 2 per cent, as compared to a 9 per cent success rate for men (Mahon 1991b). Among the thirty-six respondents from the lower grades interviewed, 75 per cent had never been promoted, 56 per cent of whom had between 12 and 19 years of service. When there were internal or confined competitions, the chance of promotion from the lowest grades was almost non-existent. Further, in competitions which did arise, their lack of success using a proportionate criteria indicated that they were likely to be discriminated against. The majority of women in the lowest grades felt that women did not have the same promotional opportunities as men and that perception was supported by an empirical analysis of competitions. In terms of equal opportunties, then, there were considerable differences between women located in the higher grades and

173

those in the lower grades. Mothers in the lower grades were 'stuck' with little or no chance of promotion and constituted an underclass.

Career breaks

In addition to equal treatment initiatives, family-friendly polices were simultaneously introduced. They included career breaks for domestic or childcare purposes and job-sharing. While career breaks were open to both men and women, the reasons for career breaks varied between men and women. In the case of career breaks for childcare purposes the majority of those who take them up are women. However, their uptake among women varies by grade. Women in the lower grades were far more likely to take a career break for childcare purposes than women in higher grades. While official figures gave a breakdown by gender rather than by motherhood status, data collected for the study indicate a predominance of mothers located in Clerical Assistant grades.

Job-sharing

Job-sharing is not actively promoted or facilitated. In fact, some departments are etremely reluctant to agree to job-sharing. Each department is free to decide on what grades can avail of job-sharing and many are opposed to job-sharing in the higher grades. The task of organising job-sharing lies with the individual civil servant who has to personally seek a job-sharing partner. Far more women would like to job-share than are accommodated. Part II of this book showed the importance and prevalence of part-time work among mothers. Job-sharing in the Civil Service offers mothers the advantages of part-time work, without the disadvanatages of insecurity, lack of permanency and lower pay. It affords mothers time with their children and halves their childcare costs, while reducing their net income by approximately a third. Women in the lower grades are more likely to seek job-sharing and to take a career break than their sisters in the higher grades. Job-sharing was a very attractive option for women whose children were older and who had to bring them to school, music lessons, etc. As job-sharers, they could share such tasks with other mothers, and this reciprocal arrangement helped them to offset their double burden in the weeks they worked.

Actual job-sharing arrangements varied; some took one week on and one week off, others three days work one week followed by two days work the following week. In only one instance was it a daily part-time work arrangement. There were, therefore, considerable savings in time and transport costs. Women who job-shared were very happy with the arrangement, they had as they said 'the best of both worlds'. Job-sharing arrangements were originally made for just one year, but later they had to be three-year contracts. The level at which job-sharing was available in the Civil Service varied by department. Many more women wished to job-share than were afforded opportunities to do so, and some women on career breaks would have preferred a job-sharing arrangement had it been available to them. However, the principal advantage of job-sharing was that it had the time advantages of part-time work without an employee being allocated simultaneously to a secondary labour market.

The organisation of childcare and its costs

As indicated above, the participation of mothers in the labour market declined as the number of children they had increased, and it varied by their occupational and educational status. Childcare was a necessarily incurred expense, to be deducted from parents' income. The form of childcare used by mothers varied by grade. Mothers in the two lowest grades were most likely to take up offers by their extended family – mothers and mothers in law – to provide childcare, so childcare was subsidised by their extended families. Alternatively, they used childminders and transported their children to the childminder's home each morning. None could afford nannies, home-based housekeepers or any form of paid dometic help. While the care purchased was both limited and cheap, the relative costs of childcare, as a proprotion of their small salaries, was considerable and acted as a disincentive to work for mothers in the two lowest grades. As they said, when they paid the tax, the childminder and expenses to and from work, it was simply not worth their while financially to continue to work (Mahon 1991: 45). Instead, they opted for a career break while their children were small, or they left their employment for good.

Overall, women at work in the higher grades were well integrated into their work, which occupied a central place in their lives. As compared with their age cohort nationally, they were older when they married and older when they had children. Mothers at the top of the pyramid, delegated their family responsibilities to nannies, childminders or husbands. Higher-grade jobs demanded long hours of work and often unexpected or unpredictable tasks. If mothers were to fulfil such demands – like their male colleagues – they needed flexibility in their childcare arrangements. So women in these higher grades were more likely to have home helps or childminders who came to their homes to look after children, rather than to leave their children with childminders. These childcare arrangements were of course more expensive, but were less demanding of the mothers, as there was not the same emphasis on pick-up time, etc. The higher salaries enabled them to afford this kind of childcare. In addition they did not feel obligated to do domestic work, concentrating on quality time with their children. Their career advancement and higher salaries helped them to stay at work, as did their satisfactory childcare arrangements.

They had broken new ground on the domestic fronts by delegating domestic and childcare tasks to paid help or to their husbands. Their childcare arrangements and the domestic help they could afford enabled them to delegate their familial labour to paid substitutes. Women in the higher grades have negotiated new roles within their families. Their behaviour supports Walby's (1990) primacy of work thesis, in which she argues that women's position in the labour market determines their postion in the family rather than that women's family position influences their work situation. A major aspect of that change was the employment of domestic help and private childcare. However the ability to re-arrange one's role within the family was based on earned income and on the extent to which women could afford their replacement costs. In the case of highly paid women this was not an issue as they could afford childcare, but for women on low incomes this option was not available. So mothers' earning capacity affected their childcare arrangements and the way in which they were able to reconcile family and working life. A breadwinner/housewife contract individualised the responsibility for childcare. This meant that income differences between mothers affect the way in which women can combine family and working lives, with disadvantages for low-paid workers.

Spousal support

For all mothers, spousal support was also very important. Women whose husbands had time-consuming jobs, or who were for one reason or another continually absent from home, found it difficult to combine motherhood and work, and opted either for a career break or for job-sharing, in order to reduce their total work-load. The career break option reinforced the traditional breadwinner/housewife model as women returned to a traditional role of full-time housewife. Job-sharing afforded an innovative intermediate response as women experienced the 'best of both worlds', like part-time workers. Mothers in the higher grades earned as much and in many cases more than their husbands'. In the case of the three mothers in the highest grades (to which mothers in the sample study had been promoted) their careers were more important than their husbands. For instance, one husband had resigned from the Civil Service, retrained as a speech therapist and worked part time so he could care for their daughter. A second had remained in Dublin and curtailed his career development so he could devote more time to raising their two sons. One was a house-husband and cared for their young daughter while his wife worked full time. So these practices indicated new divisions of labour in some families. The breadwinner gender contract facilitated this reversal of roles.

While mothers in the lowest grades were more likely to take career breaks for financial reasons, women in middle and higher grades took them because they felt overworked. The double burden of work and family was too much. When such couples' division of labour was analysed it transpired that those women who opted for career breaks had husbands who invested a lot of time in their jobs or were pursuing further education. These husbands were simply not available to help with childcare and domestic chores. The result was that these working mothers were over-burdened as they could not afford paid domestic help or home-based childcare. Travel on public transport extended the length of their working day.

Given the low pay of mothers in the two lowest grades, and their limited promotional prospects, why do some mothers continue to work full time while others don't? While we have indentified class differences between mothers, we also need to know what factors differentiate between women in the same class. The case study showed that mothers who continued to work full time and did not make use of family-friendly policies were distinctive in three ways. They made a greater contribution to total family income and were more likely to be principal bread-winners. Second, full-time working mothers' jobs were more secure than those of their husbands and were highly valued as such. This was especially important in the case of women whose husbands worked in trades or jobs which were suscep-tible to unemployment. Third, women enjoyed working and valued the social contact it afforded them.

Given the emergence of both between- and within-class differences in the use of equal opportunity policies versus family-friendly policies, the next issue is to examine the interaction between the gender contract and equal opportunity policies.

Sainsbury examined the way in which the gendered division of labour pre-scribed by the breadwinner model has been codified into the legislation in different countries (Sainsbury 1996: 49). A number of dimensions identified by her as signifiant in social policy are also important to women as paid workers. In a male breadwinner model, a joint taxation system operates with deductions (or allowances) for dependants, employment and wage policies give priority to men, the sphere of care is primarily private and caring work unpaid (Sainsbury 1996: 42). In terms of familial ideology, there is a strict division of labor with husband as earner and wife as carer. These dimensions are all part of the dominant gender contract in Ireland. However Sainsbury also argued that in some states women's entitlements have been derived from either their status as wives or as mothers. In particular she identified a fundamental divide between benefits accorded on the basis of principle of care and awarded to the mother as contrasted with the principle of maintenance which was conferred upon the father. This distinction is particularly important when examining the gendered implications of the Irish taxation system.

A male breadwinner taxation system

In the absence of state-sponsored childcare, the taxation system is the only redistributive mechanism which can be used to promote fiscal family policies. In conservative/liberal economies the taxation system is very important, and as Irish taxation policies have altered over time, they have had an impact on net family income. Human capital theorists suggest that labour market outcomes are the consequence of rational choices and that the household unit is the unit of decision making (Mincer 1985; Becker 1993). This implies that there is a house-hold work strategy. Becker argued that it was in the interest of the household as a unit for one of its adult members to concentrate on domestic work, and one on paid work. It was more efficient to have a specialised division of labour than for both spouses to do some of each. Joint taxation arrangements between couples reflected the male breadwinner contract. Within family taxation policy women were treated as wives rather than as mothers. Until 1980, the income of a wife was considered that of her husband's and classified as 'additional employments' subject to taxation at the husband's highest tax rate. Wives received a working wife's allowance of £400 and simply paid tax on all their income at the tax rate their husbands paid. This practice was constitutionally challenged in 1980, when it was argued in the *Murphy v. the Attorney General* case that it was more profitable for couples to remain as two separate earners and live in sin instead of getting married. This arrangement, it was argued was anti-family, and so unconstitutional. After the Murphy case the system was changed. It was still a family-based one. Each married couple, irrespective of whether one or both of them worked, was allocated twice the single person's tax allowances. The total tax and personal allowances of two single earners were combined and allocated to each married couple. This procedure meant that the allowances and bands were transferable between married partners making the tax situation of one-earner and two-earner families identical. This had the positive effect of maximising family income in one-earner families but if the husband's income was high enough to fully utilise all the tax allowances, their wife's additional income would be taxed at the higher rate of 48 per cent. So taxation was family-based rather than individualised and very consistent with a breadwinner/housewife contract.

While this familistic taxation regime is designed to maximise income to families, the real beneficiaries of this arrangement are married men who get double tax allowances and double taxation bands and thereby reduce their tax liability and increase their net income. Marriage to a non-earning wife represented a tax bonus. Because men are still considered the major breadwinners in the family in Ireland, these 'married' tax allowances are usually given to men. If their wives work the only additional allowance they can claim is the PAYE allowance of £850. The system favours the one-earner family and indirectly the male breadwinner contract.

For mothers employed in the higher grades, their high taxation rate was offset somewhat by their high salaries. In dual-worker families, where both husband and wife work, they can share the tax allowances between them if they wish.

Who pays for childcare

The familial ideology that accompanies the male breadwinner contract treats childcare as the responsibility of the family, more specifically of the mother. One consequence of this is that women took the responsibility for childcare payments and deducted them as an incurred expense against their incomes. In calculating the financial benefits of work, mothers deducted their childcare expenses from their net income and wondered whether or not it was financially worth their while to work. For low-paid mothers with husbands in secure jobs, it was not simply that they withdrew from their employment and returned to their domestic role but that it was economically more expedient for them to do so. In practice, for that group of mothers, a familistic taxation policy and its implementation functioned to reinforce patriarchal patterns of labour force participation. The present family-based taxation system promotes a sexual division of labour in working-class households. Low-paid wives have no financial incentives to work if they have to pay for childcare.They are therefore more likely than their middle-class counter-parts to take up family-friendly policies.

The option of job-sharing is a family-friendly policy that is not as problematic as career breaks. For job-sharers the working week is halved, but the net income decreased only by a third, as the remainder would have been paid in tax. This is financially a rational choice, combining work and family life. However job-sharing is likely to impede career development and is still a personalised reponse to the reconciliation of family and working lives. But it must be noted that job-sharing is still not available to all who would like to take advantage of it, as contrasted with a career break which is non-problematic for the organisation.

The interaction between gender contract and equal opportunities

The introduction of both equal opportunity policies and family-friendly policies simultaneously has different implications for women in different class positions. Liberal equal opportunities policies do not differentiate between women and men (Mahon 1991b). However, as indicated earlier, vertical segregation persists and women are still overwhelmingly concentrated in the lowest grades. The benefici-aries of liberal equal opportunity policies were women who were in a position to adopt male norms of working life and entered the Civil Service as graduates. They were proportionately as successful as men in promotional competitions. But liberal equal opportunity policies ignore gender differences and, in particular, do not take children into account. In the Civil Service, the only concession to women with children were family-friendly policies which reinforced traditional gender roles.

As noted already, the male breadwinner contract in Ireland incorporated women as wives rather than mothers. The Irish report on childcare services revealed that Ireland had the lowest level of provision of childcare in the EU (McKenna 1988). The absence of state-supported childcare and the lack of any tax allowances for childcare expenditure has had an effect on the take-up of family-friendly policies. Mothers are treated as wives rather than mothers so the system embodies a breadwinner contract designed to promote a male main-tenance model rather than a mother care model of the breadwinner/housewife contract. Ireland never developed what Siim (1993) refers to as the 'second stage of the welfare state', 'the cornerstone of which was the increase in the public production of services, especially childcare and other services for children and young people, and the elderly' (Siim 1993: 32). In a report by Moss on mothers and employment in Europe, state support or provision of childcare was the most important explanatory factor advanced (Moss 1986).

179

The result of this neglect is that class and income differences between mothers are ignored and traditional gender roles are reinforced. An alternative approach would be the introduction of policies which were mother-friendly, such as state-sponsored childcare or subsidies for low-paid mothers who wish to pay for child-care. This would still be a family-based policy but mother centred. This would reduce the class differences between mothers as regards the choices they are able to make regarding work and family life. The extension of job-sharing rather than career breaks would also be a positive development within the Civil Service to faciliate new gender roles, especially if fathers took advantage of it.

The emphasis on mothers has been central to social democratic states where childcare has formed part of the second stage of social welfare. In this case, children are not simply seen as a private personal responsibility but are an expense on the community in general, just as education is. The state would provide, support and subsidise childcare. This would reduce the sexual division of labour by shifting the burden of domestic work to public services and to men (Orloff 1993: 314). However, this approach would also redistribute childcare costs between the highly paid and the low paid. It would leave mothers free to make a choice between work and family without the economic restraints of the present male breadwinner model. In addition, the taxation system would become an individualistic one as has occurred in Sweden. This system would expect every-one, including women, to work but would offer some paid parental leave to both parents. Further, as workers women would enjoy all the entitlements that accrue from employment.

Conclusion

The Commission's European Social Policy (Commission of the European Communities 1993b) recommends that it undertake an economic assessment of the job creation and reflationary potential of child and dependant-care infrastructures and services. This is to be welcomed. So too is its proposal that the directive on parental leave be adopted. However, the individualisation of rights, while a legitimate ideal in terms of liberal equality, is insufficient to promote mothers' (or parents') participation in the labour force. Such a strategy must be accompanied by a recognition of the demands of care and the establish-ment of social, community and fiscal support for such care work. The present Irish arrangements are neither gender- nor child-neutral, they reify patriarchal relations and serve to dampen the positive effects of equal opportunities in employment. They also augment class differences between mothers in regard to employment continuity, which in turn will have an impact on their future rights as citizens. State policy can to a large extent facilitate the participation rate of mothers in the labour market. As we move towards the completion of an internal European labour market, mother- and parent-friendly policies must be promoted in all states.

Note

1 The newly elected government has promised fiscal support for childcare expenses in the form of tax allowances for childcare and additional tax allowances for spouses who are full-time carers.

17

WORKING PARENTS

Experience from the Netherlands

Els Veenis

Introduction

Men and women combining work and childcare seems to be an appealing ideal to many parents. The majority of the Dutch people support the idea that men and women both have the right to work and that fathers should be involved in childcare. The number of families with two working parents is on the increase, but remains low compared to other EU countries. In 1990, 36 per cent of Dutch mothers with children under 4 were in paid employment (Sociaal Cultureel Planbureau voor de Statistick 1993) and in 1996, 65 per cent of Dutch parents with young children were dual-earner families (Centraal Bureau 1996). Despite these changes, Dutch women still seem to be stuck in the vicious circle of work and family. As a consequence of being more responsible for the caring work at home, the vast majority of Dutch mothers work part time. Their jobs are often low-paid, dead-end jobs, which, in fact, tends to encourage the traditional division of responsibilities of work and care between the sexes.

How can this gap between the egalitarian ideals of the Netherlands and their more traditional practice be explained? First of all, Dutch ideas are not as modern as they look at first sight. The image of the self-effacing mother was dominant until the late 1960s. For a long time the policy of the government was to enable men to earn a living for their families while mothers stayed at home. These ideas were deeply rooted in the Dutch culture as can be seen, for example, in the popular women's magazines of that time. After the 1960s the image of the mother developed from self-effacement to self-development: care was no longer seen as a burden which she had to carry without complaint, but as a way of 'expressing herself'. Having a (part-time) job was no longer an offence against motherhood but was seen as a choice – as long 'as the children don't suffer in any way' (Morée 1992). Second, in recent years, the Dutch government has created and improved some facilities for working parents such as childcare and parental leave, but these measures are rather limited; at the same time there are more financial benefits for families with a breadwinner and a housewife than for families with two working parents. The basic assumption of the government is that the improvement of facilities for working parents is a matter of negotiation between employers, unions and parents.

In this chapter I focus upon the ways that employers have adjusted to the wishes of their employees with children. Do corporations take the lead in breaking down the 'double hierarchy' between men and women, work and care? I will discuss my research on the position of working parents in two Dutch retail companies. In theory, many Dutch employers and employees support a more equal division of tasks between men and women, in daily practice at work they still think and act in terms of the breadwinner/housewife model: a male employee should be exempt from care, a female employee is expected to give priority to the caring work at home.

A comparative case study of two companies in one segment of the labour market is, of course, limited. The position of working parents in other segments may be different, so my conclusions cannot be generalised to the situation throughout the entire labour market in the Netherlands, yet useful inferences can be drawn from this case study. This kind of research can increase our insight into the (power) processes between men and women, employers and employees. In this way we can learn a lot about the rather puzzling Dutch situation: about the implications of the ambiguous Dutch governmental policy; the paradoxes working parents face; and the myths employers and employees cherish in order to cope with the changes from a 'familial gender regime' towards an individualistic gender regime. Finally, it leads to an exploration of the possibilities for improving European social policy, the 'initiatives which might contribute to . . . reconciling men's and women's roles in the context of sharing economic and social responsibilities' (see Introduction).

Theoretical framework and methodology

In my research I adhere to the ideas of the Dutch psychologist Komter (1990, 1991). She applied the so called 'power hypothesis' of Schuyt (1973) to analyse the power differences between men and women in companies. Schuyt postulates that the rights of persons with a strong power-position are given as global, diffuse and comprehensive, whereas their duties are stated more specifically and limited; on the other hand the rights of persons with a weak power-position are specific and limited, while their duties are more comprehensive. While Schuyt concentrates on the functioning of power through formal rules, Komter extended the formal level to the informal level of the organisation (the unwritten rules of behaviour in the company on how men and women should behave) and into the subjective level of how men and women experience rights and duties, both at work and in their family. Komter shows that it is precisely at this informal level and in the experience of the employees that the gender difference is not just reproduced as a difference but is rendered as inequality.

The two companies I researched were a large chain of supermarkets with almost 38,000 employees with a relatively low educational level and a small group of bookshops with approximately 550 employees with a very high educational level, in which parents are in a minority. In the supermarkets, 12 per cent of the female employees and 22 per cent of the male employees are parents of at least one child younger than 13 years of age, and in the bookshops the proportion of parents is 21 per cent (female) and 37 per cent (male) respectively. In both companies women are over-represented in the lower functions and are almost absent in the higher positions. In the supermarkets the majority of fathers are the breadwinners of the family; their wives are at home taking care of the children; the majority of mothers work part time while their husbands have full-time jobs. In the bookshops this way of combining work and care is dominant for the fathers as well.

In the research I combined quantitative and qualitative research methods. The first step was a postal (written) questionnaire sent to 500 employees in each company. According to the questionnaires, 54 per cent of the employees with young children (70 per cent of the mothers and 41 per cent of the fathers) face some problems with combining work and care, varying from very concrete and manifest organisational problems and overload to more hidden, latent problems such as (often unspoken) wishes for more egalitarian ways of combining work and care. Women do face more problems with overload and problems with their career, while men more often express feelings of guilt that they are less involved in childcare than they would like to be.

The second step consisted of personal interviews with 25 employees from each company with children under 13 years of age, mothers and fathers, about the ways in which they combine work and care, the problems they experience and the way they cope with these problems. I was not looking for the 'truth' about their situation, but analysed the ways they reflected upon their present and past, the words they used to express their feelings and thoughts. In the analysis the terms rights and duties in work and care and the power thesis of Schuyt and Komter were used as sensitising concepts (Glaser and Strauss 1967). For these interviews I made a selection as diverse as possible from the respondents to the questionnaire; the sample was a deliberately biased sample – exceptions such as female full-time workers were consciously sought. This means that the conclusions may be more 'positive' and unrepresentative of the Dutch situation in general who tend to be more conservative than the parents in my sample. The third step consisted of a postal questionnaire to the managers of the parents I interviewed about the social policies operating in their companies.

The social policy of the supermarkets and the bookshops

In recent years, in both companies, a number of formal facilities for working parents have emerged and been developed: arrangements for day-care, unpaid maternity and paternity leave, and extensions of maternity and confinement leave. In addition, the companies also have more informal arrangements: employees must discuss with their boss and colleagues what is and what is not possible. This includes part-time work, flexible working hours, emergency leave and priority for parents in holiday periods.

In both companies the way things are handled differs from shop to shop. In most bookshops the floor managers are quite cooperative, in the supermarkets this is often not the case. In most of the bookshops the floor managers seem to trust their employees not to abuse measures, for example by not taking a day off in busy periods. In return the employees can expect a flexible attitude from their managers. The employees in the supermarkets are less positive about the attitude of their employers, who feel flexibility has to come from the workers' side only. Their managers have a tendency to say 'no' without considering different possibilities. Often, there is no proper replacement for women who are on maternity leave: colleagues are supposed to take over the work and to work overtime.

In both companies senior management seems to be rather hesitant with regard to flexible working hours and part-time work in higher functions. In shops, part-timers and flexible workers are needed to work in shifts and to fill in the gaps when other workers are ill, but the full-timers are the core of the company. Management strives for a proper balance between the number of full-time and part-time employees and seems to be afraid of creating precedents: if they allow one father or mother in a senior position to work part-time or on flexible hours, 'the fences are down'.

In spite of the fact that the intention behind parental policy is to improve the position of women, the facilities (with the exception of maternity and confinement leave) are open to both women and men. In practice it is mainly women who make use of the facilities. Women are more often made aware of the facilities available by bosses, women are more prepared to go from one facility to the next, part-time work and confinement leave are more readily acceptable for women.

The corporate culture of the supermarkets and the bookshops

In both companies the parents do not talk much about their children, it is considered a private issue which one talks about with relatives and friends. Sometimes parents together talk about the children, relate funny anecdotes or discuss educational problems, but they do not talk much about the way they combine work and care. Employees seem to be rather careful not to offend one another about the subject of working mothers; there are no discussions about childcare. The way colleagues share tasks at home is regarded as one's own choice that has to be respected. However, the employees do have some hidden thoughts about each other and some jokes are made to parents.

It is mainly in the supermarkets that colleagues are not expected to notice that an employee also has caring tasks. This is expressed in rather informal support from colleagues given to working mothers and caring fathers. The situation of working parents is not disapproved of, but is considered with mixed feelings, varying from scepticism to admiration. Moreover, an (implicit) distinction is made between men and women. In the first place, and definitely in the super-markets, it is expected that women take upon themselves the greater part of the care at home. A mother who often phones in ill arouses the suspicion that it is actually her child who is ill. In the second place, the expectations are that a mother will work part-time; since the caring tasks are mainly attributed to women the combination of full-time work and motherhood is considered to be too great a burden and there is a fear that women (if they choose that option) will rely too heavily on the support of their colleagues. In the third place, the situation of working parents is seen as one of personal choice, and that the parents must be responsible for the consequences of their situation. Women with children may continue working provided the company does not suffer in any way. Considering the caring tasks of women, part-time work for women is considered as self-evidently suitable, but at the same time it is just as self-evident that part-time workers are not able to move on to higher functions. If a man wants to work part-time, then it is his business, but colleagues do not consider it an attractive option because in the eyes of his colleagues he is 'opting' for fewer opportunities at work.

The perception of rights and duties from employees with children

It is not only managers and colleagues who allocate different rights and duties to fathers and mothers, parents themselves also do it. Parents are aware of the danger of being noticed if they are different from the others, and they are aware that, due to themselves, colleagues are additionally burdened and the company incurs damage if they are too involved with their family.

Men and work: self-evident ambitions

Men are unanimously in favour of their right to work – it forms an essential part of their life. It means responsibility, challenge, protecting the family, and personal development. The significance of work is almost always referred to in positive terms, even by the men who are not too happy with their job. Unemployment and needing to receive disability benefits are the worst scenarios, followed by becoming stuck in a function without a future, or being a house-father.

The men have a strong sense of duty with respect to their work, they consider that they work hard, particularly in peak periods, and they make sure that the company is bothered as little as possible by the fact that they have a family. Fathers link this duty to the opportunities that the company offers them: they apply for interesting, managerial functions, with considerable freedom and positive career prospects. For men, the duty of work means that they are available a great deal of time; however, it is noticeable that at work they delineate their own tasks fairly stringently, they do not take on any tasks that are not officially part of their function, unless they particularly enjoy doing so.

Women and work: dutiful part-timers

The women are less unequivocal than the men about their right to work. On the one hand they dismiss the idea that a woman has less of a right to work than a man, and on the other hand they put that right into perspective by entertaining a double scenario: that of the housewife and that of the overburdened mother who has no time for herself or for the children. They can understand that a mother stops working because she prefers to be with her children and because the combination is too much. They also consider this option to be the last resort, as they consider 'just sitting at home all day' as being unattractive. Part-time work is the best solution: it is possible to be involved in the care of the children, and work has only a limited claim on time and responsibilities. For the women, being in paid employment means an important supplement to the work at home, it gets them out of the tedium and the isolation.

The women also have a strong sense of duty with respect to their work: compared with men their working time is limited, but their ambitions to do their work well are not. They often delineate their tasks less than the men do, and do not link their efforts so clearly to the facilities that the company offers them: even in the less senior functions with no future prospects they work hard.

Men and care: cuddling breadwinners

For the men fatherhood is linked to being a breadwinner, even for those whose wives also work outside the home. They feel responsible for the financial well-being of their family, for creating the conditions under which the children can thrive. For men fatherhood means that they have to settle down: they now feel not just responsible for themselves, but also for their wives and children. This also involves a different attitude towards their work: on the one hand, their job makes it possible for them to fulfil this new responsibility, but, on the other hand, it prevents them from being at home a great deal. They want to be a father who, outside working hours, is there for his family, who takes his wife's place if she is not able to be there and who builds up his own ties with the children. They take their work seriously, but put the idea of constant availability for their job into perspective – since they have children they do not want (any longer) to be so singularly involved in their careers.

Women and care: the priority of the duty to care

The women consider it self-evident that they start working less when children arrive, they want to be 'involved' with the child as much as possible. Motherhood means being responsible for the daily well-being of the children; for women the duty to care encompasses numerous practical tasks and a considerable investment of their time. As well as for the men, the arrival of children, for women, means farewell to their youth, but this tends to manifest itself as a (temporary) adjustment

187

to their ambitions at work and getting used to the idea that tasks of caring are their primary responsibility. The women in the bookshops make more effort than the women in the supermarkets to share the caring with their husband. They are also more positive towards day-care. The worst scenario for the women in the bookshops is of 'the man who does nothing at home', and for the women in the supermarkets it is 'the crèche-baby' and the 'latch-key child'.

Conclusions and discussion

According to my research in the Netherlands, the 'double hierarchy' between work and care, men and women, while under attack, is still very much alive and kicking. Implicitly most employers and employees, even those with egalitarian ideas, make a distinction between men and women. The caring tasks at home are seen as being the duty of the mothers, and for fathers priority is given to the right to work and to a career. It is more readily expected and accepted of women that they take on the caring tasks and therefore use the facilities available. At the same time, it is the norm that the company should be bothered as little as possible by the fact that employees have children. The way parents solve their problems with the combination of care and work is their own choice and responsibility. The thought that the organisation of work could be modified to the principle that every employee has caring tasks, is, in the current company culture, still almost blasphemous.

Both men and women consider and refer to paid employment in terms of rights, and care is referred to in terms of duty. Work is seen as something you can claim, care as something that can lay claim on you. This points to a difference in status, where work is ranked higher than care. The men tend here to show a stronger feeling of right than the women, and among the women there is an element of a strong awareness of duty, both for their work and at home. In the light of the hypothesis of Schuyt, we can postulate that most men, both at work and at home, have a stronger power position than their female colleagues and partners. For men, the duty to work involves a greater investment in time, but, more so than for the women, it is delineated into tasks that do and do not have to be carried out. The duty to care is, for men, delineated into time and tasks, but is therefore also vague and general, and that of women is wide ranging, both in time and content.

At this moment there are currently two possibilities open to Dutch women with children: they can claim their right to care by taking up a position as a mother or they can claim equal opportunities at their work precisely by not taking the position of mother-with-caring tasks. The first strategy is usually used by the less qualified women and the advantage of it is that overload is combated and that the women are able to fulfil their duty to care. The disadvantage is that these women are not able to move to the core of the company as they are required to modify their career aspirations, at least temporarily. The more highly qualified women tend to use the second strategy more. The advantage is that there is still time for their career aspirations to be fulfilled. The disadvantage is that the women usually take on two duties, one on top of the other – their duty to care and a strong sense of duty as employee. Moreover, they must compete with men who have a limited duty to care and a less overwhelming sense of duty to work. The possibilities are also limited for the men with children: they can take part in the large group of fathers who combine work and care as 'cuddling breadwinners' or they can (temporarily) give their caring tasks more priority. This results in a not too attractive special position for fathers in the company.

What light does this shed on the situation in the Netherlands with its gap between the ideal and practice? The idea that mothers may work 'as long as their children do not suffer at all' seems to be less strong. But it has been replaced by the fear that companies get into difficulties if mothers and fathers really start to claim their right to work and care. One pillar of the double hierarchy is beginning to wobble, that is, the premise that men have more right to work than women. The other pillar is still, however, very firmly anchored: the difference in duty to care between men and women is less subject to erosion just as is the ultimate superior ranking of work over care and the ideas about 'good care'. This also puts the right of women to work into perspective: they may work as dutiful part-timers, but must give up their aspirations for a career to be a good mother.

On the one hand, you can say Dutch women are more privileged than other European women – with the exception of the Scandinavians: most mothers are allowed to make the choice as to whether they want to work outside the home or not and they can also choose the part-time option of combining work and care without becoming overburdened. On the other hand the domains of work and care are deeply separated and gendered. To break down this situation the government has to take a more active role to stimulate the integration and 'degendering' of work and care. This means that a switch must be made towards a combined model of work and care.

In my research I have shown that employers and employees often consider that there is equal treatment if men and women are given the same opportunities, provided that they act as an employee without caring tasks. The organisation of labour is not under discussion. In a combination model different patterns of work and care should be developed so that the right of every employee to care and the right of every carer to work are guaranteed, this would form the core of the action.

Currently in the Netherlands, the government, employers and unions are playing the ball back and forth on matters relating to who is responsible for parental policy. However, encouraging integration between work and care does not form one of the immediate economic interests of companies; it is somewhat naïve to assume that labour organisations are keen to encourage men to take on more caring tasks. The reorganisation of the organisation of labour must, it is true, take place in companies, but it requires a vision of care that is wider and more focused on the long term than that of the employers and unions. It is wider because care should not be thought of only in terms of money and economy, but

18

ARE FATHERS CHANGING?

Comparing some different images on sharing of childcare and domestic work

Dino Giovannini

I know that 'the same' object must necessarily show different aspects to each of us. First, because the world in my reach cannot be identical with the world in your reach, etc.; because my here is your there; and because my zone of operation is not the same as yours. And, second, because my biographical situation with its relevance systems, hierarchies of plans, etc., is not yours and, consequently, the explications of the horizon of objects in my case and yours could take entirely different directions.

(Schutz and Luckmann 1973: 59)

The vast social changes that have come about as regards the structural organisation of daily routine have changed radically, above all in northern Italy, the man/ woman, parent/child relationships. Such changes have not occurred, qualitatively or quantitatively, however, in relation to the sharing of the workload or looking after the children, the weight of which rests mainly on the woman's shoulders (Bimbi and Castellani 1990).

In what way should we go about making changes and what initiatives should be undertaken so that men take on more responsibility in childcare and the education of their children? This chapter presents some results from wider research carried out to find out the meaning of being fathers today (Giovannini and Ventimiglia 1994, 1997). The research has been supported by the Emilia-Romagna Region and it is a part of a wider transnational project, done in collaboration with the EU, on the themes of larger involvement of men in childcare.[1]

One of the reasons that led to the region getting involved directly in this field is shown by the high percentage of women with small children who work full time. In 1991 about 70 per cent of women with children under the age of 10 were employed. At present of 100 women in the 14–55 age group, excluding students, about 75 per cent work. Furthermore, the Emilia-Romagna is one of the best equipped regions for infant services both at national and European level.

Although this situation is quite representative of northern Italy, it is not true of the south.

In this study we considered different topologies of fatherhood; their behaviours, role and the social images they represent. We also analysed the perceptions and representations that children have of the image and the role of father and mother. Finally we tried to identify assonances/dissonances concerning the reconstruction made by each partner of their own role.

In this chapter some results based on a sample of 43 childcare workers and 44 parental couples of pre-school children (fathers and mothers) are discussed. The childcare workers and the couples separately participated in discussion groups which were organised in eight meetings, over a time span of six months. In total we organised nine groups, three for each specific role; the meetings were held in three towns in the Emilia-Romagna Region. All of the parents had volunteered to participate in the study and, of course, the samples cannot be considered as representative of the whole father–mother–childcare workers' population.[2]

However, the aim of a qualitative analysis is not to gather statistically sound data, but rather to assemble points of discussion on relevant issues. It should be noted that we found marked differences in family organisation and task sharing for the couples taken into consideration. In order to present these differences, we will examine two points in particular: (a) sharing of family responsibilities by couples; (b) the reconciliation of family and work.

Comparing one's own and other peoples' perceptions

In relation to what it means 'to be a father today' this research has now produced quantitative and qualitative data. The results take the form of images, representations, opinions and beliefs that the various social 'actors' involved (fathers/mothers; husbands/wives; childcare workers; children) have expressed at various times and at different levels.

In essence, they are concerned with different perceptions regarding everyday behaviour carried out by individuals who are seen, defined and analysed simultaneously as *fathers* and as *men*. These *subjective* modes of reconstructing reality often appear to differ, as in the case of the differences that one encounters, for example, between the two partners about their respective educational and interpersonal roles (Giovannini and Molinari 1994).

The divergent perceptions relating to the time for oneself, for housework and the children, discovered during the interviews and meetings with the couples reflecting on the same experiences, are certainly a very important result. But it is even more important to identify the significance that fathers, mothers, children and childcare workers attribute to the behaviour specifically relating to the role of father. It is by interpreting these contents and meanings that we come to fully grasp whether social practices relating to fathers' involvement in the care of their children depend on interaction/negotiation between parents.

In general, participants in the discussion groups have tried to investigate and study the possible significance that specific figures, such as fathers/mothers, husbands/wives and childcare workers, may attribute to the concept of *fatherhood*. Several conceptual tools were used by the discussion groups in order to define better the psycho-social context in which today's fathers move; we have given priority to the concepts of behaviour (action), attitude and image or representation.

Sharing of family responsibilities

Fathers talk about themselves

It is not an easy task to summarise briefly the qualitative results of the group meetings held with fathers, and this chapter outlines a few fundamental points. There are so many different ways to be a father, and each one of them is linked to one's personal history and individual traits such as personality, beliefs, experiences. Among these variables, one of the most important is the relationship with one's partner and children.

'To be a father' is not considered a natural 'innate' instinct, but instead a cultural behaviour, linked to individual experiences: most fathers seem to describe themselves more on the basis of 'the ways they differ from somebody else' (*'I try to be a totally different father than my own; he was never there, he never cared much for the family or us children'*) than the intrinsic features pertaining to the father role. Another significant remark relates to the importance attributed to social expectations in general, as they are conveyed by the mass media and social interactions with other parents.

They feel inadequate as fathers, partly as a consequence of well-ingrained stereotypes; therefore, they tend to define their personal way to be a father only in relation to their partners and on the basis of their individual traits. Here we may introduce the concept of searching for a father identity structured by a *comparison with* and *difference from* something that lies outside one's sphere. This way of characterising the search for an identity is put into practice through representations and self-perceptions of reality which have positive connotations.

On the basis of the representations given by fathers, there seems to be more help being offered in and around the house, which increases with the birth of a second child; emotional closeness to the partner during her pregnancy and at childbirth; an increased presence at home with the family during the weekend; more emotional involvement and dialogue with children. The reasons that brought about such changes reside, as clearly stated by respondents, in the changes that have taken place within our society and especially in the woman's role; in higher standards of living, which bring about the necessity for people to fulfil their relational and affective needs more than their material ones, as a sort of compensation for the coldness and lack of human relationships which seem to permeate today's society; and most of all 'because this is what I mostly lacked when I was a child'.

What conditioning factors affect the self-definition as fathers? Respondents mention the relationship between family and society and also stress the fact that it is very difficult to find different and alternative ways of definition; as regards the father's role, there is a strong need for differentiation and the typical behaviour of the 'old paternal' model is rejected. They feel uncertain because, if on the one hand they have totally rejected the old paternal model, on the other hand they seem unable to find viable alternatives to the 'old father figure', and therefore they look for individual solutions to this dilemma according to their personal beliefs and attitudes.

As regards the aspects pertaining to 'upbringing and education', we notice a clear lack of steady trends. The authoritarian, cold and detached model has been discarded and replaced by a more loving and affectionate behaviour based on increased closeness and dialogue with one's children. The transmission of those values which are considered important depends each time on the constant evaluation of their application and feasibility, even though fathers are well aware of difficulties, partly due to the general lack of clear reference values and a sort of educational permissiveness.

Mothers speaking about fathers

This section outlines, from the mothers' point of view, some of the differences which arose in family organisation and task sharing between the 44 couples studied.

The first element that mothers underlined during the meetings is the general willingness of their partners to care for their children after they come home from work. This attitude is often seen as a preference by fathers for playing with their children, or in some cases, as a real sharing of responsibility as regards children's physical care. This widespread willingness is often combined with two conditions which seem to hamper its practical benefits, in other words: (a) the fact that often fathers spend extremely long hours at work, and, as a consequence, their presence with children is necessarily short during work-days; (b) the real difficulty that fathers have in participating in family work, apart from caring for their children.

Therefore, according to Molinari (1994a), there are four significant variables for definitions of the modes of family organisation: (1) fathers play with their children; (2) provide physical care of the children; (3) time actually spent by fathers at home; (4) sharing of family responsibilities. From a combination of these four variables Molinari (1994a) has identified four types of couple relations, which are defined according to the degree of fathers' participation in family routine and domestic work.

The involved father

The first type of relationship, which includes, for the most part, working couples, is characterised by an active participation by both parents in the tasks necessary for the smooth running of the family. In some cases, this task sharing finds its rationale in the couple's well-established experience of living together before the birth of the child, while for others, this attitude has grown progressively with the birth of the first or second child, which seems to foster an increased awareness by fathers to listen and respond to their spouse's needs.

In couples falling within this category, we find some women who are deeply involved in their careers, and they express different opinions regarding their personal and professional involvement (*feeling guilt or blaming ourselves, that's just something we have to forget*). The motivations given to explain this attitude can also be somewhat ideological and these motivations seem also to be widely shared by involved fathers. In other instances, the intense condition of being a working mother is experienced as a double regret, first for having to steal time away from one's family and second the inability to fully accept a role reversal which is still uncommon today, that is, when a father spends more time at home than the mother.

The involved father, in theory

The second type of couple shares some common traits with the previous group, that is the role interchangeability in caring for the children and sharing family work and organisation; but this is combined with the fact that fathers have very little free time. In these couples the husband (usually a professional or self-employed) spends very little time with his family, although he expresses his willingness to do so. Whenever the mother is also employed, her responsibility in managing family life 'on her own' becomes burdensome and her work schedule must be adjusted to this situation.

The 'guest' father

The highest number of couples are included in this third category. For the most part, the woman is employed, and works for not more than 6 hours a day. Women in this group say that their spouses are generally willing to play with or care for the children, but at the same time they delegate to women all responsibilities regarding domestic work. Therefore we can say that these couples follow a rather 'traditional' work sharing, with the father who spends some time with the children (mostly playing) after work while the mother does her domestic work when her husband is with the children. *'Daddy only works outside the house, mummy does all the house work. Daddies don't do the ironing'* (a 4-year-old child).

Other women instead feel that this arrangement is a sort of male 'privilege' which negatively affects women's relationships with their children. In many cases this arrangement is more or less accepted 'as a matter of fact' and the woman seems to adjust easily to the limited level of contribution offered by her partner, while other couples enter into open conflict about these matters.

The delegating father

The fourth type, which includes a smaller number of couples, sees the presence of a father who delegates to his partner all the tasks regarding both family organisation and children's care and upbringing. In these cases, the woman is employed for shorter hours or has even left her job because she could not reconcile her 'double role' as mother and worker; in this situation her partner has certainly felt legitimised in delegating everything to her. Here the father's absence seems to derive in particular from the father's difficulty in 'familiarising' with his children from the very beginning: for these fathers the 'achievement of fatherhood' is a slow process, and they do not have to face conflicting situations as their spouses shoulder the heavy load of caring for the children and the house without complaining too much. In these situations we sometimes find the woman has very negative feelings towards the role that mothers are called upon to play.

Difficulty in reconciling family and working life

Difficulties seem to lie in the attempt to reconcile work-related expectations with family and childrearing responsibilities.

The point of view of fathers

Fathers stress the fact that it is very hard for them to lighten their work commitment; also, despite positive attitudes towards their children, they also refer to a feeling of 'restlessness' when they think about having to spend a lot of time at home with them. We may detect here social identifications and expectations which are still deeply ingrained and very strong, reflecting the need for a father figure who has a job and is a 'provider', together with a sort of inclination by fathers themselves to conform to this model.

Generally they consider the family the most important thing even if none of them considers the possibility of leaving work to take care of the children. How important their job and their family is depends on individual values. Any new offer of a more stimulating and profitable job depends on each individual situation. Indeed, some refused such offers because of the family. In other cases, some accept an external commitment justifying it with the attempt to maintain a high level of relationship with the family itself; the reasons of this choice are psychologically and economically important to both partners.

The content analysis of fathers' meetings shows that they spent more time at work than with the family. So they are aware that work takes time away from the family and they are torn between the wish to be at home and their involvement in their work. This conflict is not so great when the job is part-time, with flexible working hours or if it is subordinate employment. It is also much easier for them to accept the fact that their wives stay at home, because this option reproduces an ingrained 'status quo' still supported by prevailing cultural models.

Fathers give other motivations for not changing their accepted behaviour by remarking that women are more patient with children in the long run; in order to find justification for the fact that they spend much of their time away from home and their children, fathers seem to emphasise the nurturing qualities and skills of their partner rather than stressing 'biological and/or innate' differences between the sexes.

In essence, concerning the career, we may underline two different attitudes: (1) the father renounces his own career less then a mother does, as a result of a negotiation process; (2) the father does not renounce his own career because it is perceived as a source of self-fulfilment. It is implicit in this attitude that it is the mother who has to renounce or postpone her own aspirations. The father is not always conscious that his wife has to renounce her career. If the aspirations of both are equally self-motivated, partners try to find other solutions, in order to resolve the conflict.

The point of view of mothers

The variables coming into play here are the type of job and work-hours of both partners. However, in many cases these variables lose the features of objectivity and stability attributed to them, because instead they come to represent the ways in which sharing and direct responsibilities for family organisation are carried out (Molinari 1994b).

It seems that these types of relations are not considered 'as a matter of fact', but more often result from an intersubjective process of shared construction between the partners. Using Molinari's typology of fathers, let us consider the first category of couples, characterised by the highest level of sharing (*the involved fathers*). We clearly see from discussions with mothers that this situation did not happen 'naturally', but was built and negotiated by both partners. The woman in this case does not place herself immediately in a subordinate position, but from the start demands from her partner that he cooperates with her in their experience as parents.

The situation regarding the second type (*the involved father, in theory*) seems more difficult to manage, because the task of reconciling work and family falls on the woman: the constant variable here is the fact that 'the amount of time fathers dedicate to their job is extremely high', and this forces the woman to go through a 'never-ending reconciliation' process.

But where do these differences in direct involvement and family time sharing come from? How does it happen that one partner comes to delegate to the other almost the total load of responsibilities for family work, while theoretically both partners should be fully interchangeable in their roles regarding children's care and upbringing and family organisation?

Molinari (1994b) considers that in this case also, the key element seems to be, at least in part, in women's hands, in other words in the fact that women tend to take full responsibility for the organisation of the family, thus leaving less room for fathers. In essence, women are the first 'to renounce, to take parental leave, even before they are asked to do so' and this legitimises their partners to organise their work schedules on their own.

The point of view of childcare workers

There is a strong belief by the childcare workers[3] that fathers' participation in family life is still limited and partial: the organisation of the house is still a mother's job; even when there is cooperation, it is still the woman who plays the leading role. In other words, we see the emergence of a father figure who lacks autonomy, depends on his partner to carry out his role, and is willing to cooperate but in a 'passive' way.

Childcare workers also reported a difference in the way parents speak and relate to them: generally, fathers tend to show a lower degree of interest, which depends on circumstances, while the behaviour of mothers is more consistent and responsible. However, childcare workers still believe that fathers are strongly committed to their work, which takes up most of their time and energy, and therefore reduces their participation in family life. Reconciling work and family is still a distant goal.

Childcare workers also remark that whenever a choice has to be made, the mother is still the one who gives up work, although they have underlined the fact that the issue of reconciling work and family needs further study, since a transactional symbolic framework and value models are still lacking. As a mother/childcare worker said: '*the father figure is a growing image, not a finished product. We have sown the seeds of growth, I see differences, notice different aspects, I don't know in which direction we are going.*'

Conclusions

The main goal of our study was to provide us with data that would make us thoroughly understand not so much whether there is a 'new' way to 'be a father', but rather the true reasons behind the different and increased involvement/participation of fathers in the care of their children and what can contribute to these changes. The theory is that today paternity constitutes an exploration into the specificity of the male identity, which has still to be defined between resistance and a tendency towards change (Giovannini 1993).

The analysis of available data offers us a complex set of information about the ways used by fathers themselves to explain their role. The comparison between motivations and descriptions given by fathers and the ones given by mothers/wives, by childcare workers and children themselves – although to a much lower degree – raises several interesting points. The results of our research show there is no equal sharing either of childcare or of family work. The father is a support, a prop, but does not share. Usually he perceives and admits the inequality of sharing the workload by showing understanding and admiration for what his partner does.

The important thing to point out is a different grading of values which is given to being a father on the one hand and being a husband on the other. In fact, men, on the one hand, say that they are satisfied with the present division of roles with regard to family work and think it is not necessary for them to be more involved in domestic work. On the other hand, as regards play time with their children, they say they would like more. The perception does not even arise that the father's role in its qualitative and quantitative dimension cannot take place outside and independently of the qualitative and quantitative dimension of the couple's relationship.

Acknowledgement

The research and writing of this chapter was supported by a Consiglio Nazionale delle Ricerche.

Notes

1 See the Report of the International Seminar organised by Emilia-Romagna Region 'Men as Carers: Towards a Culture of Responsibility, Sharing and Reciprocity between the Genders in the Care and Upbringing of Children', Marina di Ravenna (Italy) 21–22 May 1993.
2 As regards the selected sample, the fathers participating in the meetings ranged between 25 and 46 years of age (median age 36 years; age range for the most part 36–46 years), and held a middle–high level school qualification (28 had a diploma and 7 a university degree). The mothers ranged between 30 and 40 years of age for the most part (middle age 33 years), and held a middle–high level school qualifications (36 had a diploma or a university degree); as regards their jobs, 5 mothers did not work outside the home, while the majority of them (25) were employed. Of the couples, 45 per cent had only one child and only 4 (10 per cent) had 3 children. Almost all of them said that their political preference lay with the left.
3 In the discussion groups 43 childcare workers were involved with between 16 and 20 years of work experience in the childcare services (general mean 13.1 years). The average age was 38.4 years and for the most part the representative ages ranged between 41 and 50 years (39.5 per cent) and 31 and 40 years (37.2 per cent). The majority of the selected sample had two children (60.6 per cent), 36.4 per cent one child and the 3 per cent three children. Only 13.9 per cent were not married. (Please note that great majority of childcare workers in Italian services are women.)

19

FAMILY ORIENTATION AMONG MEN

A process of change in Sweden

Ulla Björnberg

Men, family and work

In Sweden, over at least three decades, there has been a political commitment to sustaining equality between men and women within the family and in society (see Chapter 3). The purpose has been to strengthen the participation of men in family life and make them more family oriented.

Women have been encouraged to participate in the labour market. Extensive and affordable public childcare and paid parental leave for both mothers and fathers have been the most important measures to implement a modern companionate family form in Sweden.

In this chapter I reflect on the effects of these policies on men. It is based on an empirical study of employed fathers with 5-year-old children.[1] They are classified as work-oriented and family-oriented respectively. These classifications are explored further in the chapter.

The family orientation among women is taken as a point of reference for an understanding of family orientation among men. It is assumed that men as breadwinners identify strongly with their job and that men are bound to experience role strain not unlike the strain suffered by full-time employed mothers (Robinson and Barret 1986; Sandquist 1993).

Often women have been portrayed as role models for men when constructing a new father's role. Research on men as fathers suggests that men's own fathers have provided negative role models and that the men themselves want to develop new types of relationships with their children (Holter and Aarseth 1993). In my analysis I argue that changing orientations towards fatherhood and partnership ought to be analysed with reference to men and conceptions of masculinity in society at large.

Work and family orientation among Swedish fathers

A recent study on career orientation among male non-manual employees, a replication of a similar study done in 1962, revealed that men have become increasingly family- and child-oriented, while their career ambitions had taken on a different direction (Nilsson 1992). These results are in line with my study where results suggest that the men saw great disadvantages for the family or themselves if they engaged more in their work. Over half of the men adapted their work to their families, by reducing their working hours or changing jobs for the sake of the children, or refraining from accepting career promotions.[2] Compared with data from other countries in the study, a higher proportion of Swedish fathers indicate that their family lives would suffer if they decided to put more efforts into their jobs.

The results also indicate that a majority of the men consider that their primary identification lies with family and private life and not with employment and professional life. More Swedish men than men in other countries in the study have their identity based on their family life. The data suggests that the children are the primary motivation for men to adjust their professional activity to their family lives. On the other hand, men's involvement in household work and in childcare is low compared to that of women. Men do a third of what their wives do, even when both have full time jobs (Rydenstam 1990). Thus, men tend to be child oriented but less motivated to do housework.

Work-oriented and family-oriented men[3]

What is actually meant by 'family orientation' or 'work orientation'? Could we for instance suppose that men who claim to be family oriented are more involved in the household and family matters than the men who consider themselves to be more work oriented? With the goal of analysing the implications of 'work and family orientation', the men in the study were classified into two groups: family oriented and work oriented. An exploration of the categories reveals that work-oriented men tend to be somewhat older than family-oriented men. They are more likely to belong to the upper classes than family-oriented men (68 per cent work oriented versus 41 per cent family oriented). More of the work-oriented men than the family oriented men have a university education. Work-oriented men also work longer hours as compared with family-oriented men (22 per cent and 10 per cent respectively). In terms of their views on ideal family forms – traditional or companionate – differences between the two groups were negligible.

Work-oriented men have obtained more flexibility in their working conditions to a much higher extent than family-oriented men. Work-oriented men have reduced their working hours as a strategy, to a higher extent than family-oriented men.

Occupational status probably explains part of these differences. For example, a comparison between production workers and civil servants shows that the latter have adopted these measures to a greater extent: 10 per cent more civil servants have obtained flexible working hours or reduced their working hours. Manual production workers are more likely than service workers to have adopted these measures (a difference of 10 per cent).

It was expected that more family-oriented men would have cut down on over-time compared with work-oriented men, but this was not the case. Neither have they refused offers of promotion more frequently. Work-oriented men have made slightly more changes concerning increased work commitment compared to family-oriented fathers, but the difference is not great. More work-oriented fathers claim that they do not succeed in balancing family and work very well, 30 per cent of work-oriented fathers compared to 18 per cent of family-oriented ones. Work-oriented fathers have more stressful jobs and feel negative (tired, weary, stressed) on returning home from their jobs compared to family-oriented fathers. They also tend to be more critical of their share of responsibility for the children than family-oriented men.

Insecure paternal identities?

Do work- and family-oriented fathers differ in their attitudes towards their father roles? How secure are they in their roles as fathers? The discourse concerning parenthood, fatherhood and motherhood in a modern cultural context empha-sises insecurity and ambivalent attitudes (Björnberg 1992). In several articles, it is said that many 'new' fathers claim that their own upbringing serves as a model for their own parental role to a very limited extent (Holter and Aarseth 1993). Their own experiences are not adequate or sufficient in many new types of situations which they face as fathers but which their own fathers were not confronted with. For instance, one significant change is that the family is, in its everyday dynamics, characterised by democracy and regard for the individual. Old models of author-ity have collapsed and are replaced by models of mutual negotiation. Another change is that emotional relations are given a central position in family life. Individual needs and demands have increased for all individuals in the family. The parents are counsellors and even friends to their children and no longer dominate and exert overt power.

Modern society demands a high degree of achievement, which in combination with decreased actual control over the children's development, strengthens inse-curity and leads to anxiety and stress (Beck-Gernsheim 1992). This ambivalence in parenthood can be reinforced by the fact that mothers and fathers have different views on what responsibility for the children means.

In order to shed some light on experience of parental identity parents were asked some questions about the way they satisfy their children's needs in the family. One indicator used was whether they felt dominated by their children's needs, or whether they managed to balance children's needs against their own. Approximately a quarter of the men stated that they give in to the children's needs. The majority claimed that they managed to sustain the balance between the needs of the children and their own needs.

An interesting observation, however, is that the family-oriented men feel dominated to a larger extent. More family-oriented men experienced conflicts with their partners concerning responsibility for children: 24 per cent of the family-oriented men versus 15 per cent of the work-oriented men claimed to have frequent conflicts with their partners concerning childcare. The family-oriented men also had more frequent conflicts concerning childrearing (15 per cent versus 10 per cent). Another interesting difference between the groups of men concerns their feeling of having to compensate the child for the time which they do not spend at home. Family-oriented men felt such a need regularly and more frequently than work-oriented men. More than half of them felt such a need on a daily or weekly basis compared to about a quarter of the work-oriented men. In household matters, family-oriented men experienced conflicts about money more often than work-oriented men. This may be due to the fact that work-oriented men lived in a relationship where they had split the responsibilities for different expenses in the household.

Equality: men's family orientation and changing fatherhood

In general the results show that the differences between the categories are not as wide as could have been expected. There are, however, differences between the groups in attitudes. The results indicate that men who identify themselves with work also have ambitions for their family lives, but they are unable to live up to the demands they experience as fathers and equal partners. Their work makes them exhausted and less keen on doing housework or taking care of the children on a daily basis.

The comparison between the categories suggests a higher sensitivity concerning the children among family-oriented fathers. Men who identify themselves with the family also seem to be more engaged with the children and at the same time they feel insecure in their roles as fathers. They often feel ruled by the children and claim to feel obliged to compensate the children for the time they do not spend at home. Family-oriented men have more conflicts with their partner concerning their relationships with the children. These insights into a complex area suggest that the ways in which men are involved in family life are not necessarily moving in the same directions.

What do different men mean when they indicate that their primary identity is mainly anchored in the family? For example, men with a traditional view of the family could reveal a family identity, suggesting that the family is a symbol of men's status as adult men. Wives and children constitute the traditional symbols of their ability to sustain a family. This view has no implications for men's ambitions to be involved as fathers or husbands who share the household tasks. To another group of men, family identity could mean that they have an idea of the family as a project which presupposes their active participation. For yet another group of men, their primary identification with the family means that the family circle means most for their sense of security and comfort. These men might not link their own involvement in family matters with what family life means to them. Family orientation is therefore a vague concept which can have many connotations.

In a recent Norwegian study on men, four patterns of family orientations were differentiated (Holter and Aarseth 1993). Two of these patterns are of particular interest for this study, since they are considered to be examples of new trends in male family orientation. One was called 'career-extending style', a style of viewing children and family as an important part of a career. The men with this orientation were primarily focused on their children and were keen on developing relationships with their children because of new insights concerning social relationships. By having greater involvement in interpersonal aspects of family life they develop more skills in social behaviour outside family life. This type of man seems to correspond to the pattern found among the work-oriented men in the study.

The other style was labelled 'the caring man'. This style implied an upgrading of traditional family values, especially the female parts of family life. A cosy atmosphere in the home was emphasised along with high values given to family ambience, comfort, emotional relations and aesthetics. Home-baked bread, high quality food, reading and watching television together were important elements. This type of family orientation might be closer to the group of men who have been labelled as family-oriented in this study.

The other two types of family-oriented men were 'the justice man' and the 'family idealising man'. The 'justice man' considered equal sharing to be an ideal goal to strive for. He took on a practical attitude towards sharing the jobs in the household and tried to do duties which he judged to be his 'fair share'. In sharing housework he should do the same duties as his partner. Time sharing was not considered as important as performance of duties.

The 'family idealising man' made strict divisions between family and work. While he took on an idealising attitude towards the family – it being very important to him – in practice the family was devalued and not given priority by the men in this group. But these men often had feelings of guilt towards their family and had a strong sense of not being able to balance family and work.

These examples show various patterns in orientations towards work and family, and that many men live with ambivalent attitudes. My hypothesis is that most of those who indicated the middle position on the scale when replying to the question on where their identities lay, are in reality very ambivalent and searching for a way to regard work and the family. This group consists of those who consider work as important as the family, and who must find solutions in everyday life that combine ambitions and demands from both spheres reasonably well.

The modernisation of childhood

Men's orientation towards children, partners and family life is part of a process of change which has its roots in several different spheres of society. The modernisation of society has implied a weakening of patriarchy and parenthood in general. During recent decades in Sweden, the state shouldered a greater part of the responsibility for children, particularly regarding financial support, education and socialisation. The parents' roles are still of the greatest importance for the development of the children, but there has been a movement towards the integration of parenthood into society, especially in those areas where the traditional concept of fatherhood had greatest legitimacy. These include changes in the family law which took place between 1965–85. I am mainly referring to the way these decades saw the legal erosion of the patriarchal family system – systems based on fatherhood, and not on the male sex in itself (Dahl 1991). The erosion of fatherhood has become an unavoidable consequence of this development and men lack role-models when it comes to developing a modern idea of fatherhood (Björnberg 1992).

The French sociologist Sullerot has described the change in institutionalised fatherhood in terms of the weakening of fathers' legal and social positions during the late 1980s in most countries in Europe. Her thesis is that a patriarchal family system has also been undermined by demographic movements during the same period. She suggests that women have taken control of reproduction because women are able to control their own fertility by the use of modern contraceptives and liberalised rules on abortion (Sullerot 1992). In addition, divorce laws in most European countries have been simplified during this period, and it is easier for women to request and obtain a divorce. After divorce, it is normally the woman who gets the legal and practical custody of the children. One implication of this development is that fatherhood, from the male point of view, has become conditional in a way that it never was before. Fatherhood depends entirely on the mother, her will and her relationship to the father. Children born outside the marriage belong to the woman. Mothers have a stronger position than fathers in legal terms (Sullerot 1992). The erosion of patriarchy in the family has brought about a diminution of fatherhood, with a consequent weakening of the proper father–child relationship.

Fatherhood in Sweden

Recently, a movement towards emphasising biological fatherhood has taken place. This has been made possible because of enhanced genetic techniques. In previous legislation, the father's biological fatherhood was not the crucial issue, but rather whether the child was born into a marriage or not. Thus it was marriage that regulated fatherhood (Frost 1993). A legal change during the post-war era gave extra-marital children rights of inheritance. These children became the equals of children born in marriage. This change can be interpreted as a step towards a more direct link between father and child.

Compared to international laws, Swedish family law differs in some important ways. One difference is the recognition of the child's right to both its parents. The reference point is hence that the child is entitled to know its biological origin, the right to know who its father and mother are. It means that adopted children have the right to know that they are adopted and, if possible, who their parents are. Anonymity in connection with donation of sperm is not allowed according to Swedish law. The child must have knowledge of who the donor is. In divorce, the basic rule is that the legal custody is split between the parents. The parent with the practical custody of the child must allow access to the other parent, otherwise custody may be lost. This rule has also been formulated in terms of the right of the child to its parents.

Parental leave for fathers, and their rights to take time off to care for sick children are further points marking the child's rights to have a father, or vice versa, the father's rights to exercise his fatherhood. This is a regulated framework whereby fatherhood is socially constructed, an expression of Swedish society in which fatherhood is to be understood as more than a breadwinning and an authority role. Fatherhood is expressed through direct social relationships with the child. One consequence of this development is that men demand greater access to their children. Both men and women strive to attain equality in their rights to exercise parenthood. Arguments for equal parenthood are related to visions of equal partnership and shared devotion to all aspects of family life.

Visions of the growth of a new family form, on the basis of an equal partnership with two breadwinners, creates expectations for men who develop an active father-role to become more family-oriented in other respects: an active father is also expected to be an equal partner, a husband who is engaged in an equal marriage. These expectations stem from an interpretation of motherhood – an interpretation that gives a significantly wider meaning to motherhood than solely the focus of mother–child relations. Motherhood also includes such things as care, giving birth, creating a home – which all connect to the social picture of the woman's place in the family.

Conclusion

In comparison to motherhood, fatherhood has never had this wide meaning of care and creating a home. Men regard household labour and childcare as leisure activities, whereas women tend to regard these activities as a responsibility for the home and the family (Horna and Lupri 1987). Women view the relationship between work and the family as a conflict between two areas of responsibility.

When men in modern society wish to develop their relationships to their children, many of them have other motives. When men have been asked about their motives to become more active fathers, they often refer to a wish to develop as persons. They expect that contact with little children will help them to find new insights into themselves and help them to develop aspects of their personality, particularly the emotional side. In a comprehensive literature review of fatherhood, Lamb and Oppenheim (1989) have come to the conclusion that fathers' engagement is inspired by curiosity and a wish to have contact with their children. Equality in parenting, or the ideal of an equal marriage, have had little effect on men's attitudes and activities. These conclusions also need to be set alongside the fact that much research shows that on the whole men play with the children, and engage less in organising other matters concerning the child. There are therefore reasons to suppose that men have a more differentiated picture of family orientation than women. The pressures behind men's development towards an active fatherhood can therefore not be interpreted as a primary wish to develop equality in family life, but partly as a wish to gain control over reproduction, and partly as a wish to be able to develop as individuals via closer contact with the children.

As researchers, especially feminist researchers, we have to be aware that men who choose to be involved fathers do not necessarily also have a motivation to become equal partners. Men's motives to be active fathers are based on other types of rationality compared with those of women. I want to emphasise the importance of men and their experiences with family life being understood through theories which focus on men and masculinity. The male notion of fathering and fatherhood is different from mothering and motherhood. Men's motives to create better relationship with their children are linked to their working lives, whereas the links for women are more strongly associated with the home and the family.

Notes

1 The study was conducted in co-operation with other European countries: West and East Germany, Poland, Russia, Hungary. The Swedish study is based on personal interviews with 670 randomly sampled mothers and fathers of pre-school children.

2 Reduction of work hours is granted by law for parents with children below eight years.

3 The two categories of men have been compared on questions concerning family and work. The empirical measurement in the study used the question about the importance of family and job for the image of the self. Those men who have scored 1–2 on a 5-point scale (from 'Family' to 'Work') have been categorised as 'family oriented', and the remaining ones as 'work oriented'.

BIBLIOGRAPHY

Acker, J. (1990) 'Hierarchies, Jobs, Bodies: A Theory of Gendered Organizations', *Gender and Society* 4, 2: 131–158.

Afsa, C. (1996) 'L'Activité féminine à l'épreuve de l'APE', *Recherchés et Précisions*, 46: 1–8.

Allardt, E. (1986) 'Representative Government in a Bureaucratic Age', in S. Graubard (ed.) *Norden – The Passion for Equality*, Oslo: Norwegian University Press.

Allen, Sheila and Wolkowitz, Carol (1987) *Homeworking: Myths and Realities*, London: Macmillan.

Andersen, D. and Holt, H. (1990) *Fleksibel arbejdstid i den statslige sektor*, Copenhagen: Socialforskningsinstitutet.

Arbejdsministeriet, *et al.* (1989) *Hvidbog om Arbejdsmarkedets Strukturproblemer*, København: Arbejdsministeriet.

Arber, S. and Ginn, J. (1992) '"In Sickness and in Health": Caregiving, Gender and the Independence of Elderly People', in C. Marsh and S. Arber (eds) *Families and Households*, Basingstoke: Macmillan.

Atkinson, (1985) *Flexibility, Uncertainty and Manpower Management*, IMS Report No. 89, Falmer, Sussex.

Balls, E. and Gregg, P. (1993) *Work and Welfare: Tackling the Jobs Deficit*, London: Institute for Public Policy Research.

Beck, B., Dallinger, U., Naegele, G. and Reichert, M. (1995) *Betriebliche Mabnahmen zur Unterstutzung pflegender Arbeitnehmerinnen und Arbeitneheme*, Scientific Report for the Bundesministerium fur Familie, Senioren, Frauen und Jungend, Bonn.

Beck-Gernsheim, E. (1992) 'Everything for the Child – For Better or for Worse?', in U. Björnberg (ed.) *European Parents in the 1990s. Contradictions and Comparisons*, New Jersey: Transaction.

Becker, G. (1993) *A Treatise on the Family*, Cambridge, MA: Harvard University Press.

Berry Lound, D. (1994) *Help the Aged Senior Care Survey*, London: Help the Aged.

Bielenski, H. (1992) *New Forms of Work and Activity*, Dublin: European Foundation for the Improvement of Living and Working Conditions.

Bimbi, F. and Castellani, G. (1990) *Madri e padri*, Milano: Angeli.

Bjerring, B. and Emerek, R. (1990) 'Hvornaar har vi tid til at gaa paa arbejde? (Do we ever have time to work?), in *Aarbog for Arbejdsmarkedsforskning*, Aalborg: Aalborg Universitetsforlag.

Björnberg, U. (1992) 'Parenting in Transition: An Introduction and Summary', in U.

Björnberg (ed.) *European Parents in the 1990s. Contradictions and Comparisons*, New Jersey: Transaction.

Bjurstrøm, H. I. (1993) *Deltidsansattes rettigheter. En komparativ studie av Danmark, Norge Storbritannia og Tyskland.* Oslo: Institute for Social Research.

Blackwell, J. (1989) *Women in the Labour Force*, Dublin: Employment Equality Agency.

Blank, R. and Freeman, R. (1993) '*Evaluating the connection between Social Protection and Economic Flexibility*' NBER W.P. 4338.

Blau, D. and Kahn, F. L. (1992) 'The Gender Earning Gap: Learning from International Comparison', *American Economic Review* 82, 2: 533–545.

Blossfeld, H. P. (1994) *Family Cycle and Growth in Women's Part-time Employment in Western European Countries*, Final Project Report, January.

Boh, K. (1989) 'European Family Life Patterns – A Reappraisal', in K. Boh *et al.* (eds) *Changing Patterns of European Family Life: A Comparative Analysis of 14 European Countries*, London: Routledge.

Boh, K. *et al.* (eds) (1989) *Changing Patterns of European Family Life: A Comparative Analysis of 14 European Countries*, London: Routledge.

Borchorst, A. (1994) 'Welfare State Regimes, Women's Interests and the EC', in D. Sainsbury (ed.) *Gendering Welfare States*, London: Sage.

Boris, E. and Prugl, E. (eds) (1996) *Homeworkers in Global Perspective. Invisible No More*, New York and London: Routledge.

Bradshaw, J., Ditch, J., Holmes, H. and Whiteford, P. (1993) *Support for Children: A Comparison of Arrangements in Fifteen Countries*, London: HMSO.

Brannen, J. (1989) 'Childhood and Occupational Mobility: Evidence from a Longitudinal Study', *Work, Employment and Society* 3: 179–207.

Bradshaw, J. *et al.* (eds) (1996) *The Employment of Lone Parents: A Comparison of Policy in 20 Countries*, University of York: Social Policy Research Unit.

Brannen, J. (1991) 'Money, Marriage and Motherhood: Dual Earner Households after Maternity Leave', in S. Arber and N. Gilbert (eds) *Women and Working Lives*, Basingstoke: Macmillan.

Brannen, J. and Moss, P. (1990) *Managing Mothers: Employment and Childcare*, London: Unwin Hyman.

Brannen, J. and Moss, P. (1991) *Managing Mothers: Dual Earner Households after Maternity Leave*, London: Macmillan.

Brannen, J. and Wilson, G. (eds) (1987) *Give and Take in Families: Studies in Resource Distribution*, London: Unwin Hyman.

Brannen, J., Meszaros, G., Moss, P. and Poland, G. (1994) *Employment and Family Life: A Review of Research in the UK, Research Series No. 41*, London: Department of Employment.

Brechling, F. P. and O'Brien, P. (1967) 'Short-run Employment Functions in Manufacturing Industries: An International Comparison', *Review of Economics and Statistics* August: 1–12.

Brett, A. (1991) 'Why Gender is a Development Issue', in T. Wallace and C. March (eds) *Changing Perceptions. Writings on Gender and Development*, Oxford: Oxfam.

Bridgwood, A. and Savage, P. (1993) *General Household Survey 1991*, London: HMSO.

Briggs, A. and Oliver, J. (1985) *Caring Experiences of Looking after Disabled Relatives*, London: Routledge and Kegan Paul.

Callan, T. and Farrell, B. (1991) *Women's Participation in the Irish Labour Market*, Dublin: National Economic and Social Council.

Callender, R. (1990) 'Women and Work: The Appearance and Reality of Change', *Labour Market Review* 1, June: 17–36.

Carlsen, S. *et al.* (1994) *The Equality Dilemma: Reconciling Working Life and Family Life, Viewed in an Equality Perspective*, Ligestillingsraadet (The Danish Equal Status Council), Copenhagen.

Central Statistics Office (1984) *Labour Force Survey 1983*, Dublin: Stationery Office.

Central Statistics Office (1991) *Family Spending: A Report on the 1990 FES*, London: HMSO.

Central Statistics Office (1991) *Labour Force Survey 1990*, Dublin: Stationery Office.

Central Statistics Office (1992) *Labour Force Survey 1991*, Dublin: Stationery Office.

Central Statistics Office (1996) *Labour Force Surrvey 1995*, Dublin: Stationery Office.

Central Statistics Office (1997) *Census 1996: Principle Demographic Results*, Dublin: Stationery Office.

Centraal Bureau voor de Statistiek (1996) *Sociaal Economische Maandstatistiek*, Voorburg/Heerlen: CBS.

Chen, M. and Sebstad, J. with O'Connell, L. (1996) *Towards a New Economic Orthodoxy: The Case of Homeworkers*, Cambridge, MA: Harvard Institute for International Development.

Clancy, P. (1991) 'Irish Nuptiality and Fertility Patterns in Transition', in G. Kelly and V. Richardson (eds) *Family Policy: European Perspectives*, Dublin: Family Studies Centre.

Cochrane A. and Clarke, J. (eds) (1993) *Comparing Welfare States*, Milton Keynes: Open University.

Cockburn, C. (1991) *In the Way of Women: Men's Resistance to Sex Equality in Organizations*, Basingstoke: Macmillan.

Commission des Communautés Européennes (1992) *L'Europe dans le mouvement demographique'*, Brussels: CEC.

Commission of the European Communities (1990) *Childcare in the European Communities 1985–1990, Women of Europe*, Supplement, 31, Brussels: CEC.

Commission of the European Communities (1993a) *Europeans and the Family: Results of an Opinion Survey*, report by N. Malpas and P. Lambert, Brussels: Eurobarometer 39.

Commission of the European Communities (1993b) *European Social Policy: Options for the Union*, Luxembourg: OOPEC.

Commission of the European Communities (1994) *The Major Issues of European Demography, Joint Report by Independent Experts*, Brussels: CEC.

Corti, L. and Laurie, H. (1993) *Caring and Employment*, unpublished report from the ESRC Research Centre on Micro-social Change, University of Essex.

Council of Europe (1991) Seminar on Present Demographic Trends and Lifestyles in Europe, Strasbourg 18–20 September 1990, Strasbourg: Council of Europe.

Council of Europe (1996) *Recent Demographic Developments in Europe*, Strasbourg: Council of Europe.

CREDOC (1995) *Prestations familiales, modes de garde et relations parents/grands enfants*, Collection des Rapports 156, Paris: CREDOC.

Daatland, S. (1990) 'What Are Families For? On Family Solidarity and Prevalence for Help', *Ageing and Society* 10, 1.

Dahl, T. (1991) 'Likestilling og fødselsrett' (Equality and laws on reproduction), in R. Haukaa (ed.) *Nye Kvinner Nye Menn* (New Women, New Men), Oslo: Ad Notam.

Dale, A. and Glover, J. (1990) *An Analysis of Women's Employment Patterns in the UK, France and the USA: The Value of Survey-based Comparisons*, Department of Employment Research Paper No. 75, London: HMSO.

Dallago, B. (1990) *The Underground Economy in Italy*, Cambridge: Cambridge University Press.

Danmarks Statistik (1992) *Statistisk Oversigt 1992* (Living Conditions in Denmark), Compendium of Statistics, Copenhagen.

Danmarks Statistik (1995) *50-year Review,* Copenhagen.

Danmarks Statistik (1996) 'Befolkningens arbejdsløshed 1995', in *Statistiske Efterretninger, Arbejdsmarked 1996: 25,* Copenhagen.

DARES (1995) 'L'Évolution des emplois familiaux de 1992 à 1994', *Premières synthèses* 109.

Davidoff, L. (1991) 'The Rationalisation of Housework', in D. Leonard and S. Allen (eds) *Sexual Divisions Revisited,* Basingstoke: Macmillan.

Davies, R. B., Elias, P. and Penn, R. (1992) 'The Relationship Between a Husband's Unemployment and His Wife's Participation in the Labour Force', *Oxford Bulletin of Economics and Statistics* 54, 2: 145–171.

Del Boca, A. and Rota, P. (1995) 'How High are the Costs of Hiring and Firing in Italy?', Discussion Paper 35, London: University College.

Del Boca, D. (1987) 'Wage Discrimination in Italy', *Ricerche Economiche* 1.

Del Boca, D. (1993) Offerta di lavoro e politiche pubbliche la nuova Italia', *Scientifica Roma 1993.*

Del Boca, D. (1996) 'Intra-household Allocations and Labor Supply', in I. Parsson (eds) *The Economics of the Family,* London: Routledge.

Delphy, C. (1991), 'Continuities and Discontinuities in Marriage and Divorce', in D. Leonard and S. Allen (eds) *Sexual Divisions Revisited,* London: Macmillan.

Dex, S. (1987) *Women's Occupational Mobility: A Lifetime Perspective,* London: Macmillan.

Dex, S. and McCulloch, A. (1995) *Flexible Employment in Britain: A Statistical Analysis,* Manchester: Equal Opportunities Commission.

Dex, S. and Shaw, L. (1986) *British and American Women at Work,* London: Macmillan.

Dex, S., Clark, A. and Taylor, M. (1993a) *Household Labour Supply,* unpublished report from the ESRC Research Centre on Micro-social Change, University of Essex.

Dex, S., Walters P. and Alden, D. (1993b) *French and British Mothers at Work,* London: Macmillan.

Ditch, J., Barnes, H., Bradshaw, J., Commaille, J. and Eardley, T. (1996) *A Synthesis of National Family Policies,* European Observatory on Family Policies, University of York.

Doumanis, M. (1983) *Mothering in Greece: From Collectivism to Individualism,* New York: Academic Press.

Dretakis, M. (1994) 'The Reduction in Income Resulted in a Reduction in the Birth Rate', *Eleftherotypia* (Greek daily), 21 September, Athens.

Drew, E. (1990) *Who Needs Flexibility? Part-time Working: The Irish Experience,* Dublin: Employment Equality Agency.

Drew, E. (1992) 'The Part-time Option? Women and Part-time Work in the European Community', *Women's Studies International Forum* 15, 5/6: 1–8.

Drew, E. (1995a) 'Demographic Change in Europe: Reproducing Gender Inequalities', Working Paper No. 2, Dublin: Centre for Women's Studies, Trinity College.

Drew, E. (1995b) 'Employment Prospects of Carers for Dependent Relatives', *Health and Social Care in the Community* 3: 5–11.

Drew E. (forthcoming) 'Reconciling Divisions of Labour at Home and at Work', in S. Duncan and B. Pfau-Effinger (eds) *Gender, Economy and Culture in the European Union,* London: UCL Press.

Drew E., Emerek R. and Mahon, E. (1995) *Families, Labour Markets and Gender Roles: A Report on a European Research Workshop,* Dublin: European Foundation for the Improvement of Living and Working Conditions.

Eardley, T., Bradshaw, J., Ditch, J., Gough, I. and Whiteford, P. (1996) *Social Assistance in OECD Countries: Synthesis Report,* London: HMSO.

Elias, P. and Hogarth, T. (1994) 'Families, Jobs and Unemployment: The Changing Pattern of Economic Dependency in Britain', in R. Lindsey (ed.) *Labour Market Structures and Prospects for Women*, Manchester: Equal Opportunities Commission.

Ellingsæter, A. L. (1987) 'Ulikhet i arbeidstidsmørnstre', in *NOU 1987: 9b*. Vedlegg til arbeidstidsutvalgets innstilling.

Ellingsæter, A. L. (1990) *Fathers Working Long Hours. Trends, Causes and Consequences*, Working Paper 2, Oslo: Institute for Social Research.

Emerek, R. (1987) 'Om Maalinger', in U. Kock, *et al.* (ed.) *Køn og Videnskab*, Aalborg: Aalborg Universitetsforlag.

Emerek, R. (1991) *Timeløn og arbejdsomfang i den enkelte ansættelse* (Time rate and workload), Arbejdsnotat nr. 31, Danmarks Statistik.

Emerek, R. (1995) 'On the Subject of Measuring Women's (and Men's) Participation', in *FREIA's paper series*, No. 23.

Emerek, R. *et al.* (1990) *IDA – en integreret database for arbejdsmarkedsforskning*, Danmarks Statistik.

Emerson, M. (1988) 'Regulation and Deregulation in the Labour Market', *European Economic Review* 32: 775–817.

Ermisch, J. (1990) 'Demographic Aspects of the Growing Number of Lone-parent Families', in OECD, *Lone-Parent Families: The Economic Challenge*, Paris: OECD.

Esping-Andersen, G. (1990) *The Three Worlds of Welfare Capitalism*, Cambridge: Polity Press.

Eurolink Age (1995) *Caring for Older People: A European Issue*, Report from a Eurolink Age seminar, Bonn 1994.

European Commission (1993a) *Growth, Competitiveness, Employment: The Challenges and Ways Forward Toward into the 21st Century*, Luxembourg: OOPEC.

European Commission (1993b) *European Social Policy: Options for the Union*, Luxembourg: OOPEC.

European Commission (1995) *Employment in Europe*, Luxembourg: Office for Official Publications of the European Communities.

European Commission (1996) *Employment in Europe*, Luxembourg: Office for Official Publications of the European Communities.

European Commission Network on Childcare (1993) *Mothers, Fathers and Employment 1985–1991*, London: European Commission Network on Childcare.

European Commission Network on Childcare (1994) *Leave Arrangements for Workers with Children*, Brussels: European Commission, (DG V).

European Commission Network on Childcare and other Measures to Reconcile Employment and Family Responsibilities (1995) *Family Day Care in Europe*, Luxembourg: European Commission.

Eurostat (1991) *Labour Force Survey 1989*, Luxembourg: Office for Official Publications of the European Communities.

Eurostat (1992) *Labour Force Survey 1990*, Luxembourg: Office for Official Publications of the European Communities.

Eurostat (1992b) *Women in the European Community – A Statistical Portrait*, Luxembourg: Office for Official Publications of the European Communities.

Eurostat (1993a) *Demographic Statistics 1993*, Brussels: Eurostat.

Eurostat (1993b) *Rapid Reports: Women in the European Community*, No. 10, Luxembourg: Office for Official Publications of the European Communities.

Eurostat (1993c) *Digest of Statistics on Social Protection in Europe, Vol. 4: Family*, Luxembourg: Office for Official Publications of the European Communities.

Eurostat (1994a) *Europe in Numbers*, Luxembourg: Office for Official Publications of the European Communities.

Eurostat (1994b) *Rapid Reports: Households and Families in the European Union*, Luxembourg: Office for Official Publications of the European Communities.

Eurostat (1994c) *Rapid Reports: The Population of the European Economic Area on 1 January 1994*, No. 4, Luxembourg: Office for Official Publications of the European Communities.

Eurostat (1994d) *Labour Force Survey 1992*, Luxembourg: Office for Official Publications of the European Communities.

Eurostat (1995a) *Demographic Statistics 1995*, Brussels: Eurostat.

Eurostat (1995b) *Labour Force Survey 1994*, Luxembourg: Office for Official Publications of the European Communities.

Eurostat (1995c) *Yearbook '95*, Luxembourg: Office for Official Publications of the European Communities.

Eurostat (1996a) *Demographic Statistics 1996*, Brussels: Eurostat.

Eurostat (1996b) *The European Union Labour Force Survey, Methods and Definitions 1996*, Luxembourg: Office for Official Publications of the European Communities.

Eurostat (1996c) *Labour Force Survey 1995*, Luxembourg: Office for Official Publications of the European Communities.

Evandrou, M. (1990) *Changing the Invisibility of Carers: Mapping Informal Care Nationally*, STICERD, Paper No. WSP/49.

Evers, A. and Leichsenring, K. (1994) 'Paying for Informal Care', *Ageing International* March: 29–40.

Fagnani, J. (1993) 'Bref aperçu sur les systèmes de protection sociale de la famille en Europe', *Solidarité Sante-Etudes statistiques*, No. 4 (Oct.–Dec.), Paris: Ministère des affaires sociales de la santé et de la ville.

Fagnani, J. (1995) 'L'Allocation parentale d'éducation: effets pervers et ambiguités d'une prestation', *Droit Social* 3: 287—295.

Fagnani, J. (1996a) *Family Policy in France in 1995: A Historic Turning-point? Developments in National Family Policies in 1995*, Brussels: Employment and Social Affairs, Commission of the European Communities.

Fagnani, J. (1996b) 'Family Policies and Working Mothers: A Comparison of France and West Germany', in D. Garcia-Ramon and J. Monk (eds) *Women of the European Union: the Politics of Work and Daily Life*, London: Routledge.

Fagnani, J. (1996c) 'Retravailler après une longue interruption: le cas des mères ayant bénéficié de l'allocation parentale d'éducation', *Revue Française des Affaires Sociales*: 129–152.

Ferrera, M. (1996) 'The "Southern European Model" of Welfare in Social Europe', *Journal of European Social Policy* 6, 1: 17–37.

Finch, J. and Mason, J. (1993) *Negotiating Family Responsibilities*, London: Routledge.

Fine, B. (1992) *Women's Employment and the Capitalist Family*, London: Routledge.

Flipo, A. and Hourriez, J. M. (1995) 'Recourir à une femme de ménage', *INSEE Première* 411.

Folbre, N. (1994) *Who Pays for the Kids? Gender and the Structures of Constraint*, London: Routledge.

Frankenberg, R. (1991) 'Sex and Gender in British Community Studies', in D. Leonard and S. Allen (eds) *Sexual Divisions Revisited*, Basingstoke: Macmillan.

Freeman, R. (1994) *Working under Different Rules*, NBER, New York: Russell Sage.

Frost, L. (1993) 'Det retlige faderskap' (Fatherhood according to law), in P. Blume and H. Petersen (eds) *Retlig Polycentri* (Polycentric law), Akademisk Forlag: Koepenhamn.

Georgas, J. (1989) 'Changing Family Values in Greece', *Journal of Cross-Cultural Psychology* 20, 1: 80–91, Western Washington University.

Gerson, M. (1989) 'Tomorrow's Fathers. The Anticipation of Fatherhood', in S. Cath, A. Gurwitt and L. Ginsberg (eds) *Fathers and their Families*, Hilsdale Hove and London: The Analytic Press.

Giddens, A. (1984) *The Constitution of Society: Outline of the Theory of Structuration*, Cambridge: Polity.

Ginsburg, N. (1992) *Divisions of Welfare: A Critical Introduction to Comparative Social Policy*, London: Sage.

Giovannini, D. (1993) 'Fatherhood and the Sharing of Children: The Problem of Fathering Today', in *Report from Conference on Parental Employment and Caring for Children: Policies and Services in EC and Nordic Countries*, Copenhagen: The Danish Ministry of Social Affairs.

Giovannini, D. and Molinari, L. (1994) 'Fathers' and Mothers' Involvement in Childcare as a Factor of Intersubjective Relationships', paper presented at the Conference 'Social Practices and Symbolic Mediations', Neuchatel, March.

Giovannini, D. and Ventimiglia, C. (eds) (1994) *Paternità e politiche per l'infanzia: essere padri oggi* (Fatherhood and childcare policies: to be father today), unpublished report of research, Regione Emilia Romagna, Assessorato Formazione Professionale, Lavoro, Scuola e Università, Bologna.

Giovannini, D. and Ventimiglia, C. (eds) (1997) *Padri in contro luce* (Fathers against the light), Milano: Angeli (in press).

Gittins, D. (1993) *The Family in Question: Changing Households and Familiar Ideologies*, Basingstoke: Macmillan.

Glaser, B. G. and Strauss, A. L. (1967) *The Discovery of Grounded Theory: Strategies for Qualitative Research*, Chicago: Aldine.

Glasner, A. (1992) 'Gender and Europe: Cultural and Structural Impediments to Change', in J. Bailey (ed.) *Social Europe*, London: Longman.

Glendinning, C. (1988) 'Dependency and Interdependency: The Incomes of Informal Carers and the Impact of Social Security', *Journal of Social Policy* 19, 4: 469–497.

Goodman, A. and Webb, S. (1994) *For Richer, For Poorer: The Changing Distribution of Income in the United Kingdom, 1961–1991*, London: Institute of Fiscal Studies.

Graham, H. (1983) 'Caring: A Labour of Love', in J. Finch and D. Groves (eds) *A Labour of Love Women, Work and Caring*, London: Routledge and Kegan Paul.

Green, H. (1988) *Informal Carers*, London: HMSO.

Gregersen, O. (1991) *Flekstid*, Copenhagen: Socialforsksningsinstitutet.

Gregg, P. and Wadsworth, J. (1995) 'More Work in Fewer Households?', in J. Hills (ed.) *New Inequalities*, Cambridge: Cambridge University Press.

Gregson, N. and Lowe, M. (1994) 'Waged Domestic Labour and the Renegotiation of the Domestic Division of Labour within Dual-Career Households', *Sociology* 28: 55–78.

Hakim, C. (1987) 'Grateful Slaves and self-made women: fact and fantasy in women's work orientations', *European Sociological Review* 7, 2: 101–121.

Hall, R. (1993) 'Europe's Changing Population', *Geography* 78, 338: 3–15.

Hantrais, L. and Letablier, M. T. (1996) *Families and Family Policies in Europe*, London: Longman.

Harrop, A. and Moss, P. (1994) 'Trends in Parental Employment', *Work, Employment and Society* 9, 3: 421–444.

Hartmann, H. (1976) 'Capitalism, Patriarchy and Job Segregation by Sex', in *Signs: Journal of Women in Culture and Society* 1, 3 (Spring): 162–163.

Hernandez, D. J. (1993) 'America's Children: Resources from Family, Government and the Economy', *Census Monograph Series. The Population of the United States in the 1980s*, New York: Russell Sage Foundation.

Hernes, H. M. (1987) 'Welfare State and Woman Power', in *State Feminism*, Oslo: Norwegian University Press.

Hernes, H. M. (1992) 'Women and the Welfare State: The Transition from Private to Public Dependence', in A. Showstack Sassoon (ed.) *Women and the State*, London: Routledge, pp. 72–92.

Hirdman, Y. (1990a) 'Genussystemet', *Demokrati och makt i Sverige*, SOU: 44.

Hirdman, Y. (1990b) *The Gender System: Theoretical Reflections on the Social Subordination of Women*, The Study of Power and Democracy in Sweden, Report No. 40, Maktutredningen, Uppsala, Sweden.

Hirdman, Y. (1992) 'Utopia in the Home', *International Journal of Political Economy, A Journal of Translations* 22, 2.

Hirdman, Y. (1994a) 'Social Engineering and the Woman Question: Sweden in the Thirties', in W. Clement and R. Mahon (eds) *Swedish Social Democracy A Model in Transition*, Toronto: Canadian Scholars Press Inc.

Hirdman, Y. (1994b) *Women – From Possibility to Problem? Gender Conflict in the Welfare State. The Swedish Model*, Research Report No. 3, Stockholm: Arbetslivscentrum/The Swedish Centre for Working Life (Now Insitute of Working Life).

Hobson, B. (1994) 'Solo Mothers, Social Policy Regimes, and the Logics of Gender', in D. Sainsbury (ed.) *Gendering Welfare States*, London: Sage.

Hoem, J. M. (1990) 'Social Policy and Recent Fertility Change in Europe', *Population and Development Review* 16, 4: 735–748.

Hoffmann-Nowotny, H. J. and Fux, B. (1991) 'Present Demographic Trends in Europe', in Council of Europe, *Seminar on Present Demographic Trends and Lifestyles*, Strasbourg September 1990, Strasbourg: Council of Europe.

Højgaard, L. (1990) *Vil kvinder lede?*, Copenhagen: Equal Status Council.

Højgaard, L. (1991) *Vil mænd lede?*, Copenhagen: Equal Status Council.

Højgaard, L. (1993) 'Køn og løn i pengenes verden', in J. Wiik (ed.)*Kvinnaloennas Mysterier – myter og fakta om lønsdannelsen*, Copenhagen: Nordic Council of Ministers.

Højgaard, L. (1994) 'Decentralisering og loenforskelle mellem kvinder og maend', in *Arbejdsmarkedspolitisk Aarbog*, Copenhagen: Ministry of Labor.

Holland, S. (1993) *The European Imperative, Economic and Social Cohesion in the 1990s*, A Report to the Commission of the European Communities, Nottingham: Spokesman Press for Associate Research in Economy and Society.

Holter, Ø. (1991) 'Kjønn og klasse i et formanalytisk perspektiv', *Sosiologi i dag* 4: 3–31.

Holter, Ø. and Aarseth, H. (1993) *Menns Livssammanhang* (The male world), Oslo: Ad Notam.

Homenet Bulletin (1996) Special Issue on the ILO Convention, No. 4.

Hopflinger, F. (1991) 'The Future of Household and Family Structures in Europe', in Council of Europe, *Seminar on Present Demographic Trends and Lifestyles in Europe*, Strasbourg, September 1990, Strasbourg: Council of Europe.

Horna, J. and Lupri, E. (1987) 'Fathers' Participation in Work, Family Life and Leisure: A Canadian Experience', in C. Lewis and M. O'Brien (eds) *Reassessing Fatherhood*, Hilsdale Hove and London: Sage Publications.

Humphries, J. and Rubery, J. (1992) 'Women's Employment in the 1980s: Integration, Differentiation and Polarisation', in Michie, J. (ed.) *1979–1991: The Economic Legacy*, London: Academic Press.

Humphries, J. and Rubery, J. (1995) *The Economics of Equal Opportunities*, Manchester: Equal Opportunities Commission.

Huws, U. (1984) *The New Homeworkers: New Technology and the Changing Location of White Collar Workers*, London: Low Pay Unit.

Huws, U. (1995) *Action Programmes for the Protection of Homeworkers: Ten Case Studies from Around the World*, Geneva: ILO.

Huws, U., Hurstfield, J. and Holtmaat, R. (1989) *What Price Flexibility? The Casualisation of Women's Employment*, London: Low Pay Unit.

Hyman, R. (1991) 'Plus ça change? The Theory of Production and the Production of Theory', in A. Pollert (ed.) *Farewell to Flexibility*, Oxford: Blackwell.

ILO (1995) *World Labour Report No. 8*, Geneva: International Labour Office.

Ipsen, S. (1993) *Kvindelige Arbejderes Arbejdstid*, København: CASA.

Jani-Le Bris, H. (1993) *Family Care of Dependent Older People in the European Communities*, Luxembourg: Office for Official Publications of the European Communities.

Jani-Le Bris, H. (1994a) *L'Aide familiale aux dépendants agés en milieu Rural*. Paris: Clerippa (unpublished).

Jani-Le Bris, H. (1994b) 'Working and Caring: Developments at the Workplace for Family Carers of Disabled and Elderly Persons', Background Paper for the International Conference European Foundation for the Improvement of Living and Working Conditions and the German Ministry for Family Affairs and Seniors, November, Bonn.

Jani-Le Bris, H. and Luquet, V. (1993) *Perte d'autonomie et soutien familial*, Paris: Clerippa.

Jensen, A. M. (1989) 'Reproduction in Norway: An Area of Non-Responsibility?', in P. Close (ed.) *Family Divisions and Inequalities in Modern Society*, Basingstoke: Macmillan.

Jenson, J. and Sineau, M. (1995) 'Family Policy and Women's Citizenship in Mitterand's France', *Social Politics* 2, 3: 244–269.

Jenson, J., Hagen, E. and Reddy, C. (eds) (1988) *Feminization of the Labour Force*, Cambridge: Polity.

Jhabvala, R. and Self-Employed Women's Association (1994) 'Organising Women by Struggle and Development', in S. Rowbotham and S. Mitter (eds) *Dignity and Daily Bread: New Forms of Economic Organising among Poor Women in the Third World and the First*, London: Routledge.

Jhabvala, R. and Tate, J. (1996) *Out of the Shadows: Homebased Workers Organise for International Recognition*, New York: Seeds Pamphlet Series.

Joshi, H. and Davies, H. (1993) 'Mothers, Human Capital and Childcare in Britain', *National Institute Economic Review* 146: 50–59.

Karlsson, G. (1996) *Fraan broderskap till systerskap. Det socialdemokratiska kvinnoförbundets kamp för inflytande och makt i SAP* (From brotherhood to sisterhood. The political struggle of the Social Democratic Women's League for influence and power) Arkiv.

Kennedy, S., Whiteford, P. and Bradshaw, J. (1996) 'The Economic Circumstances of Children in Ten Countries', in J. Brannen and M. O'Brien (eds) *Children in Families: Research and Policy*, London: Falmer Press.

Knijn, T. and Verheijen, C. (1988) *Tussen plicht en ontplooiing. Het welbevinden van moeders met jonge kinderen in een veranderende cultuur*, Nijmegen: ITS.

Komter, A. (1990) *De macht van de dubbele moraal. Verschil en gelijkheid in verhouding tussen de seksen*, Amsterdam: Van Gennep.

216

Komter, A. (1991) 'Gender, Power and Feminist Theory', in K. Davis (ed.) *The Gender of Power*, London: Sage.

Kouvertaris, Y. and Dobratz, B. (1987) *A Profile of Modern Greece: In Search of Identity*, Oxford: Clarendon Press.

Kumar, V. (1993) *Poverty and Inequality in the UK: The Effects in Childcare*, London: National Children's Bureau.

Lamb, M. and Oppenheim, D. (1989) 'Fatherhood and Father–Child Relationships', in S. Cath, A. Gurwitt and L. Ginsberg (eds) *Fathers and their Families*, Hilsdale Hove and London: The Analytic Press.

Lambiri-Dimaki, J. (1983) *Social Stratification in Greece: 1962–1982*, Athens: Sakkoulas.

Lane, C. (1993) 'Gender and the Labour Market in Europe: Britain, Germany and France Compared', *The Sociological Review*: 274–301.

Lazcko, F. and Noden, S. (1992) 'Combining Paid Work with Eldercare: The Implications for Social Policy', *Health and Social Care in the Community* 1.

Leichsenring, K. (1994) 'Shifting Money', paper presented at the international meeting 'Payments for Care', Helsinki.

Leira, A. (1992) *Welfare States and Working Mothers. The Scandinavian Experience*, Cambridge: Cambridge University Press.

Leira, A. (1993) 'The "Woman-Friendly" Welfare State? The Case of Norway and Sweden', in J. Lewis (ed.) *Women and Social Policies in Europe*, London: Edward Elgar.

Leira, A. (1994) 'Combining Work and Family. Working Mothers in Scandinavia and the EC', in P. Brown and R. Crompton (eds) *A New Europe: Economic Restructuring and Social Exclusion*, London: UCL Press.

Leira, A. (1995) 'Defining Family Obligations in Norway', in J. Millar and A. Warman (eds) *Defining Family Obligations in Europe*, Bath: Bath Social Policy Papers.

Lewin, K. (1951) *Field Theory in Social Science*, New York: Harper & Row.

Lewin, K. (1994b) 'Motherhood, Fatherhood and Sharing of Childcare', paper presented at the International Congress Changes in Family Patterns in Western Countries, Bologna (Italy), October.

Lewis, J. (1992) 'Gender and the Development of Welfare Regimes', *Journal of European Social Policy* 2, 3: 31–48.

Lewis, J. (1993) *Women and Social Policies in Europe*, Aldershot: Edward Elgar.

Lewis, R. (1986) 'What Men Get Out of Marriage and Parenthood', in R. Lewis and R. Salt (eds) *Men in Families*, London: Sage.

McBride Stetson, D. and Mazur, A. (eds) (1995) *Comparative State Feminism*, Thousand Oaks, CA: Sage.

McDevitt, D. (1987) 'Marriage, Maintenance and Property', in C. Curtin, P. Jackson and B. O'Conner (eds), *Gender in Irish Society*, Galway: Galway University Press.

McGrath J. (1990) 'Gender Inequality in Employment: Discrimination or Rational Choice?', *Labour Market Update 4*, September, pp. 2–3, Dublin: FAS.

Macintyre, S. (1991) 'Who Wants Babies?', in D. Leonard and S. Allen, (eds) *Sexual Divisions Revisited*, Basingstoke: Macmillan.

McKenna, A. (1988) *Childcare and Equal Opportunities*, Dublin: Employment Equality Agency.

McLaughlin, E. (1993) 'Ireland: Catholic Corporatism', in A. Cochrane and J. Clarke (eds) *Comparing Welfare States*, Milton Keynes: Open University.

McLaughlin E. and Glendinning, C. (1994) 'Paying for Care in Europe: Is there a

Feminist Approach?', in L. Hantrais and S. Mangen (eds) *Family Policy and the Welfare of Women*, Cross National Research Papers, University of Loughborough: 52–69.

McRae, S. (1986) *Cross-Class Families*, Oxford: Clarendon Press.

McRae, S. (1991) *Maternity Rights in Britain: The PSI Report on the Experience of Women and Employers*, London: Policy Studies Institute.

McRae, S. and Daniel, W. (1991) *Maternity Rights in Britain: First Findings*, London: Policy Studies Institute.

Mahon, E. (1987) 'Women's Rights and Catholicism in Ireland', *New Left Review* 166 (Nov./Dec.): 53–78.

Mahon, E. (1991a) 'Equal Opportunities in the Irish Civil Service: An Interim Review', *Equal Opportunities International* 10, 2: 1–10.

Mahon, E. (1991b) *Motherhood, Work and Equal Opportunities: A Case Study of Irish Civil Servants*, Dublin: Stationery Office.

Mahon, E. (1991c) 'Women and Equality in the Irish Civil Service', in E. Meehan and S. Sevenhuijsen (eds) *Equality, Politics and Gender*, London: Sage.

Mahon, E. (1994) 'Ireland: A Private Patriarchy', *Environment and Planning* 26: 1277–1296.

Mahon, E. (1995) 'Ireland's Policy Machinery: The Ministry for Women's Affairs and the Joint Directors Committee for Women's Rights', in D. McBride Stetson and A. Mazur (eds) *Comparative State Feminism*, Thousand Oaks, CA: Sage.

Maier, Frederike (1991) *Women and Employment Restructuring: Part-time Employment*, Paris: OECD.

Marchand, O. and Thélot, C. (1991) *Deux siècles de travail en France*, Paris: INSEE.

Marshall, T. E. (1965) *Class, Citizenship, and Social Development*. New York: Anchor Books.

Marten, M. H. and Mitter, S. (eds) (1994) *Women in Trade Unions: Organizing the Unorganized*, Geneva: ILO.

Martin, J. and Roberts, C. (1984) *Women and Employment: A Lifetime Perspective*, Report of the 1980 DE/OPCS Women and Employment Survey, London: HMSO.

Maruani, M. (1992) 'The Position of Women on the Labour Market: Trends and Developments in the Twelve Member States of the European Community 1983–1990', *Women of Europe Supplement*, No. 36, Brussels: Commission of the European Communities.

May, M. and Brunsdon, E. (1996) 'Women and Private Welfare', in C. Hallett (ed.) *Women and Social Policy*, London: Prentice Hall/Harvester Wheatsheaf.

Meehan E. and Sevenhuijsen, S. (1991), *Equality Politics and Gender*, London: Sage.

Meeting of Experts on the Social Protection of Homeworkers, 1–5 October 1990, ILO Office, Geneva.

Meulders, D., Plasman, R. and Stricht, V. (1991) *Position of Women on the Labour Market: Developments between 1983 and 1989*, Department of Applied Economics, Free University of Brussels, DUBLEA.

Meulders, D., Plasman, O. and Plasman, R. (1994) *Atypical Employment in the EC*, Hampshire: Dartmouth.

Mincer, J. (1985) 'Intercountry Comparisons of Labour Force Trends and Related Developments: An Overview', *Journal of Labour Economics* supplement, 3, 1, Part 2: 21–32.

Mitter, S. (1986a) *Common Fate, Common Bond: Women in the Global Economy*, London: Pluto Press.

Mitter, S. (1986b) 'Industrial Restructuring and Manufacturing Homework: Immigrant Women in the UK Clothing Industry', *Capital and Class* 27 (Winter).

Mitter, Swasti (ed.) (1992) *Computer-aided Manufacturing and Women's Employment: The Clothing Industry in Four EC Countries*, London: Springer-Verlag.

218

Mogensen, G. Viby (ed.) (1990) *Time and consumption, Time Use and Consumption in Denmark in Recent Decades*, Copenhagen: Danmarks Statistik.

Molinari, L. (1994a) 'Le mamme raccontano' (Fatherhood told by mothers), in D. Giovannini and C. Ventimiglia (eds) *Paternità e politiche per l'infanzia: essere padre oggi* (Fatherhood and childcare policies: to be a father today), unpublished report of research, Reggione Emilia Romagna, Assessorato Formazione Professionale, Lavoro, Scuola e Università, Bologna.

Molinari, L. (1994b) 'Motherhood, Fatherhood and Sharing of Childcare', paper presented at the International Congress Changes in Family Patterns in Western Countries, Bologna (Italy), 6–8 October.

Morée, M. (1992) *Mijn kinderen hebben er niets van gemerkt. Buitenshuis werkende moeders tussen 1950 en nu*, Utrecht: Jan van Arkel.

Morris, L. (1989) *The Working of the Household: A US/UK Comparison*, London: London School of Economics.

Moss, P. (1986) 'Childcare and Equality of Opportunity: Consolidated Report to the European Commission', Brussels: Commission of the European Communities.

Moss, P. (1988) *Childcare and Equality of Opportunity: Consolidated Report to the European Commission*, Brussels: CEC.

Myrdal, A. (1941) *Nation and Family. The Swedish Experiment in Democratic Family and Population Policy*, New York: Harper.

Myrdal, A. and Klein, V. (1956) *Women's Two Roles*, London: Routledge.

Naegele, G. and Reichert, M. (1995) 'Eldercare and the Workplace: A New Challenge for Research and Social Politics in Germany', in J. Phillips *Working Carers: International Perspectives on Caring and Working for Older People*, Aldershot: Avebury.

Nilsson, A. (1992) 'Den nye mannen – finns han redan?' in J. Acker *et al. Kvinnors och Mäns liv och Arbete* (The new man – does he already exist? Work and life of men and women), Stockholm: SNS.

Norris P. (1987) *Politics and Sexual Equality*, Sussex: Wheatsheaf.

Norvez, A. (1990) *De la naissance à l'école. Santé, modes de garde et préscolarité dans la France contemporaine*, Paris: PUF–INED.

NOSOSKO (1995) *Social Security in the Nordic Countries*.

Nyberg, A. (1989) 'Tekniken – kvinnornas befriare? Hurshaallsteknik, köpevanor, gifta kvinnors hushaallsarbete och förvärvsdeltagande 1930 talet, 1980 talet', Dissertation, Sweden: University of Linköping.

O'Connor, J. and Ruddle, H. (1988) 'Caring for the Elderly. Part II: The Caring Process: A Study of Carers in the Home', in *National Council for the Aged Report 19*, Dublin.

OECD (1980) *Women and Employment: Policies for Equal Opportunities*, Paris: OECD.

OECD (1992) *Employment Outlook*, Paris: OECD.

OECD (1995) *Employment Outlook*, Paris: OECD.

OPCS (1991) *General Household Survey 1989*, London: HMSO.

Orloff, A. S. (1993) 'Gender and the Social Rights of Citizenship: The Comparative Analysis of Gender Relations and Welfare States', *Am. Soc. Rev.* 58: 303–328.

Ostner, I. and Lewis, J. (1995) 'Gender and the Evolution of European Social Policies', in S. Liebfried and P. Pierson (eds) *European Social Policy*, Washington, D.C: Brookings.

Pahl, J. (1989) *Money and Marriage*, London: Macmillan.

Pahl, R. (1984) *Divisions of Labour*, Oxford: Basil Blackwell.

Papadopoulos, T. (1996) 'Family, State and Social Policy for Children in Greece', in

J. Brannen and M. O'Brien (eds) *Children in Families: Research and Policy*, London: Falmer Press.

Papadopoulos, T. (1998) 'Welfare Support for the Unemployed: A Comparative Analysis of Social Policy Responses to Unemployment in the European Union Countries, D Phil thesis, University of York.

Parker, G. (1990) *With Due Care and Attention: A Review of Research on Informal Care*, 2nd edn, London, Family Policy Studies Centre.

Pateman, C. (1988) 'The Patriarchal Welfare State', in A. Gutman (ed.) *Democracy and the Welfare State*, Princeton, NJ: Princeton University Press.

Payne, J. (1987) 'Does Unemployment Run in Families? Some Findings from the General Household Survey', *Sociology* 21: 199–214.

Pearson, M. (1994) *Experience, Skill and Competitiveness: The Implications of an Ageing Population for the Workforce*, Dublin: European Foundation for the Improvement of Living and Working Conditions.

Petmezidou, M. (1991) 'Statism, Social Policy and the Middle Classes in Greece', *Journal of European Social Policy* 1, 1: 31–48.

Petmezidou, M. (1996) 'Social Protection in Southern Europe: Trends and Prospects', *Journal of Area Studies* 9: 95–125.

Phillips, J. (1995) *Working Carers: International Perspectives on Caring and Working for Older People*, Aldershot: Avebury.

Phizacklea, Annie (1983) *One Way Ticket*, London: Routledge and Kegan Paul.

Plantenga, J. (1995) 'Part-time Work and Equal Opportunities: The Case of the Netherlands', in J. Humphries and J. Rubery (eds) *The Economics of Equal Opportunities*, Manchester: Equal Opportunities Commission.

Pollert, A. (1987) '"Flexible" Patterns of Work and Ideology', Industrial Relations Research Unit, Warwick University.

PP II (1973) *Perspektivplan-redegørelse 1972–1987*, København: Statens Trykningskontor.

Princess Royal Trust for Carers (1995) *Carers in Employment, A Report on the Development of Policies to Support Carers at Work*, London: The Princess Royal Trust for Carers.

Robinson, B. E and Barrett, R. (1986) *The Developing Father. Emerging Roles in Contemporary Society*, New York: The Guilford Press.

Rose, K. (1992) *Where Women are Leaders: The SEWA Movement in India*, London: Zed Books.

Rowbotham, S. (1993) *Homeworkers Worldwide*, London: Merlin Press.

Ruben, G. (1975) 'Traffic in Women', in R.R. Reiter (ed.) *Towards an Anthropology of Women*, New York: Monthly Review Press.

Ruggie, M. (1984) *The State and Working Women*, Princeton, NJ: Princeton University Press.

Ruxton, S. (1996) *Children in Europe*, London: NCH Action for Children.

Rydenstam, K. (1990) *Undersökning om Kvinnors och Mäns Tidsanvändning* (Investigation of women's and men's time usage), 1990/91 Stockholm: Statistiska Centralbyreuen.

Sainsbury, D. (1994) *Gendering Welfare States*, London: Sage.

Sainsbury, D. (1996) *Gender, Equality and Welfare States*, Cambridge: Cambridge University Press.

Salvage, A. (1995) *Who Will Care: Future Prospects for Family Care of Older People in the European Union*, Dublin: European Foundation for the Improvement of Living and Working Conditions.

Sandquist, K. (1993) *Pappor och Riktiga Karlar. Om Mans- och Fadersroller i Ideologi och Verklighet* (Fathers and Real Men. On Male and Father Roles in Ideology and Reality), Stockholm: Carlssons.

Sassoon, A. S. (1992) *Women and the State*, London: Routledge.

Schmidt, V. H. (1992b) 'Households and Working Time Arrangements', in C. Marsh and S. Arber (eds) *Families and Households*, Hampshire: Macmillan.

Schneekloth, U. and Pothoff, P. (1993) 'Persons in Private Households Needing Help and Care', in D. Trent (ed.) *Promotion of Mental Health*, Vol. 1, Aldershot: Avebury.

Schutz, A. and Luckmann, T. (1973) *The Structure of the Life-world*, Evanston, IL: Northwestern University Press.

Schuyt, C. J. M. (1973) *Rechtvaardigheid en effectiviteit in de verdeling van levenskansen*, Rotterdam: University Press.

Second Commission on the Status of Women (1993) *Report to the Taoiseach*, Dublin: Stationery Office.

Self-Employed Women's Association and HomeNet (1996) *Recognition of Homebased Workers at the International Labour Organisation*, Ahmedabad, India: SEWA.

Self-Employed Women's Union Launched (1994) *Community News, Izindaba*, 4, 3.

Siim, B. (1987) 'The Scandinavian Welfare States. Towards Sexual Equality or a New Kind of Male Domination?', *Acta Sociologica* 30, 3/4: 255–270.

Siim, B. (1993) 'The Gendered Scandinavian Welfare States: The Interplay Between Women's Roles as Mothers, Workers and Citizens in Denmark', in J. Lewis (ed.) Women and Social Policies in Europe, Aldershot: Edward Elgar.

Sociaal Cultureel Planbureau (1993) *Sociale Atlas van de vrouw. Deel 2: Arbeid, inkomen en faciliteiten om werken en zorg voor kinderen te combineren*, Den Haag, Vuga.

Stathopoulis, P. and Amera, A. (1992) 'Care of the Elderly in Greece', in I. Kosberg (ed.) *Family Care of the Elderly*, London: Sage.

Stenvig, B., Andersen, J. and Laursen, L. (1993) 'Statistics for Work and Family in Denmark and the EC', in S. Carlsen and J. Elm Larsen (eds) *The Equality Dilemma*, Copenhagen: Munksgaard International.

Sullerot, E. (1992) *Quels Pres? Quels Fils?*, Paris: Fayard.

Symeonidou, H. (1994) 'Full and part-time employment of women in Greece. Correlations with life cycle events', *quoted in Blossfeld*.

Tansey, J. (1984) *Women in Ireland: a Compilation of Relevant Data*, Dublin: Council for the Status of Women.

Tate, J. (1995): *Social Europe: Homeworking in the European Union*, Report of the ad hoc Working Group, Luxembourg: European Commission, Employment, Industrial Relations and Social Affairs.

Tate, J. (1996) *Every Pair Tells a Story*, Report on a Survey of Homeworking and Subcontracting Chains in Six European Countries in the European Union Brussels: European Commission Directorate General V, Employment Industrial Relations and Social Affairs.

Tester, S. (1996) 'Women in Community Care' in C. Hallett (ed.) *Women and Social Policy*, London: Prentice-Hall Harvester Wheatsheaf.

Thomas, M., Goddard, E., Hickman, M. and Hunter, P. (1994) *General Household Survey 1992*, London: HMSO.

Tinker, A. (1994) 'Future Prospects for Family Care and Employment', unpublished paper at the Working and Caring Conference, Bonn.

Titmuss, R. M. (1971) *Commitment to Welfare*, London: George Allen and Unwin.

Tronto, J. C. (1993) *Moral Boundaries: A Political Argument for an Ethic of Care*, New York: Routledge.

Tsoukalas, K. (1987) *State, Society and Work in Post-war Greece*, Athens: Themelio.

Twigg, J. (1994) *Carers Perceived*, London: Macmillan.

Ungerson, C. (1983) 'Why Do Women Care?', in J. Finch and D. Groves (eds) *A Labour of Love Women, Work and Caring*, London: Routledge and Kegan Paul.

Ve, H. (1989) 'The Male Gender Role and Responsibility for Childcare', in K. Boh *et al.* (eds) *Changing Patterns of European Family Life: A Comparative Analysis of 14 European Countries*, London: Routledge.

Waerness, K. (1989) 'Caring', in K. Boh *et al.* (eds) *Changing Patterns of European Family Life: A Comparative Analysis of 14 European Countries*, London: Routledge.

Waerness, K. (1990) 'Informal and Formal Care in Old Age', in C. Ungerson (ed.) *Gender and Caring: Work and Welfare in Britain and Scandinavia*, Hemel Hempstead: Harvester Wheatsheaf.

Wagner, D. L. and Hunt, G. G. (1994) 'The Use of Workplace Eldercare Programmes by Employed Caregivers', *Research on Ageing* 16, 1: 69–84.

Walby, S. (1986) *Patriarchy at Work*, Cambridge: Polity.

Walby, S. (1990) *Theorizing Patriarchy*, Oxford: Basil Blackwell.

Walby, S. (1997) *Gender Transformations*, London: Routledge.

Walsh, T. (1991) 'Flexible Employment in the Retail and Hotel Trades', in A. Pollert (ed.) *Farewell to Flexibility?*, Oxford: Basil Blackwell.

West Yorkshire Homeworking Group (1990) *A Penny a Bag: Campaigning on Homework*, Batley, Yorkshire: Yorkshire and Humberside Low Pay Unit.

West Yorkshire Homeworking Unit for Leeds County Council (1992) *Outwork in Leeds*.

Whatmore, K. (1989) *Care to Work: National Carers Survey*, Vol. 1, London: Opportunities for Women.

Whitting G. (1992) 'Women and Poverty: The European Context', in C. Glendinning and J. Millar (eds) *Women and Poverty in Britain in the 1990s*, Hemel Hempstead: Harvester Wheatsheaf.

Wignaraja, P. (ed.) (1992) *New Social Movements in the South: Empowering the People*, London: Zed Books.

Wilensky, H. L. and Lebeaux, C. N. (1958) *Industrial Society and Social Welfare*, New York: The Free Press.

Wolfe, A. (1989) *Whose Keeper? Social Science and Moral Obligation*, Berkeley: University of California Press.

Yearbook of Nordic Statistics, NORD 1995: 1, Stockholm.

Yorkshire and Humberside Low Pay Unit (1991) *A Survey of Homeworking in Calderdale*.

INDEX